Dance Appre

Dance Appreciation is an exciting exploration of how to understand and think about dance in all of its various contexts. This book unfolds a brief history of dance with engaging insight into the social, cultural, aesthetic, and kinetic aspects of various forms of dance. Dedicated chapters cover ballet, modern, tap, jazz, and hip-hop dance, complete with summaries, charts, timelines, discussion questions, movement prompts, and an online companion website all designed to foster awareness of and appreciation for dance in a variety of contexts. This wealth of resources helps to uncover the fascinating history that makes this art form so diverse and entertaining, and to answer the questions of why we dance and how we dance. Written for the novice dancer as well as the more experienced dance student, *Dance Appreciation* enables readers to learn and think critically about dance as a form of entertainment and art.

Amanda Clark is a Professor and Dance Program Coordinator at Western Kentucky University, where she teaches all levels of jazz and tap dance technique, along with dance theory coursework. She received an MFA in Dance from the University of Oklahoma and a BPA in Dance Performance from Oklahoma City University. Amanda's choreography has been presented nationally and internationally and encompasses a mix of classical and contemporary approaches within the jazz and tap dance genres. Amanda's primary research interests lie in the history and pedagogy of jazz and tap dance.

Sara Pecina is the Director of Dance at Berry College. She received her MFA in Dance from the University of Oklahoma and graduated with a BA in Dance from Western Kentucky University. She has presented research on the history and pedagogy of jazz and tap dance both nationally and internationally at various dance conferences, including both the National Dance Education Organization and the Dance Studies Association annual conferences. Sara is a certified mat Pilates instructor and has also trained to teach Dance for Parkinson's Disease with Mark Morris Dance Group and is in the American Tap Dance Foundation's Rhythm Tap Teacher Program.

Dance Appreciation

Amanda Clark and Sara Pecina

Routledge
Taylor & Francis Group

LONDON AND NEW YORK

First published 2021
by Routledge
2 Park Square, Milton Park, Abingdon, Oxon OX14 4RN

and by Routledge
52 Vanderbilt Avenue, New York, NY 10017

Routledge is an imprint of the Taylor & Francis Group, an informa business

British Library Cataloguing-in-Publication Data
A catalogue record for this book is available from the British Library

Library of Congress Cataloging-in-Publication Data
A catalog record has been requested for this book

ISBN: 978-0-367-18400-1 (hbk)
ISBN: 978-0-367-18403-2 (pbk)
ISBN: 978-0-429-06137-0 (ebk)

Typeset in Univers
by Newgen Publishing UK

Visit the companion website: www.routledge.com/cw/clark

Contents

■ Contents

Contents

Preface

Dance surrounds us in our daily lives no matter who or where we are. Humans naturally express themselves through movement in endless ways with nuances that reflect our cultures, beliefs, and individual experiences. As we commence our study of understanding dance, let us first consider what dance means. What is dance to you? How would you define dance to others? Try to construct your own working definition of dance. What might it include? What phrases capture the essence of this activity in ways that are meaningful and relevant to you? To the world around you?

Now consider your definition. In what ways might your definition exclude a group of people, limit the type of motivation, serve only a certain purpose, or restrict the dance to particular movement, accompaniment, modes, or settings? Dance can mean many different things to different people; yet, at its core, <u>dance is expression through movement.</u>

Dance is human, visceral, complex, exciting, multi-faceted, and ever-evolving. There is great power in dance, whether one participates as performer or spectator, creator or researcher. Dance has the capacity to connect individuals across generations, nationalities, and geographies. It can extend beyond language, racial, and gender barriers. It can make us laugh or make us cry. Upon viewing a dance performance, we may find ourselves mesmerized or challenged to think in new ways. The study of the art form can foster understanding of the relationship between culture and art. We can develop an appreciation for the unique differences and perspectives of humankind and are exposed to an alternative means of entertainment, modes of thinking, and perspectives of the world and life around us. The benefits of this great art form are immeasurable.

This textbook has been designed to introduce the non-dancer within the United States and the United Kingdom to the diverse world of dance. As dance education continues to expand within higher education curricula, courses that focus on fostering an understanding and appreciation for dance as an art form require a broad range of needs. To cover every aspect of dance equally would either require volumes of text or only have room for one or two sentences per topic. Instead, this book provides insight into various facets of dance to equip the reader with a broad knowledge base and understanding of dance. Specifically, readers will explore the purposes of dance, cultural influences, composition, how to view dance, various forms of dance, history, technological impacts, and the lives of dancers.

While this book captures the global expanse of dance, Part II provides more detail for Western theatrical dance forms. This approach to dive into a deeper understanding of these forms was taken with the recognition that a majority of our readers' first encounters with and experiences in dance will be with these forms. It is not meant to limit the scope of dance. In no way is this meant to imply that these forms are more complex or significant than any other; rather, they are utilized as an access point to garner an appreciation and awareness of dance in a way more readily available to readers.

This textbook serves as a conversation starter, not ender. The topics included are not all that dance has to offer, but they do offer broad perspectives, relatable to the reader's immersive experience. The following chapters provide a survey of topics in dance with overarching themes of dance's ability to embrace and adapt to the global community. The exploration of these various perceptions is meant to ignite interest to pursue a greater appreciation for dance. It is the authors' intent that the material covered within this textbook will incite the reader to continue the journey into the world of dance, diving deeper into the cultural, historical, aesthetical, and kinetic relationships within dance. The impulse to move is within each individual, and the power that dance can yield is unending. Let us explore this rich art form together and uncover connections in culture that unearth our deeper relationship to one another as human beings.

Acknowledgments

As we consider those who have helped to make the writing of this book possible, we must first and foremost acknowledge the individual who helped each of us at the beginning of our dance journey. Becky Seamster was not only our first dance teacher, but also the woman who empowered us to discover the unique power of dance. We would also like to express our gratitude to Jo Rowan and her work within dance education, for it is her program that opened our eyes to the history, value, and preservation of American dance forms. We are most grateful to our editing team, including Sarah Gore and Ben Piggott, for their trust, effort, and assistance throughout the creative and production process. There are countless colleagues and friends who have supported our endeavors throughout the writing of this book; however, none have encouraged us more than our families. To Dean and Jasmine, we thank you for your patience and humor. Your support and love mean the world to us.

Part I
What is Dance?

INTRODUCTION

Close your eyes. Imagine yourself in the following scenarios:

> After much anticipation, you receive the best news of your life. What is your instinctive reaction? …
>
> You are a toddler, teetering on your toes as you hear your favorite cartoon come on the television. What do you intuitively do? …
>
> You nervously propose to the love of your life, who promptly accepts. What are your natural reactions? …
>
> Finally, imagine that you receive the worst news of your life. What might your reaction be?

It is likely that each of these imaginary responses included some form of movement. Great news is often met with a jump into the air or a raising and stretching of the arms. Young children bounce their knees, stamp their feet in place, and vigorously pump their arms in the air. Couples in love almost certainly embrace. Devastating news is often followed by a drop of the head or collapse to the knees. Movement of the human body is a natural response. We instinctively react to the world around us in a myriad of non-verbal manners. Often, movement can express what words cannot. Think back to the above examples. Elation and satisfaction are demonstrated with a leap into the air. Excitement is revealed in the bouncing motions of a child. Love and tenderness are displayed in a couple's embrace. Grief or agony is depicted in a drop to the knees.

Dance becomes the result of this range of movement actions: the human body leaping, bouncing, reaching arms out to embrace, and dropping to the floor. Dance, as the ultimate expressive form of movement, has the potential to convey a great range of emotions and ideas, the capacity to cross language boundaries and connect individuals, and the power to stir an individual both physically and emotionally. From the beginning of humankind, movement has been a means to celebrate great news or victory, to honor the dying, to tell stories, to persuade others, to heal the sick, to entertain, to demonstrate hierarchical power, or to unify a community.

Natural movements to emotion → transformed to dance

Before one can fully appreciate dance, one must understand it. Part I uncovers the art of dance and provides a basis from which readers may view and articulate their perceptions of a dance. Chapter 1 details the primary purposes of dance within a culture: ritualistic, political, social, therapeutic, and theatrical. Chapter 2 encourages readers to consider dance through a cultural lens, offering select and varied dance forms as examples. In Chapter 3, concepts of choreography, such as the elements of space, time, and energy, are introduced within the context of Western theatrical dance. The choreographic process is described, including the act of improvisation and ways in which dances can be formed. Chapter 4 then exposes readers to methods of viewing and perceiving dance. Readers are challenged to identify dance as art and entertainment and introduced to the aesthetic and kinesthetic responses one can have when observing dance.

1 Purposes of Dance

Humans have a natural instinct, an innate impulse, to move. We stretch our bodies as we awake, we jump for joy, and we slump our head and shoulders when depressed. Some of us cannot help but tap our toes to the sound of music; others cannot talk without waving the arms around in the air. Humans communicated first through the use of bodily movement. Some psychologists even suggest that this impulse to move begins within the fetal stage, as a child "performs active movements of rotation, flexion and stretching during the second half of pregnancy."[1] What began as a spontaneous human behavior was molded into a means of non-verbal communication. Through gestures and movement, humans revealed their needs, conveyed their ideas, and expressed their fears. Humans have shaped this instinctual movement beyond a natural means of communication and into a form of art to convey narrative and abstract ideas and meanings. Dance can be considered as the oldest of all art forms, preceding music, painting, and sculpture. With the human body as an instrument, dance became a medium for early humans in the communication of ideas, expression of religion, connection to nature, celebration of life and death, means of recreation or sport, and mode of social interaction.

Dance can function in a myriad of ways, and it can also offer keen insight into a given culture, exposing the viewer to the intricate ways in which humans and their civilizations differ. A society's way of life influences the reasons for which a group dances as well as the manner and style of the movements. While the use of the human body serves as a common denominator within the countless dances found around the globe, these dances may vary vastly from culture to culture. As we uncover the ways in which one dances along with the reasons for the dance, we learn about the innate similarities and unique differences among humans. Our views of what dance is are broadened, and our understanding of who can dance, along with the how and why, are enhanced. It is through this understanding that we develop an appreciation for the art form and its role in the world around us.

The purpose of dance can vary depending upon a variety of factors. Social class or political status, age, gender, and religious beliefs can each influence the reason a group may or may not dance or the manner in which one dances. For some, the practice of dance can generate concern for sexual promiscuity or an apprehension about the religious taboos against the body, while others may see dance as an aesthetic display of confidence in the human body, of femininity or masculinity, or as a sacred experience. People may utilize movement as an artistic representation of historical events or harness dance as a vehicle to assert a call to action and incite change. Dance can also serve as a form of worship, connecting performers and spectators to a higher being or power. It may delineate hierarchy and express respect and reverence for political order. Dance could generate group unity and social affirmation, creating a sense of belonging within a group. In some instances, dance can create a means of social interaction or even courtship. Individuals or groups of people may use dance as a form of recreation, fitness training, or means of healing. For others, dance can be a method of education, a profession, or in many cases an exhilarating form of entertainment.

Dance serves five primary purposes or functions; ritual, political, social, *an of which can vary greatly* therapeutic, and theatrical. Before we explore these different functions of dance, let us first take a moment and consider each purpose. What role can dance play within a formal or informal ritual? How can dance convey one's social class or political order? How can dance help heal the body and mind? What is different between those forms of dance and social or theatrical dancing? Which purpose(s) for dance do you find most often within your life?

BOX 1.1 DANCE AS COMPETITION

Comp. dance is to win, However also can have other benefits that come with

Humans are inherently competitive. It is no surprise that the impulse to move has blended with the desire to win. Dance competitions have become an industry of their own within today's global society. In these events, dancers perform – often theatrical dance choreography – for adjudication. The purpose is not to entertain, socialize, worship, or demonstrate political power. Rather, the goal is to compete, to win. The individual's or group's primary reason for participating in the activity is for competition, yet through their participation, they are developing a strong work ethic, fostering teamwork, and practicing dedication and perseverance. Dancers may also have an opportunity to earn scholarships to future competitions or training events. Perhaps, then, competition can also be considered a purpose of dance.

RITUAL DANCE — *to praise, celebrate, or commemorate*

One of the ways in which dance functions within a society is in the form of ritual. Rituals are prescribed sets of procedures or actions that are followed in a formal manner in observance of a religious or other ceremonial event. Cultures, both past and present, have incorporated dance into various forms of sacred and secular rituals. We find that the original use for dance as ritual lies deep within early cultures. Dance in prehistoric civilizations did not begin merely as a separate recreational activity within society, nor did it serve as a profession. Dance functioned as a central element of religion and played an inherent role in daily life. Belief systems, similar to those of many groups of people today, maintained that gods and spirits had powers of influence over daily life. These groups looked to gods or supernatural powers that influenced reoccurring events such as the rising and setting of the sun, the changing seasons, the growth of crops, and even their own life and death. Early **ritual dances** were designed to please or placate the gods or to ask for favor or blessing from the spirits. These events contained a group of traditionally established actions and dance. This interconnected faith between the human and the spirit world was woven throughout all facets of early humankind's existence and remains present today. As a result, various forms of ritual dance have emerged.

There are a great number of purposes for which a culture, society, group, or individual may engage in ritual. For example, some groups perform ritual dances as a means to prepare for war or promote healing among the community. While many rituals may have been originally rooted in sacred meanings, rituals today can be sacred or secular in intent. Themes can range from healing to fertility, from lifespan to war. Rituals are considered to be either specific or cyclical. **Specific rituals** are done only one time and for a very distinctive purpose, such as marriage, whereas **cyclical rituals** are more general and may be repeated each season, such as those performed at harvest time. Rituals can extend over the course of several hours or may even last many days and can occur within a central location of a community or in a designated public location, such as a hotel ballroom. Often, the circle is an important element of many rituals, as it provides a sense of unity among participants, allowing each to see the others and maintain a sense of belonging. Historically, additional elements of ritual dance have included the use of fire, which provided not only light but a focal point around which a dance was performed, along with body decorations, such as paint, feathers, colored stones, and the use of masks to further enhance the dance and the experience. Masks enable the performer to assume the identity of the god or spirit imitated. The use of masks not only helps in the performance of the dance, but in fact merges the identity of performer with that of the spirit and assists the performer as the god is summoned in order for communication to occur throughout the ritual.

As societies have evolved, the practice of many dance rituals has declined; however, cultures have preserved the tradition of certain rituals or have altered them to suit their group's needs. Following are a sampling of rituals seen throughout time and around the world. Cultures and individuals that engage in dance rituals uncover great power in dance, not only to pray humbly to their gods or to honor traditions but also as a means for social connections within the group, as recreation, and as entertainment!

Fertility Rituals

Fertility rites are performed for the abundance of food and life. Without nourishment and healthy offspring, a community would cease to exist. Plants and animals provide not only food but also shelter and clothing. For example, lumber is used to build structures; animals and plants are used for clothing. Their ample supply is essential to survival. Society relies on agriculture, and people often danced in an effort to secure necessary resources. For example, the *kagura* is a Japanese Shinto dance ritual wherein practitioners dance to ask the gods for blessing over their harvests. In some cultures, rain dances are performed in which individuals dance to ask the gods to release the rains to help the crops grow or sustain human and animal life. People still appeal to higher beings for rain; consider the 2019–2020 Australian bushfire crisis and the vast quantity of social media requests for individuals to pray for rain to end the fires. The assurance of food, favorable conditions for crops, fertility, and the reproduction of animals is just as essential for our daily lives to continue as it was centuries ago.

Hunting and Animal Rituals

Hunting and animal rituals are performed in several ways. Historically, survival for early cultures depended on plentiful animals and successful hunting. Ever respectful of the animals, these rituals enabled humans to call upon the animal spirits for protection. At other times, these rituals served as preparation for a specific hunt, providing a means of envisioning the hunt or gaining power over the animal in order to ensure the kill. Groups also danced to ask the gods to deliver favorable conditions for the hunt. The Matis, an indigenous people in Brazil, perform a dance ritual, which includes special body paint, chanting of animal sounds, and movement performed in a line, designed to attract forest pigs in preparation for a hunt. Another example can be found in the Yaqui and Mayo people of Sonora, Mexico, who have preserved their deer dance; however, their dance is now performed for educational rather than practical purposes.

Rite of Passage Rituals

Lifespan rituals are those performed to mark an event or change in life from one stage to another. The marriage ritual is a celebration dance of a couple moving into a new life phase. This ritual is aimed at ensuring a successful marriage. Historically, it was also performed to ensure the production of offspring and thus maintain the vitality of the group. Initiation rituals are often performed when boys and girls reach the age of puberty. Initially, these were done as a means to protect the individuals from harm during their transition. Various types of initiation and marriage rituals can be found in modern societies, such as the father and daughter dance at a *quinceañera*, the *hora* at *bar* and *bat mitzvahs*, and the traditional groom and bride's first dance at a wedding.

Birth and funeral rituals are those that celebrate and bless the beginning or end of life. Birth rituals can occur prior to and following the actual birth of a child. During the rites leading up to the birth, dancers request favor and blessing from

1.1
Illustration of the
Native American
bison dance.
Beeldbewerking/
Getty Images

the gods to ease the labor and ensure the health of the child and mother. Other dance rituals celebrate the healthy birth of a child. Funeral rituals are aimed at providing peace to both the living and the dead. These rites also unite the living with the dead, serving as a medium through which members can connect with their ancestors. The processional quality often encompassed within these rituals can be witnessed today in funerals as friends and family drive in procession from the church to the cemetery or walk in succession to the grave site.

A now much less common form

As cultures have evolved, many dance rituals have faded from existence or transitioned in mode or meaning. While some communities continue to practice dance rituals as part of their daily existence, others have shifted their historical dance rituals from ceremonial performance to public exhibitions and performances. Some have done this with the goal of archiving and educating the public on their cultural history, whereas others use their traditional dance rituals as forms of public entertainment. The power of dance to express with the body what words sometimes cannot, while emphasizing social bonds within the community and providing a means for worship, has been a key element in many rituals around the world since the beginning of time.

POLITICAL DANCE *- shows power, status, & priviiegdee*

The suggestion of political dance may bring to mind thoughts of political banter, governmental elections, and party divides. Yet, **political dance** explores the manner in which dance can be used as an instrument to display power and status among the ruling classes within a given society. In some cultures, this is employed through court dances performed within the governing courts. **Court dances** are ceremonial court spectacles and rituals often designed in such a way as to demonstrate hierarchy and royal authority. Historically, court dance, regardless of the culture in which it appeared, often followed a specific format. Court dances were lavish and lengthy events, some lasting hours or extending over a period of days. Due to modernizing societies, tourism, and commercialism, many court dances have been condensed in length, are performed by professional troupes, and are now made available for public viewing and considered classical dances within a given culture. Yet, court dances continue to be performed within some cultures and as part of court festivities and events today. Let us look at various examples of how dance has functioned in this political capacity.

In the late seventeenth century under the reign of Louis XIV, King of France, court spectacles flourished in his country palace at Versailles. At age fourteen, he performed the role Apollo, which earned him the nickname Sun King, wherein courtiers donned in masks circled around him like planets orbiting the sun. The symbolism of this role followed Louis XIV throughout his reign as commoners and nobility alike looked to him for ultimate authority. Crossing the lines between social and theatrical, the spectacles within the court of Louis XIV proved the potential of dance as an instrument in displaying political power.

Often within court dance, only the courtiers, nobles, chiefs, or leaders dance. In other societies, any member of the group may be permitted to join in or assigned to perform the dance. However, the ability to dance well is a requirement taken seriously by all. For example, in the Asante culture, found in central Ghana in West Africa, the ability to dance well was once a qualifying factor in the election of the Asantehene, or king. Once in power, the Asantehene dances before his people on certain occasions. He does this to display his royal power and imperial qualities among his people as well as to honor those who preceded him in power. Court dances can be a vehicle for leaders and communities to pay respect to the previous generations of rulers. By engaging in these traditional rituals within the court, the ruling class honors those who came before, thus emphasizing the sacredness of the political structure of the group.

The use of court dance to display hierarchical structure can also be witnessed in other cultures throughout history and today. The island of Java is located in Indonesia and known for its own classical version of court dance, the *bedhaya*, which is performed by nine females. Javanese court dance was not originally open to those outside the court and was only viewed and learned by a few within the palace walls. Initially performed by the sultan's female relatives, *bedhaya* was reserved for those in highest power. Here, the hierarchical structure is revealed in the setting of the dance and the costumes and the seating arrangement of the onlookers. Permanent physical structures were established within each Javanese palace, designed uniquely for court dances. The proximity in which one is seated to the ruler is dependent upon one's rank.

During the European Renaissance (fourteenth to seventeenth centuries), elaborate spectacles and royal balls became routine celebrations within French and Italian courts. These were lengthy, costly, and highly embellished affairs that featured the aristocrats and nobles as performers. Similarly to the other

Sign and celebration of power

1.2
A *bedhaya*
dancer performs
at the Sultan's
Palace Kraton in
Yogyakarta, Java,
Indonesia.
Matthew Williams-
Elli/Robert Harding/
Age Fotostock

examples discussed thus far, participation in these court dances also exhibited
to the invited spectators the performers' status within the court along with their
dependence on the royal order. These court spectacles followed a rigid structure,
beginning with an entrance designed to emphasize the order of power – those
with the highest social status danced first. Even the geometric floor patterns in
which the performers danced symbolized political status.

A final look to Japan reveals yet another court dance, known as *bugaku*. This traditional court dance was born in China, later imported to Japan, and is preserved today in the Japanese Imperial Court. Prior to World War II, *bugaku* was performed only for noble eyes. The dance served as a symbol of status in that it was reserved to be viewed by only the most powerful. It has since been made available to the public. The dance is divided into two groups, those referred to as "of the Left," which are from China, and dances "of the Right," those of Korean origin. These dances are further distinguished by the contrast of musical accompaniment, colors in which the dancers are costumed, and movement characteristics.

Court dances are typically comprised of movement derived from folk dances, those emerging among the common people. These movements were then adapted by the ruling class and often refined to suit their needs and reflect their behaviors and attributes or ideals of the culture. For example, within the Asante culture, the Asantehene dances with energy, yet his movements are slow and elegant, demonstrating a coolness and control.[2] In *bugaku*, the tempo gradually increases, yet the dancers move stately and slowly with extreme control and deliberation. Central to the tranquil *bedhaya* is the idea of the disciplined self. *Bedhaya* is performed both to glorify the ruler and to uphold the power of the courts, yet also displays ideal Javanese qualities. The nine dancers who perform the dance represent not nine individuals but, rather, nine different facets of a single individual. Emphasizing balance and a composed self, the slow-motion movements executed in unison are highly stylized. <u>Dancers show no emotion.</u> Instead, they move in a calm and dignified manner at all times, much as one would expect from a member of the noble class. Similarly, in the European court dances, the dancers' movements were fluid and controlled, extending from an upright torso that emphasized dignity. Although the speed at which the dancers

This is such an interesting routine/style

1.3
Photo of *bugaku* performed in traditional setting. Image captures the sixtieth anniversary of the emperor's enthronement at the Imperial Palace in Tokyo, Japan. Photo by The Asahi Shimbun via Getty Images

[handwritten: The emergence of Teaching!]

moved varied, their behavior consistently modeled European aristocratic ideals and behavior. To assist performers and maintain standards, dance instructors and even written manuals emerged within various cultures, guiding individuals on the proper method of executing specific steps and/or dances and the manner in which they were to be performed.

As societies evolved throughout the twentieth and twenty-first centuries, many shared the traditional dances once reserved for the court with the public. Since the economic gain associated with access to the arts was discovered, public viewing of these dance forms has become connected to tourism within these cultures. For example, performances of *bedhaya* and *bugaku* are both performed in conjunction with events of the court yet also appear in public venues. Court dance glorifies the court and serves as a dignified representation of and reverence for the hierarchical structure of a society, often emphasizing proper etiquette and aristocratic behavior. Court dance can be seen today both as a ceremonial function within the court setting as well as a theatrical performance for the public.

[handwritten: This type of dance still exists!]

SOCIAL DANCE *[handwritten: – Entertainment & Expression]*

Dance has the capacity to provide pleasure to both the performer and the spectator. Humans first found joy in movement of the body before adding layers of intent to their actions for the purpose of expressive communication. Consider the football player who has just scored a hard-earned touchdown. Often their initial instinct is to perform some movement of the body, their happy dance, in celebration of the victory. The young child in enthusiastic elation will perform fast footwork with swinging arms and a bobbing head. What is the expression on the face of the football player and the young child? A smile. Dance provides a vehicle for joy and exhilaration to be released and shared.

Humans dance for enjoyment because delight is found in the movement of the human body and the social interaction that often accompanies the dance. As we consider the social purpose behind dance, it is helpful to recognize the varied use of terms that often become interchangeable with social dance. At times, the labels of ballroom, popular, or vernacular dance may be used. **Social dance** pertains to dance that functions as a means for communal interaction or social display. Ballroom dance and popular dance, including the latest dance trends, certainly fall under the umbrella of social dance, but these terms do not paint the full picture of the purpose behind social dance. Neither does **vernacular dance**, which develops organically or naturally within a culture and is learned without the instruction of professional teachers.

Social dance may have varied intentions. It may be used as a form of recreation or exercise. We sometimes see fitness classes or videos promote social dance themes. While this may be a marketing ploy, social dance is fun and relatable to most and does ultimately get people up and moving. Dance can serve as a form of courtship. Imagine the gala where an individual is invited to take a partner's hand and is whisked around the dance floor as if in a fairytale. Dance can display cultural beliefs about gender and movement. For example, in some cultures, there are distinct modes in which the different genders may or may not dance. Finally, social dance can be intended as pure entertainment. Picture an evening out with friends at a party or nightclub where the group gathers in rhythm under pulsing lights, the dance floor at a reception where twenty young adults have lined up to do the Cupid Shuffle, or the family living room where two teenagers giggle as their hip grandparent boogies with a virtual robot.

Dance can demonstrate the communal beliefs and customs of a society, specifically in regard to gender identity within the society. In the Cook Islands, located in the south Pacific Ocean, dance is performed at all social events. Men and women perform movements identifiable to their genders, in which the focus for each remains in the lower half of the body. Men execute flapping movements of the knees, while women sway and swing their hips. Men's dances are more athletic and energetic, whereas women's dances appear fluid and graceful. These gender-specific movements and qualities are important to the integrity of the social culture of the Cook Islands. They reflect the cultural distinction made between male and female to the extent that individuals do not cross over and train in movements of the opposite sex. These gender distinctions are apparent in the Polynesian one-on-one social dance as well. Although Polynesian dance is most often performed in several alternating lines and rows of performers, they dance with a focus on and a sense of belonging to the entire group. Whether in team dancing or one-on-one dancing, there is a lack of bodily contact. Individuals do not touch in Polynesian dance, unlike European social ballroom dance or other global forms of social dance where partners may face and hold on to one another. Even after the influence of British explorers in the eighteenth and nineteenth centuries, the dance of the Cook Islanders remained constant. Although the British, shocked by

1.4
"A Night Dance by Men, in Hapaee," ca. 1774. Captain John Cook and other British voyagers were shocked by the native dancing of the islanders upon their exploration of the Pacific Islands in the 1700s.
Photo by © Historical Picture Archive/CORBIS/ Corbis via Diomedia

what they perceived to be provocative dance, were able to convert the islanders to Christianity and thus changed their religious beliefs, they were unable to persuade the islanders to abandon their dance traditions.[3] This is a reflection of how deeply dance can be integrated within a society.

Perhaps social dance is most recognizable for its social context. In America, social dance is a form of dance practiced most often by the masses merely as entertainment and enjoyment. Often the pastime at parties, nightclubs, receptions, and celebrations, it can be danced by the youngest child to the most senior adult and requires no formal training. Perhaps that is the beauty of social dance. It can be your victory dance on the ball field or your private celebration on a front porch after the end of a wonderful date. It can be found within the midst of a circle of friends gathered in a park after school as a heavy beat booms through a out of portable speakers. It can be the innocent slow dance of two five-year-old children at a wedding reception or the sweet reminder as two senior adults embrace on that same dance floor. Let us take a closer look at social dance within the United States.

is that it can be anything

BOX 1.2 THE WALTZ

Social dance has served as a tool in teaching social etiquette, which can be witnessed in the ballroom couple dances performed in European dance halls throughout the eighteenth and nineteenth centuries and even in the United Kingdom and America during cotillion and debutante balls. The waltz began as a European social dance, thriving during the nineteenth century. In the waltz, couples face one another – one hand clasped with the other placed on the shoulder or waist – as they glide across the dance floor. One partner will occasionally turn the other, as both dancers remain erect and elegant in stance. In the waltz, as was the case in early European social dances, it is customary for the male dancer to lead the female in movement. As with many social dances, the waltz is deeply connected to the music to which it is performed. Specific music in ¾ time was composed for the waltz. This music features an extended melodic phrasing, or musical idea. This enables the dance to flow around the dance floor as the clockwise circular pattern of couples creates a dynamic energy for both participants and spectators. The waltz continues today, although it now includes various versions. Like other forms of social dance, it has been adapted for the concert and theatrical stage, yet remains a classic example of social dance.

Since the nineteenth century, American social dances and popular music have been heavily influenced by the movements and rhythms of African Americans. In fact, these two forms of expression have often evolved hand in hand. At the turn of the twentieth century, ragtime music strongly influenced the social dances of the period. Ragtime music featured **syncopation** – which is an emphasis of the weak or off beats within music rather than the strong beats – and lively energy; these rhythmical patterns were quickly incorporated into the dancing of the era. The social dances that developed in the late 1800s were rooted in African American vernacular dances, many of which began on southern plantations and traveled north to dance halls. In the 1910s, animal dances emerged. These were named after the animals that the movement imitated. For example, the Grizzly Bear, the Bunny Hug, and the Turkey Trot were animal dances in which the partners would hug one another tightly and execute steps representative of the specific animals. Movements included a variety of hops, labored steps, wiggling, and flapping of the arms following rhythms borrowed from African American dances of the time. The energetic quality and close bodily contact that these dances provided suited the rebellious nature of the younger generations and contrasted with the refined European couple dances of the previous century. Social dances in the United States have been largely influenced by the rhythms and qualities of the ever-evolving music present in American society. With the shifting music genres, such as swing, rock 'n' roll, disco, and rap, new social dances emerged, matching the characteristics of the music.

– very cross-cultural

Roaring 20s societal shift

BOX 1.3 INSTRUCTION GUIDES FOR SOCIAL DANCES

– Teaching has always been a part.

Throughout time, many contributors have influenced not just the appearance of social dance but its popularity as well. Dating back to ancient Greece, instructors schooled youth in the proper way to dance. Dance masters were employed in the courts of the European Renaissance to train individuals in steps and etiquette of the dance. Dancing manuals were a part of the written collection of dances. These manuals dictated the ways in which one was to dance, with whom, where, and when. For example, Vernon and Irene Castle, American ballroom dancers famous during the early 1900s, wrote a manual entitled *Modern Dancing*, which dictated the "correct" way to dance during the 1910s. As they sought to refine and dignify the social dances of the time period, they opened their business, known as the Castle House, as a place for "proper" instruction.

Today, societies can turn to web platforms, such as YouTube, and digital applications for easy access to short tutorials on the latest dance fads and trends. Learning the newest dance craze has never been easier.

Throughout the twentieth and twenty-first centuries, social dance forms have expanded and evolved consistently within the United States. Many times, these dances have been referred to as period dances, as all are reflective in nature of the cultural time period and historical context in which they were created. Perhaps you are familiar with the dances known as the Charleston, famous during the 1920s, or the Lindy Hop of the 1930s and 1940s. Maybe you have heard of the Twist, the Frug, or the Mashed Potato, each popular dance fads of the 1960s. The Macarena and the Roger Rabbit made their debuts during the 1990s. Within each new decade, an innovative set of dances introduce themselves to the masses, becoming the next popular crazes to hit the dance floor. Many elements work together to influence each type of social dance; these include the rhythmical patterns of the movement, the musical accompaniment, the stylization of the body, the proximity to other dancers in which it is performed, and the inherent attitudes about the body.

Dance follows trends too of general society

BOX 1.4 SONG AND DANCE INSTRUCTION

Along with the rising popularity of the radio in the early to mid-1900s came radio-dance lessons, and following the advent of the television, shows featuring musicians and live performances showcased the latest popular music and social dances of the period. Throughout the twentieth and twenty-first centuries, selected songs have included dance instructions within the lyrics. Examples include "Ballin' the Jack" (1913), "Peppermint Twist" (1961), "Cha Cha Slide" (1998), and "The Git Up" (2019). Consider how media is utilized in American culture today to spread the latest trends in social dance. From Hollywood films to MTV to reality shows such as *Dancing with the Stars*, popular and social dance styles are exhibited and broadcast across the country in theaters and living rooms and via social media. This topic is discussed further in Chapter 10.

Not only does music influence the development of a social dance form, but so does society as a whole. The events occurring within the world or a given group and even social expectations can impact a natural proclivity for a certain style of movement. From the bobbed haircuts and flapping knees and elbows of individuals in the 1920s to the twisting hips of young Americans in the late 1950s, to the gyrating hips of the millennium, youth have used social dance as

1.5
Female flappers dance alongside performing musicians during a Charleston dance contest at the Parody Club. Hulton Archive/ Stringer and Getty Images

a means of individual expression and form of rebellion against societal values or notions.

Social dance is performed by people with varying skill levels, from amateurs to professionals, and in various settings. Vernacular social dances that began in living rooms, dance halls, street corners, or gymnasiums have been borrowed and adapted for use on the theatrical stage in musicals and in concert dance as well as on screen in films, television and reality shows, and documentaries. This form of dance is performed for pleasure and the pure joy of movement and as a release from the daily grind of life. Social dance offers an individual the freedom of expression through movement. In America today, we see both leisure and competitive aspects of social dance. From informal parties to hip-hop battles or swing dance challenges, social dance permeates our culture in more ways than we might realize. Cultural historian and author Julie Malnig suggests that the social bond found within the dance is not from the group itself but from the overall experience of the dancing. The setting, the energy of the people participating, and the dance itself all contribute to the overall experience.[4] It is in this experience that the social power of dance is revealed. Dance has the capacity to bring joy to an individual, to unite a group, and to display social values.

important Main idea

1.6
Individuals engage in rock 'n' roll social dancing at the *Daily Mirror*'s Bill Haley Contest at Belle Vue in 1957.
Photo by *Daily Mirror*/Mirrorpix/ Mirrorpix via Getty Images

THERAPEUTIC DANCE —to Heal

Dance is innately therapeutic and can be harnessed as a powerful device for people with various physical and mental health conditions. There are a wide variety of health benefits with dance, and both dancers and scientists have designed a myriad of programs to aid individuals with different needs. **Dance for health** is dance that is utilized as a vehicle with which to address specific health concerns and enhance quality of life. Dance programs and classes have been established to serve people with mental health conditions, autism, dementia, Parkinson's disease, brain injuries, and in hospice, as well as survivors of sex trafficking, refugees, at-risk youth, substance abuse patients, teen moms, prisoners, and many other communities. These programs may be taught by dance practitioners or certified therapists. Each serves its own specific purpose and ultimately leads to results such as an expansion of movement possibilities, enhanced mind–body connection, improved self-esteem or confidence, and strengthened communication skills.

Dance for health classes often start with participants sitting or standing in a circle, which emphasizes that everyone – including the instructor – is equal and fosters a sense of community in the group. After a warm-up and various exercises suited to the population of students, a class will usually conclude with an acknowledgment of everyone and the time that they spent together. This will often see the class return to a circle formation and may be done with bows, smiles, holding hands, or some combination thereof. While there is no one formula to suit all dance for health needs, these characteristics of an emphasized community, circle formations, human connection, and gratitude are commonly seen in a variety of programs.

fosters community between groups

One such program includes the dance classes designed for people with Parkinson's disease or similar movement disorders. Parkinson's disease is a neurodegenerative disorder, which affects the brain's ability to produce certain chemicals that help it communicate with muscles. A progressive disease, Parkinson's gradually affects an individual's ability to move, including walking, reaching, speaking, balance, and facial expression. Over time, any and every movement becomes extremely difficult or impossible. This difficulty in completing daily tasks often leads to isolation, as people affected by the disease will simply leave the house less often because it is abnormally time consuming, exhausting, and challenging, which can also lead to depression. Parkinson's is usually diagnosed in individuals over the age of fifty, though early-onset Parkinson's has been diagnosed in people as young as twenty-one. Various medications are available to combat symptoms, but there is no cure for the disease.

In 2001, the Mark Morris Dance Group in Brooklyn, New York, founded Dance for PD®.[5] This program offers specialized classes for individuals with Parkinson's or similar movement disorders and their care partners. Classes begin with students seated in a circle for a warm-up that allows them to gradually get their bodies moving without demanding balance or too much coordination at the beginning of class. The class will progress to supported standing – using

1.7
Dancers participate in a Dance for Parkinson's class.
Virginia Bridges/ *Raleigh News & Observer*/TNS via Getty Images

a chair back like a ballet *barre* for support – and then freestanding or locomotion, moving through space. Throughout class, any exercise can be modified to remaining seated for anyone in wheelchairs or having difficulty; exercises can also be modified for students using walkers or needing extra support. Students are encouraged in improvisation activities to be creative and express themselves, and interactions in groups or with partners bring a social component to the class. Furthermore, a large body of research exists, demonstrating the ways in which music aids movement for Parkinson's patients. With music being a natural component of dance, this enhances the students' abilities to move.

The Dance for PD® program is built on the foundation that dancers who are professionally trained can use their movement expertise to aid people with Parkinson's by giving them the opportunity to experience dance as an art form. These classes are not branded or marketed as therapy but instead focus on the art and joy of dance. Through this focus on dance, the classes help with posture, balance, flexibility, coordination, mind–body connection, and problem solving. Being in the classroom setting, and participating in partner or group work, creates a social environment with peers who understand the difficulty of the disease, which alleviates isolation. Music helps reestablish the natural rhythm of the body, which is lost to the disease. All these factors together help improve confidence, creativity, community, and quality of life. Additionally, the Mark Morris Dance Group holds training workshops for individuals to learn how to teach these classes, and people can become certified in their Dance for PD® method. This program has hosted trainees from countries all over the world, including Ireland, the United Kingdom, India, South Africa, Russia, Italy, Australia, and many more, bringing the healing powers of dance to countless individuals worldwide.

Another distinct dance for health program is at work in Calcutta, India, serving victims of sex trafficking. Kolkata Sanved is an organization led by women that is dedicated to healing and empowering survivors of sex trafficking and other forms of gender-based violence.[6] The founder, Sohini Chakraborty, was inspired to volunteer in shelters after seeing an anti-trafficking poster. When she realized that the girls' treatments lacked focus on the healing of their bodies, she began to fuse her passion for dance into this work. She and other practitioners utilized dance/movement therapy to help victims regain ownership and positive

This is insanely cool to me. These dance classes are healing and a form of support to these people

relationships with their bodies. In the 2017 film documentary *Little Stones*, Chakraborty explains:

> Most of the children who are trafficked into the brothels … first they cut off from their body, the disconnection. They start to hate their body. Work with the body is so important because when the exploitation, the violence, the abuse – anything that's happened, it's a tremendous physical trauma. We really do not have that much tool available to work on the physical trauma.[7]

Dance can have a huge impact on trauma

After years of groundwork, Kolkata Sanved was officially launched in 2004 and has since impacted the lives of tens of thousands of survivors worldwide. Additionally, the organization provides opportunities for survivors to become dance/movement therapists, furthering their goal of enabling women to reach their full potential and live independently. They also aim to establish a Centre of Excellence on Dance Movement Therapy in India and South Asia in order to build more opportunities for survivors in the region.

Dance/movement Therapy → Like art therapy

Dance/movement therapy (DMT) is a modality of creative arts therapy focused on dance and movement as a psychotherapeutic tool. Individuals may become registered (R-DMT) or board certified (BC-DMT) dance/movement therapists after completing specific courses of study and earning a master's degree. A small number of institutions are certified to train DMT practitioners; alternate routes to board certification are available through training with qualified teachers that includes coursework, fieldwork, and an internship. An R-DMT is considered to have completed basic training and is employable as a DMT practitioner, and a BC-DMT is considered to have earned their advanced credentials and may train others in DMT or open a private practice. There is no specific undergraduate degree recommended to pursue a master's program; however, substantial exposure to dance and psychology is recommended, including training in various forms and techniques of dance as well as performance, choreography, and dance pedagogy. Maintaining certification requires continuing education practice, and license to practice in the United States varies from state to state.

BOX 1.5 DANCE PRESCRIPTION

The United Kingdom has initiated the practice of social prescribing. Used to complement, not replace, current medications, social prescriptions assign patients to activities such as music or dance lessons, practicing sports or gardening, and similar ventures. These prescriptions may be given to patients with dementia, psychosis, lung conditions, mental health maladies, or a variety of other conditions.

proof of its actual real benefits

The American Dance Therapy Association (ADTA), founded in 1966, works to support the field of DMT by promoting education, training, practice, and research in the field.[8] The ADTA also holds an annual national conference and publishes the *American Journal of Dance Therapy* twice a year. Its website hosts links to the board certification handbook and lists approved master's programs that meet its Standards for Education and Clinical Practice. The ADTA website can also be used as a source for learning more about DMT, finding dance/movement therapists, and searching job postings in the field.

Dance for health is a growing field that consists of a wide range of techniques suited to the needs of the patients or community. It is a global movement that includes professional teaching artists as well as certified therapists working to serve special populations. Research continues to support the success of dance as a therapeutic activity. As the availability of current programs and the development of new ones continue to expand, millions of people around the globe are able to benefit from the healing power of dance.

THEATRICAL DANCE — *To entertain*

Dance becomes theatrical dancing when the focus is no longer on the needs, desires, and satisfaction of the doer but on those of the viewer. The primary purposes of dance in the Western world today are for socialization and entertainment. **Theatrical dance** is that which is performed for a non-participating audience with the intent to communicate or entertain and is supported by production elements. Theatrical dance may be composed of any dance genre, from ballet to tap dance, hip-hop dance to India's *bharatanatyam*. Choreographers mold these dance genres into stylized movement patterns with added attention given to the theatrical elements of costumes, make-up, lighting, sound, and set design. As a production package, theatrical dance serves a specific role, whether it is to entertain an audience in a commercial or musical setting or express conceptualized stories or ideas in a concert dance setting. Examples of theatrical dance can be seen on the Broadway stage, in Hollywood films, in concert dance companies, performed at theme parks and on cruise ships, and within television shows, commercials, and music videos.

focuses on all the viewer

Let us pause to clarify a couple of these terms as they relate to dance. A **genre** is the broad term used to describe a type of dance. Ballet, modern, jazz, *bharatanatyam*, tap, and Salsa are examples of dance genres. **Style** refers to the way in which a genre of dance is performed. It is the distinct movement characteristics and manner of execution that can be unique to a particular dance style or to an individual's style. Fred Astaire was a famous tap dancer from the mid-twentieth century and synonymous with the movie musical. Chloe Arnold, a contemporary tap dancer, is known for her ensemble of female performers, who often appear in the YouTube videos she produces. When comparing the two as artists, we first notice the use of the tap genre. However, Astaire danced standard tap dance vocabulary with a graceful balletic quality reminiscent of ballroom tap dance. His style incorporated a very

Ex: Genre: Tap
Style: Fred Astaire, broadway tap

erect upper body and fluid arm movements. Arnold is a contemporary tap dancer known for her incorporation of African dance-based movements and percussive pops of sassy flair with the use of her upper body and hips. While she uses many of the same tap dance steps that Astaire used, she executes them with an entirely different style. Another example can be found within the jazz dance genre. Gus Giordano and Bob Fosse were both jazz dance performers and choreographers during the mid- to late twentieth century. Giordano worked primarily in the world of concert jazz dance. His movement style maintained an earthy feel, guided by a use of deep *plié*, or bend of the knees, along with a strong and regal posture of the upper body. In contrast, Fosse performed and choreographed for musical theater productions, both on film and on Broadway. He is known for his sexually suggestive movement style, which includes pronated, or turned in, legs, limp wrists, jutting hip movements, and rolled shoulders. Both individuals choreographed jazz dance but in very distinct and stylized manners.

Theatrical dance is dependent upon attracting and maintaining audiences for its continued success. In a culture where repetition quickly leads to boredom, artists continually push for originality and innovation within choreography and the use of theatrical elements in addition to the frequent restaging of classic works of choreography. Many choreographers will even restage infamous classic works with contemporary perspectives. For example, Matthew Bourne, an English contemporary dance choreographer, is famous for his 1995 rendition of the classical ballet *Swan Lake*, which originally premiered in 1898. Bourne's contemporary version has male dancers cast in all the roles traditionally performed by females.

BOX 1.6 *THE GREEN TABLE*

In Germany in 1932, Kurt Jooss choreographed a dance that would become known as a masterpiece. With a world war looming, Jooss crafted an antiwar-themed dance entitled *The Green Table* for presentation at a ballet competition in the capital city of neighboring France. Jooss was awarded first place for his work, only to find himself a year later fleeing his home in Germany for not removing Jewish members from his company. *The Green Table*, also referred to as "The Dance of Death in Eight Scenes," opens with white male diplomats wearing masks around a rectangular table covered in green. When they pull out guns and shoot into the air, it is clear that war has been declared. The next six scenes convey various aspects of wartime, from separation of loved ones to battle itself to the survivors of the aftermath. Death appears as a character throughout the piece, portrayed as a skeleton, triumphant and hypnotic. The final scene is a return to the original setting with the diplomats, or gentlemen in black as they are known, seated around the table, suggestive of the futile effort of negotiations.

court dance	political dance	syncopation
cyclical ritual	ritual dance	theatrical dance
dance for health	social dance	vernacular dance
dance/movement therapy	specific ritual	
genre	style	

Choreographers have borrowed and continue to borrow from social dance to create culturally engaging and at times historically reflective theatrical productions. Similarly, the themes discussed in the ritual and political sections above often reappear in theatrical dance choreography as well. As mentioned previously, many of the dances that began with a ritual or political purpose have also adapted a theatrical function within their given cultures. Part II provides a deeper exploration of the development of ballet, modern, tap, jazz, and hip-hop dance as the primary theatrical dance genres of the Western world.

CHAPTER SUMMARY

There is great power both in dancing and in watching dance. Whether for the doer or the viewer, dance is an exhilarating art form that reveals much about the performers and their cultures. To some, dance is a way of life. In various cultures, dance plays a central role. In these instances, dance is a part of daily tasks, worship, enjoyment, education, and celebration. In some cultures, dance plays a peripheral role; dance is used for the purpose of social interaction and theatrical entertainment. It is an event that individuals turn to for enjoyment but not one upon which their daily lives are dependent. Dance also serves a healing purpose for some, as many turn to dance for physical and emotional support and healing.

Throughout the ages, dance has developed and evolved. Cultures have exchanged ideas and shared movement, choosing to allow their dance forms to be altered or remain traditional in movement and form. In his book *Let's Dance*, English writer Peter Buckman states, "Dance as release, dance as celebration, dance to portray life, and dance to solemnize death: these themes come down to us from the very beginnings of our society, and are still present, however diluted, in the social dances of our own time."[9] We could also add that these themes are realized in theatrical dance as well. The impulse to move is an instinct within all humans that can be realized in a myriad of ways, at various times, and for differing purposes.

Reflective Prompts

1. Consider your cultural and personal background. How do your cultural beliefs influence your view of dance?
2. Contemplate the reasons why one might dance. Perhaps you considered the use of dance as communication. But what specifically can dance

communicate or express? Do you ever use movement or gestures to communicate to others? If so, how?

3. In what ways have you been exposed to dance? What purpose/s did the dance serve? Were you aware of the purpose at the time?

4. Do you find that dance plays a central or peripheral role in your life? In your society?

5. The Asante people take into consideration an individual's dance skills when electing chiefs. What does this say about the role of dance in their society? How does this differ from the role of dance in Western society? Imagine what it might look like if United States presidential candidates were considered for their dance abilities.

6. Do you believe that men and women should dance differently? Why or why not? If so, how?

7. How can dance provide mental, emotional, or physical healing benefits?

8. Are you familiar with any social dances? Which ones and in what ways? What do you think the current forms of social dance say about today's society?

Movement Prompts

1. **Pair/Group:** Share or demonstrate the social dancing with which you are most familiar or in which you perhaps participate.

2. **Gestural Exploration:** Make a gesture that reflects how you currently feel. Now, turn to someone beside you and perform your gesture again. Did your portrayal of your gesture change? What can you tell about your neighbor from watching their gesture? How could similar exercises be utilized in psychotherapy sessions?

NOTES

1   Roderyk Lange, *The Nature of Dance: An Anthropological Perspective* (New York: International Publications Service, 1976), 48.

2   Gerald Jonas, *Dancing: The Pleasure, Power, and Art of Movement* (New York: Harry Abrams, in Association with Thirteen/WNET, 1998), 10.

3   Jonas, *Dancing*, 109.

4   Julie Malnig, *Ballroom, Boogie, Shimmy Sham, Shake: A Social and Popular Dance Reader* (Chicago: University of Illinois Press, 2009), 4.

5   "Dance for PD® About Us," Mark Morris Dance Group, accessed June 5, 2019, https://danceforparkinsons.org/about-the-program.

6   "About Us," Kolkata Sanved, accessed January 10, 2020, http://kolkatasanved.org/about-us/.

7   *Little Stones*, directed by Sophia Kruz (2017), https://tubitv.com/movies/465904/little_stones?utm_source=google-feed&tracking=google-feed.

8   "Our Mission," American Dance Therapy Association, accessed June 5, 2019, https://adta.org/our-mission/.

9   Peter Buckman, *Let's Dance: Social Ballroom & Folk Dancing* (New York and London: Paddington Press, 1978), 55.

CHAPTER 1 BIBLIOGRAPHY

"About Us." Kolkata Sanved. Accessed January 10, 2020. http://kolkatasanved.org/about-us/.

Buckman, Peter. *Let's Dance: Social Ballroom & Folk Dancing.* New York and London: Paddington Press, 1978.

Cass, Joan. *Dancing through History.* Englewood Cliffs, NJ: Prentice-Hall, 1993.

Cheney, Sheldon. *Three Thousand Years of Drama, Acting and Stagecraft.* New York: Tudor Publishing, 1929. Quoted in Richard Kraus, *History of Dance in Art and Education.* Englewood Cliffs, NJ: Prentice-Hall, 1969.

"Dance for PD® About Us." Mark Morris Dance Group. Accessed June 5, 2019. https://danceforparkinsons.org/about-the-program.

Inoura, Yoshinobu and Toshio Kawatake. *The Traditional Theater of Japan.* New York: Weather Hill, 1981.

Jonas, Gerald. *Dancing: The Pleasure, Power, and Art of Movement.* New York City: Harry N. Abrams, 1992.

Kassing, Gayle. *History of Dance: An Interactive Arts Approach.* Champaign, IL: Human Kinetics, 2007.

Kraus, Richard. *History of the Dance in Art and Education.* Englewood Cliffs, NJ: Prentice-Hall, 1969.

Lange, Roderyk. *The Nature of Dance: An Anthropological Perspective.* New York: International Publications Service, 1976.

Lee, Carol. *Ballet in Western Culture: A History of Its Origins and Evolution.* New York and London: Routledge, 2002.

Little Stones. Directed by Sophia Kruz. 2017. https://tubitv.com/movies/465904/little_stones?utm_source=google-feed&tracking=google-feed.

Malnig, Julie. *Ballroom, Boogie, Shimmy Sham, Shake: A Social and Popular Dance Reader.* Chicago: University of Illinois Press, 2009.

Nadel, Myron Howard and Marc Raymond Strauss. *The Dance Experience: Insights into History, Culture and Creativity,* 2nd ed. Highstown, NJ: Princeton Book Company, 2003.

"Our Mission." American Dance Therapy Association. Accessed June 5, 2019. https://adta.org/our-mission/.

2 Viewing Dance Through a Cultural Lens

All dance is cultural. Regardless of the genre or its geographic location, each dance form is shaped by a certain group of people within a specific environment and influenced by particular social, political, and economic factors. In addition, the group's behaviors, characteristics, perspectives, and aesthetics contribute to the development of the dance. As a result, all dance can be viewed through a cultural lens. In recent decades, the study of dance as a means of discovering insight into a culture has gained traction. The field of ethnochoreology, also known by some as dance anthropology or dance ethnology, has emerged, generating an opportunity for researchers not only to discover and share information about world cultures, including the dance forms that they practice, but also to foster awareness and celebration of and respect for human differences. Ethnochoreology is the scientific study of dance that encompasses other disciplines, such as anthropology, musicology, and ethnography, not only to focus on the dance content but also to reveal the social and cultural relationships. In this role, one studies the movement of a community and simultaneously considers the social and cultural context from which the movement derives. Dance, or, at a more basic level, structured movement of the human body, provides the power not only for humans to communicate but also to demonstrate our innate differences and provide a means for uncovering our cultural roots.

Dance anthropologists work to reveal how societies work and function, uncovering societal values and structures and highlighting the aspects that make them unique. They aim to foster a shared respect for humankind's many similarities and exciting differences. The research that they collect from a given group's dance forms helps us to develop an understanding and acceptance of the distinctions in lifestyles from one culture to the next, generating tolerance for cultural differences. When we view dance through a cultural lens, it is important that we release ourselves from our own biases and preconceptions about why people should move or in what ways it might be appropriate for individuals to move. We do not want to superimpose our own opinions of what dance should or should not be onto what we see. It would be unfair to place our own values and beliefs of what is appropriate, acceptable, aesthetically favorable, or valued onto a dance form when we know nothing of its cultural context. Rather, we should view the dance with an open mind and consider the social and historical context from which the dance form is derived rather than the context of our own lives and culture.

There is a rich wealth of knowledge that can be garnered through the exposure to and study of another culture's dance forms. As we observe and consider the ways in which a group dances, we uncover purpose and meaning behind the group's daily life. We witness religion expressed, politics at play, social classes delineated, and communal behaviors and attitudes displayed. We learn about social customs and styles of dress. The role that dance plays within that community is revealed. If one has only been exposed to dance within a Western setting, then one may be surprised by the movement type, musical accompaniment, costumes, use of the voice, and overall pacing of a traditional Turkish performance. Subject matter and storylines may be confusing when one is not familiar with the history or religion of a given group or culture. The plot of a performance, the theatrical elements or lack thereof, or even the movements themselves may not seem logical without cultural understanding or awareness. It is also important to recognize that these dance forms are each well developed and refined. They are challenging and require rigorous training to master.

As we observe various dance forms throughout the world, it is also helpful to realize that the Western use of the term "dance" is distinct from its usage within other parts of the world. In Western society, theater, dance, and music may, and often do, appear as three separate art forms. One goes to see a play where spoken word is the medium in which a story or theme is communicated; one attends a dance concert wherein movement is the vehicle for the subject matter to be conveyed; and one goes to the symphony to listen to music. With the exception of the musical theater genre, it is rare in Western art that spoken word, dance, and song are intertwined and given equal emphasis within a single production. Yet, in many other areas of the world, dance is not separated from the art of speech and song. For example, *kathakali* is a classical Indian dance drama that incorporates spoken word, music, acting, and dance. The movement is not separate from the acting; the dance is not separate from the theater.

Cultural beliefs affect how one might dance as well as why one might dance. As we look at the reasons why a group or individual dances, it is important to recognize that as the world has aged and developed, cultures have collided with one another, both borrowing from and exchanging ideas with one another. The result has been an ever-changing, ever-evolving form of dynamic movement. This chapter examines the relationship between dance and culture. Select dance forms from around the globe highlight the relationship between a culture's religion, politics, and/or social views and the resulting dance forms that developed. Rather than asking why people dance, consider the question presented by author and senior editor of *Journal for the Anthropological Study of Human Movement* Drid Williams, "What are (some group of) people *doing* (thinking, conceptualizing, etc.) when they dance?"[1]

As you read about the historical, socio-political, and economic contexts in which these dances evolved, consider what the movement and performance of each reveals about the culture. How can we observe dance with an open mind, remaining sensitive and empathetic, cultivating respect and appreciation for our unique cultural and personal differences?

BHARATANATYAM: A DANCE OF DEVOTION

The soft sound of south Indian music fills the performance space as the female soloist begins to move; she half glides, half scurries in a curved path across the stage. Ankle bracelets constructed of bells jingle as she shifts to the right and then to the left before pausing center stage with knees bent and one heel raised. Her arms are lifted in a precise angular position as if posed mid-gesture. While her stance is striking, it is her expression that the audience notices. Her well-defined eyes sharply glance up and then to the right with a playful intensity. They continue to dart in specific directions and patterns, performing a dance all their own until the body once again joins back in the movement. The gestures of the hands and stamps of the feet complement the abrupt changes in body level as the dancer lunges and drops low to the ground, only to later quickly spring into the air and then return to intricate footwork. These movements flow together in rhythmical sequence, creating a visually and aurally exhilarating work of art.

BOX 2.1 CARNATIC MUSIC

Carnatic music is the name used for the south Indian music that developed during the sixteenth century and accompanies *bharatanatyam* performance. Its compositions are intended to be vocalized even when instrumentation is involved. Instrumentation often includes flutes, stringed instruments such as the violin, a drone instrument called a *tambura*, and drums. The *mridanga* (drum) remains the only instrument that has not been influenced by the West. The guru, or teacher, serves as both singer and leader of the orchestra, which plays nearly constantly throughout the performance, offering little rest for the musicians or the dancer.

— Ritual dance

This is the classical Indian dance **bharatanatyam**, developed between 500 BC and 500 AD in the southern Indian region of Tamil Nadu. This solo art form began as a temple dance performed by a *devadasi*, or female servant of god, as part of her ritual duties within the temple. Young girls were either born into the *devadasi* tradition or offered by their families to serve the temple. Their training, which included learning the movement and technique as well as study of the Sanskrit texts, began at a young age and was led by a male *nattuvatar*, or guru.

Legit education for it

The young girl typically completed her training by the time she reached puberty and was then fully prepared to fulfill all temple duties.

All classical dance in India is religious in scope and tied to Hinduism and mythology. Whether it is folk or classical dance, it is rooted in worship.[2] Within Hinduism, there is belief in one supreme god, which is then manifested through the trinity of three gods. Dance in India is a vehicle through which the divine powers of the gods can be expressed and demonstrated. Maintaining the viewpoint that the gods are divine superhumans, individuals dance as a form of devotion to the gods. The intention, then, in *bharatanatyam* is that of spiritual expression. The thematic content of *bharatanatyam* stems from Hindu poetry, legends, and mythology. While the dancer aims to ascend to the level of the gods, it is also the desire of the dancer to draw the spectator into the performance. In this sense, the performer and the spectator experience the dance. The dancer seamlessly transitions between portrayal of mortal and deity during a performance. *Bharatanatyam* encompasses not just dance but also music, drama, and poetry.

The goal in classical Indian dance is to incite an aesthetic, spiritual, and emotional response initiated through the performers and experienced by the spectator. This is known as the **rasa theory**. *Rasa* is translated as taste or flavor.[3] This is a highly abstract concept; in performance, it encompasses the essence of the emotions that are felt by both performers and spectators. *Rasa* is an experience that is felt rather than seen. Reliant upon the dynamic between performer and spectator, *rasa* cannot be achieved without participation by the spectator.

The performance of *bharatanatyam* remained a temple ritual from the sixteenth to the twentieth century; however, during British rule (1858–1947), the *devadasis* began to perform within the royal courts. While they were still considered temple servants and resided in the temple, they would also be brought to the courts of princes to perform and even into the homes of the rich. *Devadasis* could obtain a courtesan-like status through liaisons with upper-class male patrons. Although a *devadasi* lived independently from a patron, she could still enjoy a wealthy lifestyle.

Naturally, once the dance was removed from the temple and placed within a different context, its original meaning slowly became lost. The sensual aspects of the dance, which were originally about the whole-body devotion to the gods, transposed to new imaginations. By the nineteenth century, a negative connotation was placed upon the dance, and performers were often referred to as dancing prostitutes. Social and moral reformers initiated campaigns to rid society of temple dancers and their culture. The British colony, which occupied India at the turn of the twentieth century, viewed the culture and religion of India as "backward, driven by superstition and blind faith."[4] The political powers disregarded the classical dances, and temple dancing was banned. As a result, *bharatanatyam* as an art form declined until reformers, such as E. Krishna Iyer and Rukmini Devi, fought to revitalize the traditional culture, restore the classical dances,

SO SAD!
-A once ritual dance was corrupted by uneducated outsiders

2.1
Photo depicts
a traditional
bharatanatyam
dancer.
Dmitry Rukhlenko/
Shutterstock

and bring integrity back to the traditional art forms. *Bharatanatyam* remains rooted in tradition and the culture of India, yet it has become commercialized and Westernized in many ways, as it is now often performed on the proscenium stage and incorporates many of the theatrical elements used within Western stage productions.

BOX 2.2 *NATYASASTRA*

The *Natyasastra* is an ancient Sanskrit treatise, or text, that both describes and prescribes theater in theory and practice. Sanskrit is the ancient language of India and is used within Hindu-based manuscripts and epic poems. The *Natyasastra* is believed to have been written between 3 BC and 5 AD by the sage Bharata. The story is told that the dance was revealed to Bharata by the Lord Brahma, and he then codified the information and recorded it as the *Natyasastra*, also known as the Fifth Veda or Holy Book. This undisputed and highly recognized work serves as the final authority on dance, theater, and music. Within its thirty-six chapters are 6,000 poetic verses that specify the minute details of not only the movements themselves but the music, costumes, make-up, performance space, performance order, and so on.[5]

Insanely cool

Traditionally a solo dance performed by a female, this highly rhythmical art form features movements that are smooth and fluid as well as subtly percussive. The dancer moves through traditional poses of the body, called **karanas**, which often incorporate the legs bent at an angle and the feet pointed outward. The arms and hands move through stylized and flowing gestures, known as **mudras**, that are used to convey very distinct meanings. Dancers learn these detailed single-hand and two-hand mudras, which require flexibility of the joints and control of the intrinsic muscles of the hands. The complex rhythms executed in song and dance are accented by foot beats known as *jatis*, which are made as the soles of the feet, the toes, or the heels strike the floor.[6] The rhythms of the movements are enhanced by the sound of the bells placed around the ankles.

The body positions, gestures, and foot rhythms are accompanied by strong expressions of the face, specifically through movement of the eyes. Exhaustive practice is required of the performer in order to control the finite muscles of the face in executing the exact expression of the cheek, lip, eyebrow, eyelid, nose, chin, and so on.

Big use of specific face expressions

The visual aesthetic of the dance is enhanced by the distinctive costumes and body decorations, which are inherent within all classical Indian dance forms. The female *bharatanatyam* dancer traditionally wears a silk sari draped around her torso and bound with a sash. Beneath the sari, she wears loose pantaloons. The hair is woven into a long braid, and a beaded pendant is placed around the head with a jewel that hangs at the middle of the forehead. Extensive use of jewelry includes bracelets, necklaces, earrings, and a nose ring. Make-up includes heavy black eyeliner that helps to accent the movement of the eyes. Additional body decorations include the signature marks made of a red turmeric powder called *kumkum*. These marks include the red dot that is placed in the center of the forehead. This mark, also known as a *bindi*, is traditionally worn by brides and females on other joyous occasions.[7] The palms of the hand are painted red, and the fingertips are dipped entirely in red. Finally, the soles and rims of the feet are painted red, which creates the effect that the dancer is wearing red slippers, although she remains barefoot.

Classical Indian dance is divided into three types: *nritta*, *nritya*, and *natya*. *Nritta* is dance that is based solely on the beauty of the movement and is void of specific meaning. Here, focus is given to the patterns and movements executed by the body in space. This form is abstract, lacking in narrative, and considered pure dance. In the *nritya* portions of dance, specific meaning is conveyed through the gestures of the hands, glances of the eyes, actions of the feet, and postures of the body.[8] The **natya** portions of dance include spoken word, movement, song, and scenery. Essentially, the *natya* aspect is a combination of all the elements that create the dramatic performance.[9] While the Western world requires two separate words, theater and dance, Indian culture utilizes the single word *natya* to convey the same aspect of performance.

During the mid-twentieth century, *bharatanatyam* performance transitioned from temples and courts to other performance spaces, including the proscenium stage. Traditionally, a *bharatanatyam* performance lasted three to four hours. Today, a performance is approximately two and a half hours in length and follows a codified structure. From the eighteenth to the mid-twentieth century, India was subject to British control, yet it regained independence in 1947. Along with the quest for independence came a movement by society to reclaim the country's national identity. Inherently, this mission produced a cultural renaissance during the mid-twentieth century where the once scorned arts in India, including *bharatanatyam*, were reborn and celebrated. *Bharatanatyam* is an art form well over 2,000 years in age. Although its primary ideals have remained intact, its method of presentation has altered over time to fit its surrounding and changing cultural conditions and artistic notions.

KABUKI: FROM COMMONERS TO CULTURAL TREASURE

As an actor slowly makes his way to the stage via the footbridge extending past the audience, a voice from the audience can be heard shouting out the actor's name. The performance continues while the sound of traditional Japanese music fills the air. Performers wear elaborate floor-length costumes and wigs with thickly applied make-up that appears mask-like upon their faces and necks. Their stylized movements weave between moments of pure dance and those of exaggerated acting. A true dance drama, the singing and dancing of kabuki mesmerizes all in attendance.

As is the case with most classical dance forms, a shift occurs during the dance's history, elevating the dance to a greater level of respect. Regardless of whether these dance forms throughout the world began among the lower or the upper classes, most made their way to the aristocratic level before being declared classical art forms within a country. **Kabuki**, the great Japanese dance drama, is no exception. For nearly 250 years following its first appearance, *kabuki* was regarded with a high level of disdain among Japanese rulers and upper social classes. When *kabuki* began as a popular theatrical form in the late sixteenth century, it included a mixture of acting styles yet lacked a specific format. It began among the lower classes and was considered, at times, to be abrasive and sensational, lewd and vulgar. *Kabuki* was a reflection of the tastes of the common people, and during its early history, often found itself connected to prostitution. *Kabuki* eventually fell under aristocratic control and was later deemed a classical Japanese art form. Within *kabuki,* the image of female beauty is depicted on the Japanese stage through dance, music, and drama. With the use of elaborate costumes, make-up, and scenery, along with stylized gestures and movement, *kabuki* is a theatrical spectacle.

Its interesting to me the amount of dances that at one point or another were tied to Prostitution

The first performance of *kabuki* is believed to have occurred in 1596 at a shrine in Kyoto. In a dry riverbed, a woman named Okuni performed an entertaining and suggestive dance, which quickly became popular among commoners. Okuni caused a stir by borrowing from the age-old art forms of Japanese dance and using their elements in new ways. The new dance drama of *kabuki* quickly emerged among the commoners as an entertaining spectacle that provided an opportunity for those within varying social classes to intermingle. Actors were among the lower classes, yet audiences from various positions on the social ladder visited the theater and joined the ranks of the rowdy audience. Prostitution crept into the *kabuki* theater and would soon set the path for government control of the art. As women enjoyed the income that accompanied their performance roles, they also began to develop a sense of control and power. Concerns for the welfare of the patriarchal society as well as public morality led to the banning of women from the stage by the government in 1629. Following the ban, young boys took up the performance roles so that *kabuki* plays could

2.2
A *kabuki* play is performed at the Japan Society in New York.
Linda Vartoogian/ Getty Images

continue. As fears of homosexuality emerged within the theater, the government stepped in again in 1652, declaring that only adult males could perform *kabuki*. Today, all roles within *kabuki* continue to be played by adult males.

During the seventeenth and eighteenth centuries, the reigning Tokugawa Shogunate, the military family in power, closed Japan's borders in order to isolate the country from foreign influence. The shogun control relied on moral and civil conformity. To achieve this, a four-tier social caste system was created, to which extreme obedience was demanded. The isolation of the country from the outside world, combined with the strict social order, helped to keep peace within the country for more than 250 years. The land-owning feudal lords and samurai warriors were placed at the top of the social ladder. *Kabuki* performers found themselves below the lowest portion of the social ladder.

Under the control of the shogunate, the theater as a whole was manipulated through the decree of a succession of laws. In addition to bans on who could perform, the government, fearing the increased risk of immorality and social disruption, restricted *kabuki* performers to both live and work only within a specified theater district. In the 1700s, the shogun required individuals to legally register themselves as actors of particular role types. Additional laws mandated that subject matter of plays could not be comprised of contemporary historical or social matters, although material prior to 1603, the start of the Edo Period, could be used. As you can imagine, actors found ways to circumvent this law and discreetly refer to current political issues.

The adherence to social order carried over to the theater. *Kabuki* is a hereditary art form, in that actors are either born or adopted into a theater family. Families maintain theater schools, where the familial lineage is highly regarded. Each school is controlled by a family head, or *iemoto*. Young dancers learn by imitating their instructors, who are most likely relatives. While individuals may start performing at a young age, they are only considered professional once they reach middle age and can demonstrate the maturity and true expression of a character. The name of the family head is often passed down through the generations to deserving actors. The stage placement of the actor is often determined not by his character in the play but, rather, by his social place within the school.

From the beginning, *kabuki* was mainly dance, although it soon came to incorporate musical accompaniment, song, and word. Borrowing from folk and popular dance as well as the traditional Japanese dance form of *noh*, *kabuki* movements and gestures communicate meaning in a theatrical manner. Within *kabuki*, it is general practice that movement and speaking will not happen at the same time but will, rather, occur sequentially within the play. Ensemble work is not seen on the stage as it is in Western theater. While two actors may appear in a scene together, they do not work together. Their spoken lines, which do not interact, are executed as separate actions. It is evident that in all *kabuki* plays the performer is really only a performer, regardless of experience and performance level. The audience may believe in an actor's portrayal of a character yet will see that the actor never actually cries, or he may pause to take a drink before

WILD that the discriminatory bans stuck leaving males to perform still!

Why does the govt. feel its neccessary to control it so much?

continuing his performance, thus breaking the continuity of his performance. Regardless, the performer, and not the play, is the focus in *kabuki*.

The sensual and stylized movements of *kabuki* are fluid and graceful and feature moments of static poses. In these moments, dancers remain still in a dramatic pose through which significant meaning and expression are conveyed. The movement often culminates in a codified posture, or **mie**, that the dancer will strike at a climactic moment in the performance. Here, the actor will wind up into a movement then suddenly freeze in a powerful pose; the action ceases for several seconds before the movement gradually resumes. The effect becomes a pictorial dance, a tableau of poses that the actors move through, which are visually stunning and arresting. Movement in *kabuki* is specific and directed from the waist down. The cotton socks worn on the actor's feet and the floor-length costumes that hide the feet allow the performer to appear to glide across the floor. *Kabuki* adopted and further stylized the walk found in another form of Japanese dance called *noh*, in which the feet slide along the floor creating a fluid, gliding effect. Various stylizations of the walk are then used by different character roles within *kabuki*, from the elite samurai to the feminine **onnagata**, or female impersonator. For example, the *onnagata* wears platform shoes and learns to walk by placing a sheet of paper between the knees. This causes the feet to turn in slightly and the shoulders to sway as the elbows are held close to the body.[10]

This art form makes use of elaborate make-up, costumes, and wigs. Costumes are reflective of the character role. Female roles were given to actors who were older and considered more mature in their acting abilities; thus, the art of *onnagata* emerged. Today, performance of *kabuki* by women, although no longer banned, is not preferred, as it provides too much reality within the play.

By the end of the 1600s, it had become common practice for actors to wear a wig; these, along with the numerous styles of costume, help to depict character styles and serve as an acting technique. In many plays, a character's real identity is not revealed until later in the play, thus requiring a transformation to occur. An actor can quickly transform onstage into a new character or into an evolved character by the removal of one robe to reveal a new one or by quickly changing the wig. While masks are not used in *kabuki* plays, the make-up worn by the actors may appear mask-like. Japanese culture has considered light skin representative of the upper class. Actors who depict upper-class characters apply a base of white make-up. The actors playing the roles of lower-class characters wear make-up that is darker in color.

Kabuki performances typically occur on a wide, proscenium stage, which is shared by performers, narrators, and musicians. The auditorium is rectangular in shape and features balcony seating areas on three sides. Along the auditorium lies a raised runway that connects the back of the auditorium to the left side of the stage. This passageway is called the *hanamichi*, literally "flower way," and is used by the actors as both an entrance and an exit as well as an added performance space.[11] As a result, spectators must turn their heads throughout the course of the performance in order to follow the actor as he enters and exits. The use of the *hanamichi* helps to provide an intimate connection between actor and spectator, as it allows the actor to come into close proximity with the spectator. *Kabuki* performances are designed in such a manner that the audience feels closely connected to the performers. The staging, the lighting, and the acting itself all contribute to this intimate feeling. The close connection between actor and audience continues to extend beyond the staging logistic of plays. Dating back to its inception, there has been a fascination with the lives of the actors. Audiences become enamored with certain actors; they are stars. Actors are known for their acting abilities, but more so for their lineages and appearances.

Within *kabuki* theater, the revolving stage, which allows multi-scene plays to occur through seamless scenic transitions, and trap doors, which enable performers or props to rise up or be lowered from the stage, provide dramatic visual effects. Yet, no matter how impressively the stage is designed or the dramatic effect that results from the use of the stage machinery, the scenic component must never take precedence over the actor.

Kabuki plays provide a popular form of entertainment within an informal setting. The programs create a jubilant social affair, as spectators enjoy purchased food and drink and often leave their seats to visit with one another. Lighting in the audience is not dimmed during the performance, which helps facilitate the social aspect of the program. Furthermore, the audience is not required to remain quiet during the performance and will often energetically shout out to the performers. By calling out the performers' names at appropriately timed moments during the performance, an audience member is conveying support and respect for the performers.

Kabuki is an enduring traditional Japanese dance that includes dance, music, and text. Social order and hierarchy are inherent within its structure, while its performance format encourages a social affair among audience members. Centered around spectacle, *kabuki* is ostentatious and stylized. Dance is central within the acting techniques of the performers and within the performance itself. Although its development fell under governmental control, *kabuki* has remained an art form closely connected to the people.

DAMA: SACRED RITES

Anticipation fills the atmosphere of the village square. The pounding rhythms of drums and cowbells ricochet through the air as a kaleidoscope of masks spiral in the dance arena. Dramatically striking, the variety of masks represent different animals and humans. These masks draw energy from the spirits of the deceased community leaders whom they are honoring. Brightly colored fiber skirts and accessories rustle as the performers strut, pound, whirl, and prance, embodying their masks in this sacred ritual to usher the souls of their elders into the spiritual realm.

The Dogon people live in the Bandigiara Cliff region in present-day Republic of Mali in West Africa. Their religion is rooted in three gods – *Amma*, the sky

2.3
Kanaga masked dancers in preparation to perform. Universal Images Group North America LLC/ DeAgostini/Alamy Stock Photo

god and creator of all; *Nommo*, the water god; and *Lebe*, the serpent god – and the *nyama*, or life force. The Dogon believe that the *nyama* is released from an individual at the precise moment of death, so they have strict funeral rites that they follow in order to prevent negative effects of death harming the village. The Dogon funeral consists of three phases: the cliff burial for each individual death; *nyû yana*, an annual ritual honoring all who have died; and *dama*, which features numerous specialized masked dances. For the Dogon, these rites are critical in order to protect the living from wandering *nyama* and to properly guide this life force to the next world.

This **dama** portion is a collective funeral ceremony usually performed about once every twelve years and serves to honor important men in the community, such as Hogons – the elder spiritual leaders for Dogon villages – or other important male elders. The Dogon carry out this ritual in order to guide the souls of the deceased into the spiritual world. This greatly aids the community, as the *nyama* is no longer a threat, and the deceased move to the rank of ancestor, which allows them to be conduits of communication between the supreme god *Amma* and the living. The *dama* ceremony lasts one week and requires special preparations done in secret by the **awa**, or masking society. The *awa* is exclusive to men of the community who have undergone the initiation process. *Dama* preparations are carried out in secret far away from the village to avoid unauthorized eyes. Blacksmiths carve new masks and paint old masks to be reused. Both the dancers and drummers must rehearse heavily, though secretly, in the cliffs.

Èmna refers to the masks of the *dama* ceremony, which are associated with the realm of death. For this reason, the *èmna* are considered a threat to fertility, so women can only view them from a distance and must have no involvement

very interesting!

with them. Around fifty masks or more participate in any one *dama* and include a variety of humans and animals important to the Dogon culture, such as hunters, reptiles, and birds. The masks help protect the village from negative effects of wandering *nyama*. Though the masks differ greatly, the rest of the costuming is more or less uniform. Besides their unique masks, *èmna* performers wear hoods to cover the backs of their heads and necks, a bra-like top decorated with white cowry shells, and brightly colored fiber skirts with loose cotton trousers underneath. Additional costuming includes colorful fiber armbands on the arms and wrists as well as brightly dyed hibiscus flowers, which may be used to frame the mask.

(handwritten margin note: Protect from negative effects, also praise funeral, → a Ritual dance)

The highlight of the first public performance of *dama* is the grand entrance of the *èmna* performers with energetic dancing. People from other villages come to view the spectacle, and women and children watch from afar. Drums and cowbells accompany the *èmna* as they dance into the public square, charged with the *nyama* in the masks. Each performer circles the *dani* – or dance pole placed in the center of the village's public square – counterclockwise three times before sitting around the arena in groups of their mask types waiting for their turn to perform their unique dances. Let us explore three examples.

The *tingetange* mask is one of the most physically difficult roles to perform and requires years of practice to dance on the tall stilts. The *tingetange* mask represents water birds – which the Dogon believe help keep evil spirits away from villages by flying over them at night – and also features human female characteristics. Instead of wearing heavy wooden masks, these elegant *èmnas'* faces are covered by black cloth flaps embroidered with cowry shells. Stilts emulate the water bird, while a bra of two jutting breasts made of dried baobab fruits imitate the female role. These *èmna* carry themselves regally as they use the strength in their legs to drive the stilts high in the air and prod the ground while shaking flywhisks in their hands. The towering figures weave in and out of each other as they flock together, turning their heads right and left to display their beauty. After an impressive display of strength and balance, the *tingetange* masks exit haughtily to make way for the next *èmna*.

The *kanaga* mask also represents birds, though with a deeper spiritual meaning. The mask itself features a vertical piece of wood with two parallel blades crossing it perpendicularly, one at the top and the other at the bottom. On the horizontal blades, two small wood pieces point down from the lower blade and point up from the upper blade. This intricate design symbolizes the connection of the spiritual world in the heavens with the physical world on earth. This performance features energetic upper body movements and slashes to the ground. In unison, these *èmna* circle the torso and head backward to gain momentum before launching forward to swipe the headpiece against the ground and then quickly return upright. As the large group repeats this swooping movement together, it creates a mesmerizing sound and stirs the dust from the ground. This incredible display symbolizes the journey between the realms of heaven and earth while ushering disembodied spirits toward the spirit world.

The *lebe* mask represents the snake god and is a large rectangular box with two carved eyes. Remarkably, this mask features a soaring wooden plank, sometimes nearly fifteen feet high, that is decorated with geometrical patterns of parallel and zigzagging lines and triangles. Some villages call this mask the *sirige*, which means "storied house."[12] The heavy headpiece is secured by the dancer biting into a wooden mouth grip hidden in the mask and with a tie in the back connecting to a belt. Meanings behind the geometrical decorations include the different stages of creation and degrees severing earth from the sky. The most experienced men bear this *èmna*. The defining moment of the performance of the *lebe* mask is when the *èmna* genuflect to the four cardinal points and bend forward to touch the earth with the headpiece before arching the back to touch the headpiece to the ground behind them, which requires unbelievable core and back strength and balance by the performer. This dazzling feat symbolizes bowing to all the individuals who have passed away and the link between the spiritual and human worlds.

No kidding!

Many other masks are utilized for a variety of purposes, including crowd control – making sure observers do not get too close to the *èmna*. For several more days, the masked *èmna* continue to perform in the public square as well as on the rooftops of the deceased. *Dama* concludes with all the *èmna* gathering in a "massive spectacle of dance."[13] The *tingetange* masks flock to the center on their stilts as the rest of the *èmna* spiral around them. The Dogon celebrate a successful *dama* as the souls of the dead have been led on to the spiritual world, where they rise to the role of ancestors. Benefits of a successful ceremony include plentiful crops, fertile women, and harmony within society.

very long ceremony

Unfortunately, European control and the conversion of many people to Islam and Christianity have done damage to the Dogon culture. Various regions of the Dogon are not permitted to have a Hogon leader, while others may not perform the masked dances, which does not allow younger generations to learn the *awa*'s place in the Dogon community. However, there are instances of *èmna* performing masked dances for tourists. Masks carved for these entertainment purposes do not undergo the same sacred rituals as those put to use for a real *dama*. Embracing the market of tourists has become necessary for survival in the modern world. Even though it has been taken out of context, some parts of the Dogon tradition still survive.

This is Rlly sad

LINDY HOP: BREAKING CULTURAL BOUNDARIES

In the late 1920s, segregation was rampant across the United States within schools, businesses, and entertainment venues. Ballrooms and nightclubs were popular hubs of entertainment for musicians and dancers alike. Frequented regularly by the public, these venues championed a social night-life that promoted live music, dancing, and a spirited social atmosphere for all in attendance. Many of these establishments only allowed individuals of a certain race to enter as performers or guests, while others offered separate sections for African Americans. The Savoy Ballroom, which opened in New York City's Harlem in 1926, was owned and operated by two white American businessmen, Moe Gale and Jay Faggen. Often referred to as "The Home of Happy Feet," the Savoy Ballroom became known for its interracial dancing and entertainment. Attracting locals and tourists, this upscale ballroom was considered to be more dignified than the other ballrooms and nightclubs at the time, due in part to its lavish and high-quality decorations, emphasis on etiquette, and overall size. The elongated, oval-shaped dancefloor was referred to as "the Track" and accommodated a band at either end. The bands would rotate playing throughout the night, allowing non-stop music, seven nights a week. Some of the best-known musicians played at the Savoy, including Duke Ellington, Count Basie, and Ella Fitzgerald. A host of social dances became famous at the Savoy Ballroom, including the Lindy Hop.

cool!

BOX 2.3 LINDY HOP: LEGEND HAS IT...

During the late 1920s and 1930s, dance marathons were a popular form of entertainment. As the name implies, contestants would dance until they dropped in the hopes of being the last dancer standing and winning a cash prize. It is rumored that the Lindy Hop was named during a dance marathon in 1927, the same year that Charles Lindbergh dared to "hop" across the Atlantic Ocean by becoming the first person ever to fly solo from New York to Paris. A sensational dancer named George "Shorty" Snowden performed some inventive moves near the end of the marathon. When he was asked by a reporter what they were called, his quick response of "the Lindy Hop" stuck, and a dance was born.

The **Lindy Hop**, which was first popular during the end of the 1920s and through the 1930s, was preceded by dances such as the Charleston and Black Bottom, along with the various social dances of the 1910s, known as the animal dances, all stemming from the African American vernacular dance tradition. As a result, it is an innately rhythmical, improvisational, and social dance form. The Lindy Hop is an eight-count dance that is executed at a fast pace and relies heavily on proper weight change between the feet. The Lindy Hop is known for its wild and frenetic movements, complete with kicks of the legs and bouncing steps of the feet, often contrasted with moments of cool sophistication and composure. Although the dance can appear chaotic at times, dancers find a challenge in smoothly executing the rhythmical and fast-paced movements. A key feature of the dance is found in its **breakaway**, or swing-out moments, where dance partners separate to individually improvise their own rhythmically charged moments of spontaneous movement. The breakaway, which allows partners to stretch away from one another, provided the dancers a freedom unknown to them in previous social partner dances.

lots of imbedded culture

2.4
A couple participate in a Lindy Hop competition at the Savoy Ballroom. Photo by George Karger/Pix Inc./ The LIFE Images Collection via Getty Images/ Getty Images

The energy of the Lindy Hop drew in participants and spectators alike. The free-spirited sensation of kicking the legs, twirling, side stepping, propelling through the air, and creating one's own path on the dance floor drove dancers to continue their efforts to challenge one another and share in the communal joy on the dance floor. At the same time, spectators could not help but feel the energy and vitality of the dancers. Within the walls of the Savoy, a community was created that knew no boundary of color. During a time period where segregation was present in everyday life, the Lindy Hop became a dance that burst racial barriers. Enjoyed by the masses, the dance brought people together in spite of their social differences; everyone on the dance floor could become united together in the rhythms and steps of a single dance, enjoying the power and freedom of the movement. As the United States drifted into the Great Depression of the 1930s, swing music and dance provided an escape for all Americans. Individuals traveled from near and far to visit "the Track," diverting their attention for the evening and sharing joy on the dancefloor.

Cultural historian Julie Malnig points out an additional cultural effect of the Lindy Hop. Not only did the dance help to break down racial barriers, but it also redefined gender relations within partner social dancing. Historically, European partner-dancing had maintained traditional roles of leader and follower inherent within ballroom dance. However, the Lindy Hop disregarded these roles, as dancers would continuously breakaway from one other and independently and rhythmically maintain their own movement before drawing back together. The

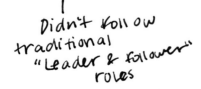

Didn't follow traditional "Leader & follower" roles

40 □

breakaway created a reciprocal dynamic between partners and demonstrated equality among dancers.

Through such mutually assertive roles of independently and jointly sustaining a combined interactive rhythmic response to swing music, the new Lindy Hoppers made a major contribution to transforming the way these dancing African Americans not only saw each other but also how other blacks and whites perceived them.[14]

CHAPTER SUMMARY

We are reminded that all dance is cultural dance. Through the research and shared findings of dance anthropologists and ethnologists, we can uncover meaning about the daily lives, behaviors, and cultural values of a given society. The ways in which socioeconomic and political factors have shaped cultures are reflected in the movement patterns and dances of a community. We have observed examples of how dance can serve a physical and visual depiction of a group's religious beliefs, political underpinnings, communal beliefs, and/or social structure.

Bharatanatyam, a south Indian classical dance, began as a ritual temple dance performed by female servants within the temple. Although the dance form has since been taken out of the temple setting and theatricalized, it continues to reflect its original intention of spiritual devotion. The importance of the Hindu influence within the culture is visible within each movement, which is deliberately and specifically crafted to convey a spiritual message and connection. *Kabuki* performances reveal the social hierarchy historically present within Japanese culture and bring awareness of how governmental control can affect the development of an art form. Within the Dogon community, the *dama* ceremony provides a means for dance to unite the community together through a funeral ritual ceremony. The viewer witnesses the group's emphasis on the use of masks to convey spiritual connection and meaning within the ceremony. Finally, the Lindy Hop demonstrated how a single dance can break racial barriers and work in opposition to the views and social behaviors of a group of people.

The dance forms discussed within this chapter serve as examples of how viewing dance through a cultural lens can foster a sense of appreciation for a given culture. As we observe the dance of a group of people, it is important that we do so with an open mind. It may be easy to watch a culture's dance with our own expectations, standards, and assumptions, but these biases will have ill effects on our understandings not only of the dance but also of the culture and the individual people. Just as dance anthropologists and ethnologists seek to learn about world cultures through the study of a group's structured human movement, we can also begin to better understand the world around us when we adjust the lens through which we view the world, including the dances that

all these dances have WAY more meanings & effects than you'd think!

awa	ethnochoreology	mudras
bharatanatyam	kabuki	natya
breakaway	karanas	onnagata
dama	Lindy Hop	rasa theory
èmna	mie	

we see. As observers, we aim to respect the unique nuances within each dance form, recognizing value within the dance and the culture, and through engaged observation, begin to understand a little more about what may be an unfamiliar culture. It is through this developed appreciation of and respect for our shared differences that we begin to generate compassion and tolerance for those with whom we encounter and interact in this global world.

Reflective Prompts

1. *Bharatanatyam* has retained its initial integrity, although aspects of the dance have been altered in some form as the culture around it has evolved. Can you think of other examples in life that have been affected by the surrounding culture? In what ways did they change or alter?
2. Look at clips of *bharatanatyam* on YouTube or through other video sources. What do you notice when watching the dance? What stands out to you and why?
3. What do you think someone from another culture might think when viewing a dance from your own culture? If your class were to create a dance that would depict the combined culture of the class, what characteristics might be included?
4. During the seventeenth and eighteenth centuries, the Tokugawa Shogunate closed Japan's borders and banned residents from leaving the country. Why would the Tokugawa Shogunate want to isolate Japan from the rest of the world? Do you think such an act helps or prohibits the development of art? Why?
5. The Dogon ceremony *dama* is rooted deep in religious beliefs of ushering the life force of the deceased into the next world. Can you think of reasons your religious beliefs call for dancing?
6. Why do you think the Lindy Hop was breaking racial barriers when discrimination was still prominent in other entertainment outlets, such as movie musicals?

Movement Prompt

1. **Bharatanatyam:** Learn the movement on the companion website. Reflect on the learning process. Did you find it easy/difficult to learn the movement? Were you surprised by any aspect of the experience? How might you view Indian dance differently after learning some basic movement?

NOTES

1 Drid Williams, *Anthropology and the Dance: Ten Lectures,* 2nd ed. (Chicago: University of Illinois Press, 2004), 13.
2 Russell Meriweather Hughes, *The Gesture Language of the Hindu Dance* (New York: B. Blom, 1964), 6.
3 Rajika Puri, "Bharatanatyam Performed: A Typical Recital," *Visual Anthropology* 17, no. 1 (2004), 58.
4 Ketu H. Katrak, *Contemporary Indian Dance: New Creative Choreography in India and the Diaspora* (New York: Palgrave Macmillan, 2011), 27.
5 Faubion Bowers, *The Dance in India* (New York: AMS Press, 1967), 14.
6 Bowers, *The Dance in India*, 28–29.
7 Patricia Leigh Beaman, *World Dance Cultures from Ritual to Spectacle* (New York: Routledge, 2018), 9.
8 Sunil Kothari, *Bharata Natyam: Indian Classical Dance Art* (Bombay: J. J. Bhabha, 1982), 31.
9 Bowers, *The Dance in India*, 24.
10 Beaman, *World Dance Cultures from Ritual to Spectacle*, 108.
11 Francis Haar, *Japanese Theatre in Highlight: A Pictorial Commentary* (Westport, Connecticut: Greenwood Press, 1971), 86.
12 Michel Huet and Jean-Louis Paudrat, *The Dance, Art and Ritual of Africa* (New York: Pantheon Books, 1978), 101.
13 Beaman, *World Dance Cultures from Ritual to Spectacle*, 165–173.
14 Karen Hubbard and Terry Monaghan, "Negotiating Compromise on a Burnished Wood Floor: Social Dancing at the Savoy," in *Ballroom Boogie, Shimmy Sham, Shake: A Social and Popular Dance Reader*, edited by Julie Malnig (Chicago: University of Illinois, 2009), 133.

CHAPTER 2 BIBLIOGRAPHY

Ambrose, Kay. *Classical Dances and Costumes of India.* London: A. & C. Black, 1965.
Arnott, Peter. *The Theatres of Japan.* London: Macmillan, 1969.
Balasaraswati. "On Bharata Natyam." *Dance Chronical* 2, no. 2 (1978): 106–116. www.jstor.org/stable/1567473.
Beaman, Patricia Leigh. *World Dance Cultures from Ritual to Spectacle.* New York: Routledge, 2018.
Bowers, Faubion. *The Dance in India.* New York: AMS Press, 1967.
Bowers, Faubion. *Japanese Theatre.* 1952. Reprint, Westport, CT: Greenwood Press, 1976.
Brandon, James R., William P. Malm, and Donald H. Shively. *Studies in Kabuki: Its Acting, Music, and Historical Context.* (East-West Culture Learning Institute.) Honolulu: University Press of Hawaii, 1978.
Chakravorty, Pallabi and Nilanjana Gupta, eds. *Dance Matters: Performing India.* New Delhi: Routledge, 2010.
Chatterjea, Ananya. "In Search of a Secular in Contemporary Indian Dance: A Continuing Journey." *Dance Research Journal* 36, no. 2 (2004): 102–116.
Davida, Dena, ed. *Fields in Motion: Ethnographer in the Worlds of Dance.* Canada: Wilfrid Laurier University Press, 2011.
Gabrovska, Galia Todorova. "*Onna Mono:* The 'Female Presence' on the Stage of the All-Male Traditional Japanese Theatre." *Asian Theatre Journal* 32, no. 2 (2015): 387–415. https://muse.jhu.edu/ (accessed May 5, 2019).

Gaston, Anne-Marie. *Śiva in Dance, Myth and Iconography*. Oxford University South Asian Studies Series. Delhi; New York: Oxford University Press, 1990.

Haar, Francis. *Japanese Theatre in Highlight: A Pictorial Commentary*. Westport, CT: Greenwood Press, 1971.

Harper, Peggy. "Dance in Nigeria." In *Dance in Africa, Asia and the Pacific: Selected Readings*, edited by Judy Van Zile, 148–163. New York: MSS Information Corporation, 1976.

Hubbard, Karen and Terry Monaghan. "Negotiating Compromise on a Burnished Wood Floor: Social Dancing at the Savoy." In *Ballroom, Boogie, Shimmy Sham, Shake: A Social and Popular Dance Reader*, edited by Julie Malnig, 126–145. Chicago: University of Illinois, 2009.

Huet, Michel, and Claude Savary. *The Dances of Africa*. New York: Harry N. Abrams, 1996.

Huet, Michel, and Jean-Louis Paudrat. *The Dance, Art and Ritual of Africa*. New York: Pantheon Books, 1978.

Hughes, Russell Meriweather. *The Gesture Language of the Hindu Dance*. New York, B. Blom, 1964.

Immoos, Thomas and Fred Mayer. *Japanese Theatre*. New York: Rizzoli International Publications, 1977.

Inoura, Yoshinobu and Toshio Kawatake. *The Traditional Theater of Japan*. New York and Tokyo: John Weatherhill, 1981.

Jonas, Gerald. *Dancing: The Pleasure, Power, and Art of Movement*. New York: Harry Abrams, in Association with Thirteen/WNET, 1998.

Kaeppler, Adrienne L. "Dance Ethnology and the Anthropology of Dance." *Dance Research Journal* 32, no. 1 (Summer 2000): 116–125. www.jstor.org/stable/1478285.

Katrak, Ketu H. *Contemporary Indian Dance: New Creative Choreography in India and the Diaspora*. New York: Palgrave Macmillan, 2011.

Kealiinohomoku, J. "An Anthropologist Looks at Ballet as a Form of Ethnic Dance." *Journal for the Anthropological Study of Human Movement* 1, no. 2 (1980): 83–97.

Knowles, Mark. *Tap Roots: The Early History of Tap Dancing*. Jefferson, NC: McFarland & Company, 2002.

Kothari, Sunil. *Bharata Natyam: Indian Classical Dance Art*. Bombay: J. J. Bhabha, 1982.

———. "Symbolism in Indian Dance." *The World of Music* 20, no. 3 (1978): 70–83.

Malm, Joyce R. "The World of Japanese Classical Dance." *World of Music* 25, no. 1 (1983): 70–79. www.jstor.org/stable/43560878.

Meduri, Avanthi. "Bharata Natyam-What Are You?" In *Moving History / Dancing Cultures: A Dance History Reader*, edited by Ann Dils and Ann Copper Albright, 103–113. Middletown: Wesleyan University Press, 2001.

Monaghan, Terry. "Why Study the Lindy Hop?" *Dance Research Journal* 33, no. 2 (Winter 2001): 124–127. www.jstor.org/stable/1477810.

Mruthinti, Harshita K. "Dancing the Divine Female: Diasporic Women's Encounters with the Hindu Goddess through Indian Classical Dance." *Journal of Asian American Studies* 9, no. 3 (2006): 271–299.

Munsi, Urmimala Sarkar and Stephanie Burridge, eds. *Traversing Tradition: Celebrating Dance in India*. New Delhi: Routledge, 2011.

Puri, Rajika. "Bharatanatyam Performed: A Typical Recital." *Visual Anthropology* 17, no. 1 (2004): 45–68.

Srinivasam, Amrit. "Reform and Revival: The Devadasi and Her Dance." *Economic and Political Weekly* 20, no. 44 (November 2, 1985): 1869–1876. www.jstor.org/stable/4375001.

Stearns, Marshall and Jean Stearns. *Jazz Dance: The Story of American Vernacular Dance.* New York: Da Capo Press, 1994.

Tiérou, Alphonse. *Dooplé: The Eternal Law of African Dance.* Paris: Harwood Academic Publishers, 1992.

Williams, Drid. *Anthropology and the Dance: Ten Lectures.* 2nd ed. Chicago: University of Illinois, 2004.

3 Crafting the Dance

When we go to a theatrical dance performance, we often do so in the hopes of being entertained, mesmerized, thoughtfully challenged, or inspired. We may notice the skill, athleticism, and beauty of the dancers on the stage purposefully moving their bodies through space. Perhaps the music that accompanies the dance, along with the costumes or lighting choices, stands out. We may even observe the details of the stage space or the theater around us. Yet, are those the aspects that mesmerize, challenge, or inspire us? Perhaps, each in its own way, but without the movements carefully selected and crafted by the choreographer, the dancers would have nothing to dance; there would be no use for costumes or lighting and no need for the theater or stage space. Choreography is an art in and of itself. We notice the dancers, but it is the voice of the choreographer speaking through the design of the movements that creates the depth behind or artistic statement of the dance.

Choreography is the purposefully selected arrangement of movement. As we have learned, dance can be crafted for various purposes. Some dances are composed for ritual or ceremonial functions; some dances are created for commercial venues; other dances are crafted for the concert dance stage. The dance genre will also require specific considerations of the choreographer. An individual will approach tap dance choreography in a distinctly different manner from the way in which one will compose a ballet or *kabuki* performance. Choreographers are mindful of these considerations. For the purpose of this chapter, Western theatrical dance will serve as the basis from which we explore the aspects of choreography.

When you see a dance performance, what is your first thought or response? Perhaps you think to yourself, "I like this!" Or, maybe you think, "This makes no sense!" What forms the basis of your opinion? The dance in general? The performance? Do you consider the choreography itself or the intent of the choreographer? While there is no formula that creates a great dance, there are certain elements that can increase the effectiveness of a dance. This chapter will define the choreographic craft, describe the choreographic process, identify the elements of dance that the choreographer manipulates, and highlight various tools a choreographer may use to compose a dance. Before we begin, take a moment and make a list of everything that you think may be involved in the choreographic process.

CHOREOGRAPHIC CRAFT

Creating choreography is a craft; it is a skill and an art. Choreographers do not merely select their favorite movements and arbitrarily put them into a sequence set to randomly selected music. Good choreography requires thought and research, trial and error. It is a process. Depending upon the individual choreographer or the constraints of the project, the process can be short, occurring within a week or less, or long, extending throughout months or even years of rehearsal. The **choreographic craft** involves carefully chosen movements patterned in aesthetically pleasing and/or purposeful sequences. These movement sequences are then sculpted into an overall form, or structure, that further enhances the choreographer's intent. A **choreographic concept** is the idea, story, or intention of the work as a whole. The concept may be story-based; it could focus on a thematic idea; or the work could be abstract.

Important to recognize prior to starting the craft

BOX 3.1 MOVEMENT EXPERIMENTATION

Take a movement and experiment with a simple gesture of the arm. Be as generic or creative in your movement choice as you wish. Perhaps you execute a simple wave of the hand or a fancy handshake. Now, try that same movement as small as you can, as large as you can; look at the gesture as you execute it; look away. What did you notice? Which version did you prefer? Keep in mind that these are just four basic ways to manipulate a simple gesture of the arm. Think of all the combinations of movements of the limbs and torso you could create. Imagine the endless options of choices!

The intent, or concept, of the choreography may be to express a specific story or plot, make a social or political statement, convey a theme, explore an abstract idea, or simply entertain. With the intent in mind, it is the choreographer's job to convey this concept to an audience. Each piece of the choreographic puzzle offers clues to help the viewer discover the meaning behind the work. The choreographer makes a series of choices throughout the creative process that include, in part, the number of dancers who will perform, what specific movement vocabulary to use within the work, how those movements should be executed, the pathways and directions in which the dancers will execute the choreography, and the musical accompaniment or lack thereof. But this is only a part of the process.

Where to Begin?

From where do ideas for a dance come? The simple answer is that they come from everywhere. Just as an author of a novel, a screenwriter of a film, or a composer of a song finds inspiration for their art within the world around them, so does a choreographer. Ideas for dances can come from an array of places: life experiences, historical events, mythical stories and legends, musical sources, plays, religion, social or political conditions, emotions, moods, or even abstract ideas such as colors and shapes. The list is endless! Artists respond to the world around them, and within that response, they strive to entertain an audience, provide a relatable experience, or challenge others to think differently. A stimulus can be defined as "something that rouses the mind … or incites activity."[1] A **stimulus** serves as inspiration for movement in general and/or a piece of choreography and provides a starting point from which a choreographer may begin to create. It can be considered as a catalyst of movement. There are five types of stimuli to which a choreographer may respond: visual, auditory, tactile, kinesthetic, and ideational.

*[margin handwriting: Similar to a Motif → motivates/ inspires whole dance *can be ANYthing!]*

A visual stimulus is that which can be seen. Pictures, sculptures, and objects are all examples of this type of stimulus. An auditory stimulus is that which can be heard. For example, music and spoken word are both forms of auditory stimuli. A tactile stimulus is that which can be touched. For example, the feel of a handful of sand as it slips between your fingers could inspire a certain movement quality that becomes the basis for a dance. A prop, such as a chair or a hat, may also serve as a form of tactile stimulus. The ways in which it can be touched, carried, and/or manipulated provide movement ideas. A kinesthetic stimulus is that which can be felt internally. Here, the movement is the focus, such as the feel of swinging-type motions or the contrasting movements of curling the body in and then stretching the limbs out into space. This kinesthetic movement idea serves as the impetus of the dance; rather than communicating a particular idea, the intent is rooted in the movement itself. Finally, an idea that extends from the mind is an ideational stimulus. This is often the more popular method of inspiration for choreography. Perhaps a personal experience will trigger a notion for a story or theme from which the choreographer will create a dance. Regardless of the type of stimulus inspiring the work, the choreographer responds to an aspect of that inspiration as a catalyst to then motivate and guide the choreographic process. The stimulus itself can narrow the scope of movement and other elements of the dance. Once a choreographer is inspired to engage in the choreographic process, it is necessary for the stimulus to evolve into a concrete concept.

[margin handwriting: I like this a lot]

How does a choreographer first decide what to choreograph? Sometimes a production itself will dictate what type of choreography is needed. For example, in a Broadway musical, the plot and narrative are prescribed, the music may be previously composed, and the specific needs of the dance sequence may already be clarified by the director, including the intent for the dance and the size of the cast. In this instance, certain boundaries have been established before the choreographer even begins the creative process. The scope of the dance has been narrowed; choreographic options have been limited. In contrast, concert dance performances most often feature several complete yet independent pieces of choreography. In this case, the choreographer may take inspiration from any number of sources, experiment with movement ideas, select cast size and the individual dancers, and conceive design ideas for the corresponding theatrical elements. The field of choices is wide open. There may be few, if any, boundaries or restrictions for the choreographer.

Improvisation

The next step in the creative process is often that of improvisation. This stage can be compared to the author's act of free writing. Here, movement ideas are explored in order for the choreographer to find a starting point and narrow the choices suitable for the work. The choreographer may engage in dance **improvisation**, the spontaneous production of movement. This enables the choreographer to realize what type of shapes or movement, such as pedestrian-like movement, technical vocabulary, high leaps, or low crawls, are most suitable for the work. With an idea in mind, whether it is a basic inspiration or a fully developed concept, the choreographer may experiment with the various movement styles and qualities to further narrow down the scope of choices and draft movement ideas.

The improvisational stage may be one that the choreographer explores on their own, although sometimes choreographers may choose to have their dancers play with movement ideas as a group, creating a collaborative effort between the choreographer and the dancers. Improvisation can be not only a means of formulating ideas for the piece as a whole but a means for developing individual movement phrases throughout the choreography. Some choreographers also utilize improvisation on the stage. This is referred to as structured improvisation. Here, the choreographer establishes a framework for the piece in which dancers spontaneously create the movement within the provided structure and parameters. The dancers continue to improvise as part of the final performance. Not all choreographers incorporate improvisation within their choreographic process or final work, yet improvisation can be a helpful tool to have within a choreographer's (and dancer's) toolbelt.

The Choreographic Process

Creating choreography is a unique process for each individual. Choreographers may take a variety of approaches in crafting a dance. There is no specific order of steps in which a choreographer must work. While one choreographer may begin with music, then determine an intent, and craft the movement last, another choreographer may start with the movement and uncover an intent and then search for appropriate music. Some choreographers enter the rehearsal setting with movement entirely planned out, whereas other choreographers create in the studio with the dancers in front of them. Regardless of the individual creative process, the choreographer must understand the elements of dance and how they work together when crafting movement into choreography.

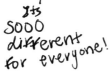
Its sooo different for everyone!

> **BOX 3.2 CHOREOGRAPHIC PROCESS: NON-TRADITIONAL METHODS**
>
> There are also a number of non-traditional choreographers who abandon conventional choreographic approaches as discussed in this chapter. For example, Merce Cunningham was an innovator in avant-garde choreography. His technique, which allowed individual movements or phrases to be placed into sequence through random acts such as the flip of a coin or roll of the dice, has often been called "choreography by chance," which is discussed in Chapter 6.

ELEMENTS OF DANCE

Dance is comprised of three primary elements: space, time, and energy. Think of it this way: movement takes up space. Regardless of where it is performed or executed, it fills the vacuum of space, just as the human body itself is tangible and takes up area. Dance unfolds over the course of a designated amount of time. A dance cannot be viewed in an instant. Unlike a sculpture, which is on display for the viewer to decide when and how long to study it, dance occurs over a specific duration of time. Finally, energy is inherent within dance. Effort and force must be applied within the human body for movement to occur. Muscles require an amount of energy to propel the body's bones through specific shapes and actions. The elements of space, time, and energy can be further divided into additional aspects that can help an audience member discover the intent behind the work and enhance the aesthetics of the piece.

Space
Space is the three-dimensional area through which a dancer can move. It is the choreographer's job to fill a void of space – the stage – with movement and/or stillness. How the choreographer chooses to do this can contribute to an effective, or ineffective, piece of choreography. It is often the spatial design of a dance that can most quickly convey to the audience the intent or meaning of the choreography. Take a moment and consider that statement. Before the dancers even begin to move, the image in space that they create can evoke certain ideas. Choreographers are deliberate about the shapes and levels through which the dancers will move, where they place dancers on the stage, and the paths in which the dancers will travel. Each aspect of the element of space is considered for both its delivery of intent and aesthetic appeal.

Maybe the most important aspect

Shape
The shapes that the dancers move through provide visual appeal as well as meaning. When considering shape, the choreographer explores both the lines

of the shape and the overall shape of a movement or position. The body lines of a shape are typically divided into two broad categories: curved and angular. Curved shapes occur when the limbs of the body are rounded in one direction or another, or the torso is curved forward, backward, or sideways, and can imply protectiveness, introversion, confidence, or spirituality depending on the ways in which the bends of the body are directed. On the contrary, angular shapes are straight or depict sharp angles. This type of body line can depict images or ideas of stillness, brokenness, extroversion, boldness, or even strength. It is important to note that most choreography does not make use of only one specific shape of body line throughout the work but will consider the conceptual needs required to convey meaning while remaining visually interesting. Furthermore, the dancer's body can make both curved and angular shapes at the same time. It is often the variety of shapes made that enhances the aesthetic appeal of the dance and helps to capture the attention of the audience. See Figure 3.1 for examples of various body shapes that include mixtures of curved and angular body lines.

[handwritten margin note: all have implic- ations]

The overall shape of the choreography can be considered in terms of symmetry or asymmetry. Here, the choreography may incorporate symmetry or asymmetry within the poses of the body or in the design of multiple bodies in space to support the work's intent. There is a formality and natural feeling of balance that accompanies symmetrical designs. Such designs can imply strength, authority, or safety. In contrast, an asymmetrical pose or arrangement of dancers does not demonstrate the equilibrium of balance from one half of the body to the other or from one side of the stage to the other. Appearing with less formality than their counterpart, asymmetrical designs adversely hint at tension or conflict. See Figures 3.2 and 3.3 for additional examples of symmetrical and asymmetrical spatial designs of dancers.

3.1
Dancers create a variety of curved and angular shapes and body lines. Photo by Jeff Smith, WKU

3.2
Dancers create a
symmetrical shape
in space with their
bodies.
Photo by Jeff
Smith, WKU

3.3
Dancers create an
asymmetrical shape
in space with their
bodies.
Photo by Jeff
Smith, WKU

The choreographer also considers the relationship of the movements within the overall space. In this regard, the choreographer is looking at how the body or bodies themselves create visual spatial design within the performance space. The size of a movement also can affect the meaning that is conveyed and contribute to the spatial design of the work. The size of a single movement can be as small or as large as possible, or any size in between.

Level

There are three primary levels – low, medium, and high – in which movement can occur, and, of course, a variety of ranges exists within each. The choreographer strives to include movement in levels that connect to the intent of the work and provide visual appeal. Just as we do not like to listen to a speaker who remains in a monotone vocal level, an audience member will lose interest if the dancers perform in only one level in space for an entire work, unless, of course, there is a specific reason and need to remain in a particular level. Additionally, it is impossible to conceive of a dancer executing only movements that are vertical and high in space – such as a big leap, arms reaching upward, and legs kicking into the air – for an entire dance. Just imagine a professor shouting an entire lecture at a high volume! The choreographer considers what spatial levels are

I like this analogy! – super important idea

52 □

3.4
Dancers
demonstrate body
positions in low,
middle, and high
levels of space.
Photo by Jeff
Smith, WKU

logical for use within the piece as well as what will provide variety in the aesthetics of the piece.

BOX 3.3 EXAMPLE OF SPATIAL LEVELS: "I WANNA BE READY"

Revelations, choreographed by renowned modern dancer Alvin Ailey, is the most well-known choreography performed by the Alvin Ailey American Dance Theater. This thirty-six-minute work, divided into three sections and eleven individual dances, offers an excellent source to analyze the elements of dance within choreography. The dance entitled "I Wanna Be Ready" provides a clear example of an effective use of spatial levels. The piece portrays an individual, both faithful and spiritual, in preparation for death. The solo dancer begins in a low-level position. After moving through various positions close to the floor, the dancer rises through the mid-level until limbs are extended high into space. The various range of levels utilized within the choreography is clearly visible throughout the dance until the soloist returns to a low-level position, and the song and dance ends. The choice of the choreographer to begin the dance in a low level, intersperse the movement with shapes that focus and extend upward, and then return the dancer to a low level suggest a heaviness that may be upon the dancer combined with the hope and longing toward the heavens that the dancer maintains.

WOAH that Meaning got deep

Areas of the Stage

In order to understand how the choreographer might use the various areas of the stage, it is important to familiarize oneself with the basic stage directions and terminology. **Downstage** refers to the area of the stage nearest the audience, and **upstage** refers to the area of the stage farthest from the audience. **Stage right** and **stage left** are named from the dancer's perspective when facing the audience.

BOX 3.4 THE RAKED STAGE

A raked stage's floor is angled, sloping upward, away from the audience. The terminology of upstage and downstage stem from the anatomy of a raked stage. This type of stage was popular in theaters during the sixteenth century, with several remaining today in Europe. By angling the stage, audience members were provided with a clearer view of the action occurring on the stage. Raked stages remained popular until they were slowly replaced by raked audience seating. Few theaters with permanent raked stages can still be found in the United States. One exception is the Ford's Theatre in Washington, DC. As you can imagine, this type of stage proves quite difficult for dancers to adapt to, as balance is immediately affected, along with transitions into and out of most jumps and leaps.

Pathways

There are many pathways in which the dancer's movement may cause them to travel throughout the stage space. Dancers can move in straight or curved pathways, in zigzags or in spirals. Pathways may be specific or meandering. Rarely do all dancers in a piece of choreography move in the exact same pathways throughout the entire choreography. The combination of the pathways enhances the visual design in space and can support the intent behind the choreography.

Time

The second element of dance is **time**, the measurable temporal intervals in which action takes place or events occur. Dance takes time. It is not a frozen snapshot, but rather, an art form that unfolds throughout a period of time. Whether it is a live performance or a filmed performance, it takes a set amount of time to watch the choreography. But the element of time encompasses more than this. In considering time, the choreographer must make choices regarding the use of tempo and rhythm.

Tempo

Tempo is the speed or pace of the beat. It is the steady pulse that drives the movement forward. The tempo of the dance is most often dictated by the selection of musical accompaniment. However, if a dance is done in silence, the movement itself will still maintain a certain tempo. Imagine the sound of a metronome or ticking clock; the steady sound of the clicks is the tempo. A tempo can be fast or slow. Many choreographic works include a varied use of tempo in which one slow section contrasts with a section of quicker tempo. Additionally, the movement within the choreography can work against the tempo of the music. The movement may follow the slow pulse of the music, or it can be done twice as fast to the same slow beat. This variety in use of tempo helps to keep the movement interesting.

Rhythm

Once a choreographer selects a certain tempo for the dance, the choice must then be made about how the movements will fit within the beats. Here, rhythm comes into play. **Rhythm** is the arrangement of the movement within the beats. Movement could occur on a single beat, or it could be stretched out so that it takes several beats to complete. Additionally, a beat can be subdivided into shorter units. Movement could occur within these shorter units, resulting in brief, quick movement. The varied use of rhythm makes the movement itself interesting to both execute and observe. Again, imagine the monotone lecturer. There is no variety in the pitch of the voice. The pace of the words is constant. Just as we do not want to listen to a monotone speaker, we do not want to watch movement that is repetitive in rhythm. Try watching a dance with the sound muted. If the movement is still interesting to watch, then the choreographer has successfully incorporated rhythm into the movement.

BOX 3.5 TAP DANCE CHOREOGRAPHY

Tap dance choreographers compose the musical notes of the rhythms. Through the percussive sounds made by the feet, tap dancers create audible rhythms of the choreography. It is interesting to note that while a jazz or modern dancer may compose a single movement that takes multiple counts to execute, a tap dancer often creates a great number of steps and sounds for a single count of music, which can make tap dance choreography very dense.

Energy

The final element of dance is energy. **Energy** is the capacity for action or the build-up of power within the body. It takes a certain amount of energy within the body to simply lift one's arm. Try reaching your arm up into the air. Notice the effort required within your body. Now, try lifting the arm as forcefully or as passively as you can. The choreographer has the same options, and more, when considering the element of energy.

energy → the power
Force → the way energy is used

Force

The **force** of a movement is the way in which energy, or power, is expended through the body. The amount of energy exerted will produce strong or gentle movement. Energy does not equal speed. It has nothing to do with the amount of time used to complete the movement, but relates to the effort and quality in which the movement is executed. Try reaching your arm up high. Be extremely lazy as you lift the arm. Now, do so with excited energy. Finally, lift your arm but try to resist the action as though another force is pulling the arm up as you try to keep it down. The lazy reach required minimal energy and could be considered a gentler action. The excited reach was most likely quicker and used a higher amount of energy. The resistant reach, while slower, also used a high amount of energy.

visual for this idea

Movement Qualities

Movement qualities are the recognizable characteristics of movement that incorporate all three elements of dance, resulting in the unique ways in which a movement can be executed. They color the movement, reinforcing the intent. As a dancer moves through space, rounded or lengthened shapes may occur. When we blend this use of space with a certain tempo and rhythm as well as a specific amount of energy, a certain quality will appear within the movement, creating dynamics within the choreography. Consider the preceding exercise of reaching the arm up high. We used the adjectives of lazy, excited, and resistant. We conveyed the characteristic of each by movement through space, at a certain tempo, and with specified amount of energy. The results produced movement recognizable as a certain characteristic.

A choreographer considers all three elements of dance – space, time, and energy – during the creative process. Aspects of these elements may be contemplated independently, but more often than not, they overlap. The key to approaching these elements is to continuously consider variety. While all aspects of the choreography must support the intent of the work, the dance would become boring to the spectator if all the movement remained on a similar level, at the same tempo, and with a consistent amount of energy applied. With this in mind, can you imagine the endless combination of options?

FORM

Structure is inherent in life. Each day consists of morning, afternoon, evening, and nighttime. We most likely have a set order in which we get ready in the morning or complete certain tasks. If we choose to be spontaneous in our approach, then there is an organic sequence at play; otherwise, we are logical in our approach. **Form** is the structure of a dance. Shaped by the intent of the work, form is what holds a piece together. Compare this idea to an essay that you may write. Words form sentences, which become paragraphs. Paragraphs begin in an introductory fashion, continue in support of the thesis statement or intent of the essay, and then conclude. When drafted together, paragraphs form a complete and thoughtful essay. Just as the words create sentences and so on, movements form movement phrases, which comprise sections of a work. The movement phrases and sections are sequenced in such a way as to provide cohesiveness throughout the work. Through effective transitions – natural shifts between individual movements, phrases, and sections of choreography – the piece, just like an essay, has a beginning, a middle, and an end, which creates unity and a sense of completeness within the dance.

Two basic examples of choreographic structures are cyclical and narrative. In a cyclical structure, the dance will end in the same way as it started. Here, the dance comes full circle by returning to the beginning pose or revisiting the initial movement phrases before concluding. In a narrative structure, the choreographer takes a linear approach to the work, and a story unfolds. The movement phrases are logically planned to sequentially further the plot or idea behind the work. Some choreographers simply choose to work from an organic framework in which the kinesthetic feel and needs of the movement itself dictate the sequence of movement phrases and order of sections.

think
saying
goodbye

think
Elvis

Within the overall form of the choreography, the choreographer must think about more than just the framework of the dance. What is the best order or arrangement of the individual movements and movement phrases? How will transitions occur between different movements, phrases, or sections? Does the choreography take longer than necessary to convey meaning, or does it end too abruptly? Regardless of the decisions that the choreographer makes when forming a dance, the goal is always to convey the intent of the choreography through choices that provide both unity and variety within the overall work.

ADDITIONAL CONSIDERATIONS

While the choreographer focuses a significant amount of energy on developing the movement, there are additional factors to consider before the movement itself is devised. These include the selection of the subject matter, the venue in which the choreography will be performed, the casting of the dancers, the musical accompaniment, and the time frame and/or schedule in which the work must be completed. The choreographer may have complete control when making decisions regarding each of these elements, or they may be dictated to the choreographer by external forces. For example, consider the subject matter. When creating the movement for a musical theater production, the subject matter is typically predetermined by a director or script. The framework in which a certain dance will take place, including the music, setting of the scene, and number of dances, has generally already been established for the choreographer. However, a concert dance choreographer most often has the freedom to self-select the subject matter for their choreography.

Venues can also present distinct challenges for the choreographer, affecting the movement choices that the choreographer may make. Not all dances occur on a proscenium stage, where the audience is located on only one side of the stage and a natural border of curtains frames the performance space. The audience may be seated on three or all sides of the stage. Additionally, site specific choreography regularly utilizes non-traditional performance venues, wherein the surface on which the dancers perform could be of any type, quality, or condition. The choreographer will make different choices regarding movement selection and the spatial design of the movement depending on the performance space.

The choreographer has many options regarding musical accompaniment. The choreographer may create movement to a pre-composed musical score, pre-recorded music, or live arrangement, or in collaboration with a musician. Some choreographers choose ambient or nature sounds, spoken word, or even silence to be used alongside the movement. Each choice delivers its own distinct set of challenges within the creative process.

Finally, casting and deadlines may dictate how the choreographer will approach the creative process. Casting may or may not be at the discretion of the choreographer. Each dancer is unique, with a different set of strengths and weaknesses, body type, and ability, and this must be taken into account when composing the movement so to present a cohesive cast and effective choreography. Limited or abundance of rehearsal space, unlimited or restricted allotment of time, schedule conflicts, and deadlines can all affect the choices the choreographer makes regarding cast selection, subject matter, movement, and scope of the choreography.

PRODUCTION ELEMENTS — *Everything else that can add to the visual*

In addition to the development of movement and design of the choreography, dance performance also requires technical elements. These include costume, make-up, lighting, scenery, and props. These technical elements support the communication of intent and meaning and enhance the production quality of the choreography.

Costumes and Make-up

The use of costumes can help to convey character roles, time periods, or other historical or symbolic aspects. The costume concept may be representational, meaning that it clearly depicts specific characteristics, or abstract. A good costume design can enhance the choreography, while a poor design can hinder the effectiveness of the choreography. Care must be given to both the design and the construction of the costume. The concept of the costume should complement the movement, not hide or restrict it; therefore, consideration must be given to the type of materials used and the manner in which it is constructed so that the dancer can appropriately move as necessary in the costume.

A specific performer may wear make-up that alludes to a whimsical or grotesque character or simply a heavier application of day-to-day make-up. Theatrical stage make-up often naturally highlights the features of the face so that the dancer's expression in performance is clearly visible to the audience.

Lighting

The design of the lights – devised by or in collaboration with either the director, the choreographer, or a lighting designer – creates an atmosphere in which the choreography can then unfold before the audience. There are many colors and options that may be incorporated into a lighting design; however, the most effective designs are those that may go unnoticed by the audience. The mood of a dance is often first established within the lighting design alone. Through the use of carefully selected color choices and the manner in which lights are focused to illuminate certain portions of the stage space, the audience members are given indications as to the tone and mood of the dance and even where to focus their attention.

Scenery and Props

Scenery may or may not be used in theatrical dance performance. Choreography may feature scenery such as hanging fabric, decorative objects, and constructed walls depicting an environment, or raised sections of flooring to enhance the visual design of the choreography or to provide additional spatial options within the movement. Props such as canes, hats, and brooms may also be used in choreography, which aid in the communication of meaning, enhance the visual design, and provide additional movement possibilities.

DANCE NOTATION

Like Miss mary's tap notes!

Dance notation – the symbolic representation of choreographed movement – has remained a persistent challenge in the dance world. While scores (written music) are ubiquitous in the art of music, dance poses particular difficulties because the instrument is the human body. Musical notes on a clarinet are definite, and while they can be played in many ways (slow or fast, loud or soft), there are simple universal terms to convey the dynamics of the material. On the other hand, the human body is an incredibly complex machine with hundreds of muscles and joints that can be moved in many directions with an infinite number of qualities simultaneously. This creates immense difficulty in capturing on paper even one movement, let alone an entire piece of choreography.

These obstacles have not stopped artists from translating movement to paper. Dance notations are utilized to archive choreographic works and enable companies to perform these works at a later date while maintaining the integrity of the choreographer's original intent. Video recordings of movement can be helpful in this effort, particularly in capturing performance qualities; however, a recording is but one interpretation of the work, and any mistakes that occurred during the performance would then be preserved in future adaptations. Additionally, technology is constantly changing. Devices used to record dance as recently as a decade prior may be obsolete, and converting film, DVDs, or digital files into more up-to-date formats is very time consuming and costly.

Many dance notation systems have been developed. Each consists of its own grammar to communicate directions, body parts, pathways, tempos, and dynamics of movement. While many creative solutions have been proposed, the complexity of the material makes any system rather inelegant. Various abstract graphics, abbreviations, pictures, and structures meticulously detail movement, but dancers and artists must receive training in order to learn to read what could be described as hieroglyphics. Even more training is required to be able to write notations, because the writer must first analyze the movement before translating it into code.

One of the most widely used current dance notation systems is Labanotation. Developed by Rudolf Laban in the 1920s, this notation system uses abstract symbols on a staff. A center line serves as the base around which various figures are drawn with different markings in them delineating body parts, direction, speeds, and dynamics. These notes are read from the bottom of the page to the top and correspond with measures in the music. Textbooks have been published about this method, and many university dance programs offer courses to provide training. The International Council of Kinetography Laban, founded in 1959, serves as the governing body regulating this intricate system.

Furthermore, since 1940, the Dance Notation Bureau has also used Labanotation to produce and archive scores of dances as well as license and stage works on dance companies every year. Though dance notation can be tedious, it does prevent artwork from fading into history and getting lost. Plus, scientists are exploring technological applications for these systems in the twenty-first century with projects such as using Labanotation to generate human-like movements in robots and animation.

CHOREOGRAPHY COPYRIGHTS

Dance was not explicitly included as a subject that can be copyrighted in the United States until the Copyright Act of 1976. Until then, dance had to be registered as a "dramatic composition" that told a story or expressed themes or emotions, which did not allow abstract dance compositions to be copyrighted. With the changes in legislature, dance is protected at the moment it is created, but unless it is then registered with the Copyright Office, there are limitations to enforcing the copyright in court. The choreography must be original and "fixed" in order to be able to register it with the Copyright Office. A piece of choreography can become fixed through a video recording or notation of the movement; Labanotation is the most commonly used notation system for this purpose.

Copyright protects an artist's right to reproduce or make a copy of the work, create adaptations or new versions of the work (such as for a movie), distribute copies of the work for sale or some form of transferred ownership like rental, perform the work publicly, and display a copy of the dance (such as on television).

In addition to the movement, artists can claim copyright of elements of dance works such as costumes, sound scores, and lighting designs. The copyright lasts for the life of the artist plus fifty years.

Even though the law is in place, there are still difficult issues surrounding dance copyrights, including works by artists across borders. Multiple cases have occurred in which American music artists seemed to have infringed upon choreographers' rights for music videos and live performances. Dancers, choreographers, and dance educators have expressed different reactions to this, ranging from outrage that dance artists are not being appropriately recognized for their work to satisfaction that these pop artists have made dance works visible to a wider audience.

THE DANCER'S ROLE

While the choreographer creates the choreography, it is the dancer who must present the work and ultimately convey the choreographer's intent and perspective. Aside from continuing to train and hone their technical abilities, dancers must be active participants throughout the rehearsal process, meaning that the dancer should be on time to all rehearsals and performances, prepared for the material previously learned, fully engaged throughout the rehearsal, and able to contribute movement ideas when necessary. Some choreographers encourage constant feedback from their dancers, such as participating in group choreographic efforts or providing the choreographer with ideas on certain movement phrases. However, this is not always the case, and it is important for the dancer to recognize when it is appropriate to voice opinions in rehearsal and when to let the choreographer make the decisions. The dancer is also responsible for the emotional portrayal within performances. Dancers must be able to invest themselves in the roles that they dance. It is not merely the choreography that can entertain or stir emotions in an audience. Rather, it is the way in which the dancers perform that brings the choreography to life. Above all, dancers should be open to the choreographer's movement ideas, conduct themselves professionally, and strive to maintain the integrity of the choreography throughout the rehearsal process and in performance. The dancer and choreographer maintain a mutual respect for one another. While their roles are distinct, their goal to bring life to the dance is shared.

CHAPTER SUMMARY

Our exploration into the choreographic craft has highlighted an array of elements and aspects that require thoughtful consideration by the choreographer. The choreographer may use the tool of improvisation to develop movement ideas for the work. As movement phrases are developed, the choreographer chooses movement for inclusion within the choreography. The dance elements of space, time, and energy are considered. The choreographer manipulates movement

choreographic concept	form	stage right
choreographic craft	improvisation	stimulus
dance notation	movement qualities	tempo
downstage	rhythm	time
energy	space	upstage
force	stage left	

through various spatial designs, differing uses of tempo and rhythm, and ranges of force and quality. Decisions must also be made on how to frame these choices into a specific form or structure to create a cohesive and complete work of art. Finally, the theatrical elements of costumes, make-up, lighting, scenery, and props are designed to complement the choreography and work as a whole. Once the work is complete, choreographers may choose to notate their dance or register the work with the Copyright Office. Throughout the creative and performance process, <u>dancers are responsible for maintaining a role of mutual respect with the choreographer.</u> *They are choreographer's bringing vision to life*

Reflective Prompts

1. At times, a production's plot and musical score are provided to the chore-ographer. In this instance, the subject matter and sound accompaniment are established, and the choreographer then creates the appropriate chore-ography. If you were the choreographer, do you think it would be easier or harder for the subject matter and accompaniment to be dictated in advance? Why?
2. Theatrical dance is often performed on a proscenium stage with a special vinyl dance flooring called Marley. Sometimes, dancers find themselves performing in various venues and environments, which can include platform stages in outdoor settings on wooden, grass, or dirt surfaces. How can the performance space or surface affect the movement options or execution of choreography?
3. A choreographer has many elements to consider when creating choreog-raphy. Do you think one element is more important than another? Why or why not?
4. If you were a choreographer, what type of dancer would you want to cast? What qualities or characteristics would you look for in a dancer? How might these choices impact the creative process?
5. View an example of claimed choreography copyright infringement. What do you think constitutes an infringement of a choreographer's intellectual and creative property? Does a movement phrase have to be repeated in exactly the same way? How long can a phrase be repeated before it is considered copyright infringement? What about costuming, spatial design, and intent?

Movement Prompts

1. **Finding Rhythm:** As a group, stand in a circle and clap a steady beat in unison. Maintain that steady beat. One individual at time will clap a creative four-count, or four-beat, rhythm followed by four more steady claps. Then the next individual will clap a new four-count rhythm followed by four steady claps. Continue until everyone has had a chance to explore a short rhythm.

2. **Learn a Phrase:** View the movement tutorial video provided on the companion website. Learn the movement phrase to the best of your abilities. What was it like to learn a movement sequence? Did you struggle with coordination? Memorization?

    Now, try that same movement phrase as slowly as you can possibly move. Try executing it as fast as you can. What happens when you perform each movement of the phrase with as much force and energy as possible? Now, try each movement with as little effort as possible. Which version did you find the easiest to perform? Which version was more difficult to execute? Which version did you prefer and why?

3. **Group Choreography:** In a small group, choreograph a short dance that conveys a specific idea or story. The movement does not need to be technical or elaborate. Feel free to keep it pedestrian based or rooted in gestures. However, challenge yourselves to be creative with the movements that you select. What structure of form will you choose for your dance?

NOTE

1   Jacquelin M. Smith-Autard, *Dance Composition,* 3rd ed. (London: Lepus Books, 1996), 20.

CHAPTER 3 BIBLIOGRAPHY

Smith-Autard, Jacquelin M. *Dance Composition.* 3rd ed. London: Lepus Books, 1996.

4 Perceiving Dance

In the twenty-first century, dance can be found within a multitude of contexts. We may notice the energetic dancers in short clips of a television commercial or a flank of dancers surrounding a vocalist in a music video as it streams on our smartphone. While visiting an amusement park or adrift on a cruise ship, we are dazzled by dancers who perform as part of the entertainment. We attend a basketball game, and at halftime, dancers fill the court. We go to a theater to see a concert dance company perform and become amazed at their sheer talent and skill. At a wedding, the happy couple share a first dance, and at a child's party, the kids collectively dance the "Hokey Pokey." Whether we take notice or not, dance happens all around us. It is typically easy to relate to social dances, but theatrical dance forms may be more difficult to discern, given the wide variety of themes and complex sequences of movements they may encompass. How do we perceive this form of dance? What lies at the basis of our perception? How do we decide what we like or do not like?

LENSES OF PERCEPTION

The intentions of a dance are unique to its purpose. In ritual dance, the movement is not meant for a spectator but rather, the performer(s). The focus is placed on either a higher power or the fellow members engaged in the ritual. A connection is formed: one that may extend between the dancers and the god(s) or among the community of performers. Social dance is targeted primarily at the joy of the participants and does not require the presence of an audience. However, theatrical dance is intended to be viewed by an audience; the energy of the movement and its meaning are shared by the performer with the spectator. Recognizing the purpose behind the dance that we see allows us to view the dance through the appropriate lens. We would not observe a ritual hunting dance with the same expectations as we would a Lindy Hop performance in a 1930s dance hall. We would not view a presentation of *bugaku*, the ancient Japanese court dance, in the same manner or mindset as we would watch a Broadway performance of the musical *Chicago*. We recognize that the intention and goals of each of these performances are different. They are designed with different meanings and for specific audiences.

The personal lens through which we view dance can also shape our perspective and opinion of the dance. Aspects specific to an individual can frame how that individual perceives the surrounding world. These can include whether one is timid or outgoing, optimistic or pessimistic, right-brained or left-brained, athletic or sedentary, and so on. These personal characteristics can affect our perception of what we see and the opinions we form. We each come from a background that is unique to us. We were not all raised in the same family environment with the same opportunities, traditions, or experiences. An individual who grows up with a single parent in the hustle and bustle of New York City will have a completely different background from the individual who is raised by two parents on a horse farm in Wyoming.

We have a particular set of standards, values, and convictions that may be shaped by religious or political views or the environment in which we grew up or reside. These can affect the way we think and feel about the world around us and even the art that we see. Intrinsic to our perceptions of art lies a set of personal experiences, standards, morals, and ethics. These can individually or collectively mold the way we view a piece of art. Even the events of a certain day can alter our perceptions. After an exhausting day of work and personal obligations, attending a dance performance may feel like sensory overload. However, another individual may find escaping to the theater to be a breath of fresh air. Our emotions can also color the way we perceive art. If you have recently experienced the loss of a loved one, you may be more affected by a dance about grief than someone who has not yet experienced that type of loss. If you are in the midst of a breakup with a long-term partner, then you most likely will not enjoy a dance performance about the joys of love.

Additionally, we embrace certain aesthetic preferences. One individual prefers rap music, another classical. One individual admires abstract non-representational art, whereas another is a fan of impressionism. Our preference for one aesthetic over another does not mean that there is not value or worth in both. As an audience member, it is imperative that we view dance, or any art form, with an open mind. By remaining receptive to new ideas and experiences and free from bias, we can begin to better understand, and perhaps even appreciate, the art we see, hear, and experience in the world around us.

Everyone has diff. preferences and what they like

DANCE AESTHETICS

Observing dance engages our senses in a variety of ways. We see the images of human bodies move through space, in and out of specific shapes, and through various levels and differing pathways, with shifting amounts of force and energy. We hear the sound of the accompaniment, whether it be music, spoken word, or abstract noise. We may even hear the footwork of the dancers or the sound of their breath connected to the movement or as a reaction to their physical exertion. Dance also engages our kinesthetic sense. We can have a physical reaction within our own bodies when we observe dance. Perhaps you have caught yourself tapping your toes or patting your leg to the beat of a song. Have you ever watched a film where you gasped and jumped in your seat? Or, maybe you looked at a piece of art that made you feel extremely uncomfortable and nervous inside. As you sit in a theater and watch a performance, have you ever noticed that you are unconsciously leaning forward or to the side, your muscles are full of tension, and goosebumps have appeared on your arms? Or perhaps you can relate to the subject matter of a dance on a personal level, and a flood of memories and emotions overwhelms you. These are all examples of kinesthetic reactions to art. Our senses are stirred as our mind begins to form opinions. Our view of the function of the dance, our understanding of the cultural aspects of the dance, our individual experiences and personal traits, and our internal and involuntary physical reactions all contribute to our overall perception of the dance.

The word "aesthetic" has been used when describing dance or its characteristics. More specifically, **aesthetic** refers to the perceived beauty that can be found within a work of art. According to the Merriam-Webster dictionary, aesthetic can mean "a particular approach to what is pleasing to the senses …" or simply "a pleasing appearance or effect."[1] However, aesthetic is often confused with beauty. One may say that a dance is aesthetically pleasing, yet that does not necessarily deem the dance beautiful. After all, what is beautiful to one person may in fact be ugly to another individual. The ballet aesthetic favors extended body lines, erect torsos, outwardly rotated legs, and stretched feet. We see the opposite in the African dance aesthetic, where the forward leaning torso, bent legs, and flexed feet are prominently used. Yet within each community, the characteristics of the specific dance are considered aesthetically pleasing and beautiful. Also worthy of consideration is the theatrical dance comprised of "ugly" movement. Should beautiful movement always be the goal? Can dance consist of raw, distorted, or grotesque movements and be aesthetically pleasing? In these instances, is the dance as a whole still intriguing and engaging to watch?

When we as the choreographer, performer, or viewer evaluate dance, we are considering a grouping of aspects that comprise the aesthetic of the work. We assess the quality of the piece, its overall value, how it is formed, and our response to it. We have an aesthetic and kinesthetic reaction when we watch dance. We will notice whether the dance is pleasing to us or not. We find the costumes, music, quality of the dancers' movements, shapes of the bodies in space, and rhythms that are produced to be intriguing, enjoyable, or satisfying. Or, in contrast, we may regard them as unattractive, unpleasant, or annoying. In either case, we are internally responding to the aesthetics of the dance. Our initial response is often either affirmation for the work ("I like this!") or one of discontentment with the work ("I do not like this!"). Whether we realize it or not, our personal response is to the aesthetics of the work. Attempting to look more deeply at the work itself will uncover the aesthetics of the dance that we admire or dislike.

Aesthetic Principles of Form

The aesthetics of art can be subjective and do not alone determine whether a dance is effective, valid, strong, or even good. What is aesthetically satisfying to one person may be unenjoyable by another person. However, there are certain guiding ideas that can work together to shape art in a more effective manner overall. Elizabeth Hayes, author and professor of dance, details within her book *Dance Composition & Production* ten aesthetic principles of form that many types of art, including dance, strive to achieve. These include unity, variety, repetition, contrast, transition, sequence, climax, proportion, balance, and harmony.[2] For our purposes, let us group these together in a slightly different sequence in order to better understand their roles within dance.

Variety, Repetition, and Contrast

The aspects of variety, repetition, and contrast can be applied within either the smaller movement phrases or the larger sections of the choreography. **Variety** refers to the multiple ways in which a movement or movement phrase can be manipulated, changed, or altered throughout a dance. There are an endless number of ways in which movement can be varied. A simple movement can be executed low or high in space, while standing on one leg or two legs, while turning or jumping, or while simultaneously executing a second movement. Some variations can convey meaning better than others. Or, a variation of a movement phrase could further address the subject matter and delineate the choreographer's intent. The use of variety within the movement can deepen the audience's understanding of intent and enhance the visual interest of the movement.

A movement or movement phrase could also be repeated for emphasis and meaning, hence the principle of **repetition**. It could become boring to watch a movement performed in the exact same manner repeatedly throughout a dance. However, this idea of repetition can also be a useful tool for a choreographer. Dance happens in an instant, and unless we are watching a film that we can rewind, we may miss something specific that the choreographer hopes to convey. The repetition of certain movements or phrases can bring attention to those ideas. This use of repetition can emphasize a desirable movement, mood, or meaning to the audience.

Contrast is similar to variety, yet distinct in that variety refers to the way the movement itself is designed within the dance, while **contrast** provides a dynamic opposition to how the subject matter or intent of the piece is treated within the work as a whole. The theme of a symphony performance may be based upon music by The Beatles. Yet, each piece performed most likely would not be at the same tempo. There might be a moderately paced song, followed by a ballad, and then contrasted with an up-tempo song. We can see this idea in fashion trends as well. A black dress may have a contrasting block of color around the waist that serves to highlight and emphasize the overall design and fit of the dress. Even a pop song does not follow a rigid pattern of verse, chorus, verse, chorus throughout. We can typically hear a contrasting section of music, called a bridge, approximately two-thirds of the way into the song. Dance includes the same principle. Sections of the dance are still connected to the overall work but may approach the intent in a contrasting way. A choreographer may contrast an upbeat section with one that utilizes a slow tempo. Another example might be a contrasting movement section wherein all of the movement is executed in a low level. When used effectively, variety, repetition, and contrast become aesthetic principles that intensify or reinforce the meaning of the piece.

Sequence, Transitions, and Climax

Sequence, transitions, and climax are principles of form that must also be cohesive within a work of art. As discussed in Chapter 3, the choreographer determines the **sequence**, or order, of individual movements, movement phrases, and choreographic sections. A sequence must be selected for the various sections of the dance to heighten the audience's understanding of the work. These sequences of movement phrases and choreographic sections must encompass logical and seamless transitions. **Transitions** are the way in which a dancer moves from one movement or movement phrase to the next and the way in which sections of choreography are connected. Imagine a dance where one movement phrase ends with the dancers positioned downstage on the floor or Point A, and the next movement phrase begins with the dancers standing in the upstage corner or Point B. The choreographer must then devise an appropriate transition to get the dancers from Point A to Point B that continues the flow of the piece and appears logical and natural to the audience. The same need for a smooth transition also occurs between sections of the piece. Perhaps one segment ends with all of the dancers posed on the stage, and the next section begins with a single dancer seated centerstage. The choreographer has many options in devising this transition. The choice made by the choreographer and the dancers' execution of that choice become an aesthetic aspect of the work. Finally, the **climax** is that point toward which the movement and energy of the piece have built. For a work to be satisfying to the audience, it should offer a sense of achievement, or arrival, toward which the work has been built. It is up to the choreographer to determine whether or not a climax is necessary for the work to deliver this feeling of wholeness or completeness.

I think this is an important idea to note

Proportion and Balance

In forming a dance, the choreographer also ponders the principles of proportion and balance. **Proportion** refers to the quantity of dancers and sections within the choreography. **Balance** is the equilibrium between sections of the choreography and within the work as a whole. Proportion deals with the number of dancers within sections of the dance, whereas balance considers stability within the work as a whole. A twenty-minute dance in which a large cast of fourteen dancers remains on the stage for each separate section of the choreography may not be as proportionately effective as if a differing number of dancers was used

How the choreo is broken up into sections

within each section. What is the effect of a dance performed by a single dancer to a large orchestral piece of music? Or a dance performed by twenty-five dancers to the music of a solo pianist? Or a dance comprised of four separate sections that features a trio of dancers performing each section? Within each example, there would be an imbalance within the overall work.

makes very diff. effect

Unity and Harmony

The final principles of unity and harmony can be met after consideration of the preceding aspects. **Unity** in a work is arrived at when all elements of the choreography work together in agreement, creating a wholeness within the dance. *makes* If all aspects of a work are appropriately coordinated, a feeling of harmony is established. These aesthetic principles can be discovered in any type of art. Study a painting, a song, a play, an architectural building, or a fashion design. Notice within any art the use of these ten aesthetic principles of form. In dance, these ideas can help the choreographer to create a more effective piece and can serve as a starting point for an audience when considering the aesthetics of a work.

ART OR ENTERTAINMENT?

The age-old debate of art versus entertainment can also affect our perceptions by establishing preconceived notions within our minds of either the art form or the experience. Some individuals view art at a high level, deeming it intellectual and thought-provoking, while entertainment is demoted to a lower level and considered frivolous or merely for show. Entertainment might be considered as a source of temporary escape from the daily grinds of life or a fleeting form of creativity, whereas art is that which should be valued and appreciated. The question then becomes whether these assumptions or determinations are accurate or fair.

The Oxford English Dictionary defines art as "the expression or application of human creative skill and imagination, typically in a visual form such as painting or sculpture, producing works to be appreciated primarily for their beauty or emotional power."[3] The same dictionary also defines entertainment with the following: "the action of providing or being provided with amusement or enjoyment."[4] Yet, the Merriam-Webster dictionary also includes that entertainment is "something diverting or engaging."[5] Let us also consider the use of the word "entertain" within the phrase "to entertain an idea or thought." In this usage, we are in fact giving consideration, thought, perhaps even appreciation to something. How, then, do we decide what is art and what is entertainment? Can art not be the same thing that entertains us? Could there be art that is entertaining and entertainment that is a true work of art?

The world of entertainment typically employs the use of the performing arts – dance, music, and theater. It is no surprise, then, that dance finds itself in the crux of the art versus entertainment debate. With the definitions in the previous paragraph in mind, do you consider dance to be art or entertainment? One could argue that we look to art to divert our attention or to engage our senses and minds. Can art not provide enjoyment? Does one attend a symphony performance simply for the opportunity to listen to art, or does one attend to also be entertained? Can we be entertained and challenged to think at the same time? Does a work of art have to make us think, or can it simply be entertaining to observe?

THE ROLE OF THE AUDIENCE

The role of an audience member can be challenging and requires careful consideration. Along with the dancer and the choreographer, the audience also plays a part in the presentation and acknowledgment of a dance performance. The most fundamental element for an audience member to realize is the importance of an open mind when viewing dance. Entering the theater with the decision that the evening will be boring, the dances will not make sense, and there is no point to the art form will leave the audience member unaffected by the performance, and the individual's experience will most likely be miserable. Rather, one should enter the space with no preconceived ideas, leaving any bias at the door and remaining open to any change that the experience may bring. This will allow the person to be receptive to a new experience, new emotions, potentially thought-provoking challenges, and hopefully an appreciation for the art.

Attending a Performance

Going to a dance performance for the first time can be an exciting or an intimidating event. You may want to research and become familiar with the production and the venue in advance. Knowing the purpose of the dance before viewing it and familiarizing yourself with the venue can prepare you mentally and emotionally for the experience. However, you may also choose to be surprised by the experience. If you are unsure what to wear, determine the venue's location and whether it will provide a formal or informal setting, so that you may dress appropriately. At a theatrical dance performance, admission is typically charged and can be pre-purchased online or by phone or immediately preceding the performance at the venue's box office. The type of dance performance will dictate the audience's etiquette during the program. If you attend an athletic event and a dance team performs during the event, it is more acceptable to stand, move around, talk, or even cheer during the performance. However, at a dance concert or musical production, the audience is expected to remain seated and quiet during the performance, though applause and laughter are appreciated by the performers when appropriate within the program. Cell phones should be silenced or turned off. Unless you are otherwise notified, you should never use any devices to record or take photos of the performance. This can infringe upon the intellectual property rights of the director, choreographer, dancers, and/or musicians and can be distracting to fellow audience members. Flash photography is also prohibited, as it can distract the performers, thus creating an unsafe performance environment.

The format of the program will differ between a theatrical musical production and a formal dance concert. Typically, in a musical, the house lights will lower as the main curtain rises on the stage, and the narrative of the show will play out in continuous scenes. An intermission will occur approximately halfway into the performance, which allows members of the audience an opportunity to stretch their legs and enjoy a refreshment in the lobby. A formal concert dance performance often includes a number of separate yet complete works of choreography. While a concert dance performance will begin in the same fashion – house lights dim and curtain rises – the remainder of the production can vary. Unless a story theme is presented, audiences can expect the main curtain to lower and house lights to rise slightly between individual dances during a dance concert. This allows a moment for the dancers to change costumes, an opportunity for the stagehands to reset the stage as needed, and a chance for the audience to peek at the program, all in preparation for the next dance. Tap dance concerts are often either emceed or staged in such a way that the action and/or sound shifts continuously without interruption except for an intermission.

It is important that the audience remember they are not just spectators but participants in the performance. For without them, there would be no reason for the curtain to rise. Dancers can sense the audience during a performance. The dancers are acutely aware of whether or not the audience is active and engaged in the performance. It is the energy of the audience that often feeds that of the dancers.

Sensory-friendly Performances

Many and various types of performances – including Broadway shows, plays, and ballets – are offered in special sensory-friendly formats. These performances include adjustments that make the shows more accessible for individuals with autism spectrum disorders, sensory sensitivities, or other disabilities. This is achieved by preparing the individuals for what to expect, reducing sensory stimulation, and allowing relaxed rules in the audience.

Parents or caregivers are given a guide to the performance that outlines the show, including the characters and any theatrical elements of which their children should be aware. Often meltdowns can be triggered by the unexpected, so sensory-friendly performances try to eliminate the unknown as much as possible. Stimuli are reduced by keeping the house lights dimmed, lowering the sound levels, and warning the audience of or eliminating sudden sound or light cues. Ear plugs or noise cancelling headphones are provided to anyone who needs them. Autism specialists and sometimes individuals with autism work with the producers of the show to make these adjustments to theatrical elements; the script or choreography is never changed, in order to maintain the integrity of the show. Usually, the cast only needs one rehearsal to prepare the differently formatted show. Additionally, audience members are encouraged to move around and make noise during the performance. Fidget toys are allowed, and anyone caught up in the action and inspired to sing and dance is allowed. This provides a judgement-free atmosphere. If anyone needs to step away, there are quiet areas set up elsewhere in the building. Professionals who have experience with autism are on staff to aid audience members and guide families through the theater.

Organizations like the Autism Theatre Initiative help facilitate these sensory-friendly performances and work with producers and donors to offer tickets at a discounted price or even for free. Some organizations work to provide experiences for people on the spectrum to engage in the performing arts directly through dance, voice, or acting classes and putting on shows. Studies have shown improvement in various effects of autism in individuals who enroll in programs such as these.

WRITING ABOUT DANCE → *HOW to write a critique*

Now that we have discussed how to view and experience dance, let us explore how to write about what we have seen. Where do we begin? What do we include, especially if we are not dancers ourselves? Great examples of dance critiques can be found in magazines and newspapers. Some of the best can be read within the pages of the *New York Times*. Published critiques of dance concerts, productions, or individual performances are most often written by individuals who have first-hand experience in and knowledge of dance. However, this does not mean that dance can only be written about by those who dance themselves. The following paragraphs will guide you through a process of creating your own version of a dance critique or reflective paper. These steps can also be considered when viewing dance in general.

BOX 4.1 PROGRAM INFORMATION

The program is your reference guide to the performance. Within the program are invaluable details about all aspects of the production. Depending on the type of performance, the specific format may vary, but the necessary information remains constant. For a typical dance concert, the following information should be listed for each dance included within the concert program:

- Title
- Name of choreographer
- List of dancers/understudies
- Composer and/or title of music
- Costume designer
- Lighting designer
- Scenic designer (if applicable)

A program for a musical will also include a plot synopsis, list of scenes, and list of characters. A program may also include biographies for directors, choreographers, designers, dancers, and musicians. Finally, program notes may be included at the bottom of the page or next to an individual dance. Program notes offer additional information about a work, such as a statement from the choreographer providing insight into the concept or a comment from the director or producer noting grant support for the work.

Describe

The first portion of your critique will include a brief description of the performance as a whole. Before you begin drafting your critique, take time to write down all of the things that you remember about the work. Be sure to keep the program to use as a reference. Consider jotting notes in your program while the house lights are up in between pieces of choreography to be able to capture more detail. Never write during the actual performance, and do not use tablets or laptops to take notes. The screens are distracting to fellow audience members. If you wish to type notes in your phone, only do so when the house lights are on and never when performers are on the stage. Whether you are reviewing the entire concert or production or just an individual dance, the program can help you to remember the sequence of dances along with titles of each piece, choreographers, music, designers, and casts. As you create a list of all that you remember, try to include as much descriptive detail as you can. Your goal is not to write a play-by-play of each and every movement, formation, and section of the choreography. Rather, you want to capture the essence of the work in such a way that someone not in attendance could understand what you saw. Consider the following questions:

- What type of performance was it?
- Who was the choreographer?
- Who were the dancers? (You do not necessarily need to include names of individual dancers, but instead include the name of the performance company as a whole.)
- What genre/s and style/s were performed?
- What did you notice about the costumes? The lighting? The scenery and/or props?

While the informative and logistical details of the performance are necessary, you want to primarily discuss and focus on the movement itself. This demonstrates attention to the choreography and offers clear context for your critique. How would you explain the movements that comprised the choreography? Do they appear technical or pedestrian-like? You do not have to be a trained dancer to offer an effective portrayal of the movement. To help provide description of the movement, break it down into two words. Use an action word to describe the movement – such as jump, roll, slither, slide, whirl – and an adjective to modify the action, such as lively, lethargically, quickly, discreetly. Rather than writing the following:

> The dancers jumped at the end of the choreography.

you could say:

> The choreography ended as the dancers energetically soared through the air, extending their bodies in an array of positions as they leapt across the entire width of the stage.

You want to use words that will help the reader to best visualize the choreography in the way that you saw it. Adjectives and adverbs can help you provide colorful descriptions to best capture the essence of the movement. Again, the goal is not to tell the reader everything that happened in the order that it occurred, but instead to offer a clear glimpse into what the performance entailed, so that the reader can then understand your following critique of the work. Through your descriptive summary, you are painting a picture for the reader to provide context for the next portion of the critique.

BOX 4.2 ALTERNATIVE PERFORMANCE TYPES

Not all dance performance occurs on a traditional proscenium stage. Performances may also be found in alternate settings such as an outdoor venue, where a makeshift platform is created in the middle of a green space. Site specific dance is that which is performed outside the proscenium stage in order to incorporate a very particular setting within the dance experience. Site specific works may be performed in libraries, on rooftops, in parks, on boats, etc. This type of performance allows a closer connection between dancer and spectator. Dance may also be performed in the air, as in aerial dance performance, or through projection with the use of technology. In each instance, the elements of space, time, and energy are altered to suit the needs of the environment. The atmosphere affects the overall production experience and therefore becomes a contributing factor to the effectiveness of the dance. The same method of describe, analyze, interpret, and evaluate can be applied in these situations as well.

Options are endless when it comes to creativity

Analyze

Following a description of the performance, it is important to offer an analysis of the elements of the dance. This portion of a critique moves beyond description to assimilate how the aspects of the dance work together. Think back to the elements discussed in Chapter 3. Dance utilizes space, time, and energy. It has structure: a beginning, a middle, and an end. It is your job to delineate how the movements you have described encompass certain choreographic elements and how those elements coordinate to create either a cohesive dance or one that is lacking in form. The following questions may prove useful:

- How is the movement designed within the performance space?
- Does the movement utilize certain levels or shapes?
- In what pathways do the dancer or dancers travel?
- If applicable, how are relationships between the dancers established?
- How does the movement utilize the element of time?
- What type of energy or energies are apparent within the movement?
- How is the piece formed? Consider how the dance begins and ends, and how the phrases or sections are sequenced.

Analysis moves beyond describing the dance. It highlights the features of the dance and demonstrates a deeper understanding of the choreographic elements. Sections of the piece may be compared or contrasted. If you have cultural or historical understanding pertaining to the work, this could be included in your analysis. If you are familiar with the choreographer or similar work, that could be shared during the analysis as well.

Interpret

The next step is to interpret the meaning of the work. By combining observations made during the descriptive and analytical stages, you can glean insight into the choreographer's intent for the work. The movement choices coupled with the choreographic choices can reveal much about the purpose behind the dance. As you ponder an interpretation of the work, consider the following:

- Does the title provide any hint of the meaning of the work?
- Are program notes about the work included within the program?
- Do the costumes or scenery offer clues to the subject matter or theme?
- Was there a mood or emotion that you could identify within the work?
- Did the structure of the dance, repetition in movement phrases, particular gestures, or noticeable relationship between dancers suggest subject matter?

Your interpretation must go beyond liking or disliking a dance. Refer to observations and statements made in your description and analysis to support your perspective. There is no right or wrong interpretation, but you must be able to point to aspects of the work to validate your opinion.

Evaluate

The last portion of the critique serves as an evaluation of the dance. Using the description, analysis, and interpretation, determine the success and effectiveness of the dance as a whole. It is important to note that a dance can be successful even if you personally do not like it. You may not prefer the aesthetics of the piece, but the choreography may still effectively convey a clear concept. Consider the following prompts:

- Has the work challenged you to think in new or specific ways? If so, in what way/s?
- What do you perceive to be the work's strengths and weaknesses?
- Could meaning be ascertained by the combination of choreographic and theatrical elements?
- Do the various elements of the dance work together and demonstrate a sense of cohesion? How or how not?
- What was the most effective aspect of the piece and why?
- What was the most ineffective aspect of the piece and why?
- If the dance was confusing, can you identify the elements that made it so?

Whether you are writing a critique of a dance performance or production or simply internally reflecting on what you see, the above steps of describe, analyze, interpret, and evaluate can help you formulate your perception of the work and uncover meaning within the dance.

CHAPTER SUMMARY

Observing dance and garnering an understanding of it can be difficult, especially if you do not have previous experience with the art form. There are many factors that affect how we perceive dance. An unawareness of the purpose of the dance could leave us misinterpreting or misunderstanding the performance; cultural barriers could also influence how we view the dance. Additionally, we each have personal experiences, morals, beliefs, and values that can shape our perspectives. Perceiving dance can be both an aesthetic and a kinesthetic experience. Our visual, auditory, and kinesthetic senses are stirred, and we can become physically or emotionally moved when observing dance. It is important for an audience member to keep this in mind and attend a performance with an open mind in order to fully experience and appreciate dance. The guiding stages of describe, analyze, interpret, and evaluate can prove helpful in critiquing or reflecting on a dance in order to develop a deeper understanding of the work.

aesthetic	harmony	transition
balance	proportion	unity
climax	repetition	variety
contrast	sequence	

Just as there are many reasons to dance and manners in which we can dance, there are as many, or more, ways in which dance can be perceived. The experience is unique to the individual. By remaining open to the possibilities, we can uncover a greater awareness of and empathy for the culture and world around us.

Reflective Prompts

1. What factors do you believe influence your perception of dance? Consider your individual, family, and cultural beliefs, personal experiences, religious background, views of the body, etc.
2. Recognizing the purpose behind the dance we see allows us to view the dance through the appropriate lens. What expectations do you have when you attend a dance concert by a professional dance company? What do you expect to see when you attend a performance of a national Broadway tour? How might these look different from the dance that you see when visiting an amusement park?
3. When we look at a piece of visual art, watch a dance, or listen to a selection of music, our senses are stirred, and we can have a physical reaction to the art. We may drum our hands on our laps in anticipation, we may tap our toes to the beat of the music, we may tighten our muscles in suspense, or we may simply find ourselves walking closer to the artwork in pure intrigue. Can you think of an example where you had a kinesthetic response to art or an experience?
4. It is possible to enjoy the aesthetics of a dance yet not like the dance as a whole. Is our perception of dance one in which we must either like it completely or dislike it completely? Can you think of a work of art that you recently viewed or experienced in which you really enjoyed some aspects but found others to be disturbing, boring, or irrational?
5. Ask a variety of people – friends, family, classmates, acquaintances, etc. – whether they believe dance is art or entertainment. Are you surprised by their answers? What about you? Do you think dance can be both art and entertainment, or must it be one or the other?
6. How do you decide whether something is art or not? In your opinion, which of these are art or entertainment or both: a Batman comic book, the novel *Pride and Prejudice*, a song performed by Johann Sebastian Bach, a song performed by Ariana Grande, the *Star Wars* movies, the painting *Black Circle* (1913) by Kasimir Malevich?
7. You have plans to attend a performance of the Martha Graham Dance Company at a prestigious theater in your town. Do you prefer to research

the company and specific performance in advance? Is it better to find out what others have said about the performance before seeing it yourself? Why or why not?

8. Select a work of choreography that you can watch in its entirety. Perhaps you can view a video in your school library or locate a dance on YouTube. Can you use the method of describe, analyze, interpret, and evaluate to formulate a response to the work as a whole?

NOTES

1 Merriam-Webster Dictionary, s.v. "aesthetic," accessed May 20, 2019, www.merriam-webster.com/dictionary/aesthetic.

2 Elizabeth R. Hayes, *Dance Composition & Production*, 2nd ed. (Pennington, NJ: Princeton Book Company, 1993), 11–21.

3 Oxford English Dictionary, s.v. "art," accessed May 20, 2019, https://en.oxforddictionaries.com/definition/art.

4 Oxford English Dictionary, s.v. "entertainment," accessed May 20, 2019, www.lexico.com/definition/entertainment.

5 Merriam Webster Dictionary, s.v. "entertainment," accessed May 20, 2019, www.merriam-webster.com/dictionary/entertainment.

CHAPTER 4 BIBLIOGRAPHY

Hayes, Elizabeth R. *Dance Composition & Production*, 2nd ed. Pennington, NY: Princeton Book Company, 1993.

Oliver, Wendy, R. *Writing about Dance*. Champaign, IL: Human Kinetics, 2010.

Royce, Anya Peterson. *The Anthropology of Dance*. Bloomington and London: Indiana University Press, 1977.

Steele, Shauna and Kristen Farmer. *Experiencing Dance: A Creative Approach to Dance Appreciation*. Dubuque, IA: Kendall Hunt, 2011.

Part II
Exploration of Western Theatrical Dance Forms

INTRODUCTION

Most likely you have been to some type of event in which dance was a featured part of the entertainment. Perhaps it was a music concert, and the lead singer appeared flanked by an ensemble of dancers moving in unison to the rhythm of the music. Or, maybe you attended a local rendition of *The Nutcracker* ballet in which you saw the Nutcracker lead Clara through the Land of Sweets. You may also have scrolled through the channels on the television, landing on a reality series in which individuals were energetically vying for the revered mirrored ball by performing different types of dances in the hopes of winning the votes of the millions of Americans tuned into the show. Or perhaps, while surfing through YouTube, you discovered timeless video clips of dancers bouncing their knees, kicking their legs, and tossing their partners through the air to the swinging tunes of Benny Goodman or Duke Ellington.

You may have noticed dance happening around you in various settings and situations. You even may have participated in dance at times. Yet, have you ever wondered what these forms of dance are? From where did they come? What makes one unique? What has influenced the various dance types, and what effect do they have on culture?

Part II identifies five primary dance genres of the Western world: ballet, modern dance, tap dance, jazz dance, and hip-hop. Chapters 5 through 9 emphasize the ways in which each dance genre is distinct, highlight the various stylistic differences within each genre, and depict the relationship between each dance genre and the culture in which it developed.

5 {Ballet}

In a small studio, a dozen small children chassé across the floor with their arms rounded in front of their giggling tummies. As they reach the end of the room, they stop and stretch one leg out behind them while opening their arms wide. They turn their smiling faces toward the mirror that hangs on the wall in front of them as if to say, "Look what we did!"…

Across the world, the curtain rises for a classical performance to reveal a vibrantly lit stage full of dancers in soft tutus standing in poses that resemble a much more polished version of the positions the previous youngsters had attempted to make. The leading male dancer swiftly enters the stage, performing a series of turning leaps and ending on one knee. The female soloist emerges on the diagonal with a grand leap, soaring through the space, and runs to the male dancer. She steps up onto the tip of her pointe shoe and extends her other leg high into the air behind her, perfectly balanced for several seconds …

Perhaps these are the images that come to your mind when one mentions ballet. Perhaps you, yourself, have encountered these very experiences. Or, maybe you picture or recall something entirely different. Just the idea of ballet can conjure an array of ideas and meanings. Some individuals envision the quintessential ballerina, clouded in a fluffy tutu, hair slicked into a bun, satin *pointe* shoes upon the feet. Others may picture the classical ballet *The Nutcracker* with the party scene of aristocratic guests, the battle scene between soldiers and mice, and the dancers performing diverse variations while in the fantastical Land of Sweets. Still others may recall a more contemporary example with dancers wearing only leotards while energetically weaving through space to a hip-hop beat by artists Jay-Z and Kanye West. Ballet may be considered exciting and dynamic, a dance form that mesmerizes its audience with every turn and leap; yet it may also be regarded by some as slow, boring, and lacking in meaning. This chapter will uncover the ways in which ballet has evolved to become an expressive and powerful art form, rich in history and diverse in approach.

BALLET AS A DANCE FORM

Ballet is a genre of dance that is both traditional and contemporary, elegant and edgy, fluid and vibrant. The technical foundation of ballet lies in European court dance of the sixteenth and seventeenth centuries. The seeds that were planted during that period grew and strengthened throughout the centuries. While new vocabulary and stylistic approaches have been added, the technical tradition remains at the heart of ballet. In the last century, artists have incorporated contemporary approaches to this technique, resulting in diverse choreography that may emphasize the tradition and elegance of classical ballet or the modern edginess of contemporary ballet. The movements within ballet emphasize verticality. The erect spine of classical ballet, the use of the *pointe* shoe, and the elevation within the jumps and leaps of the vocabulary support the notion of the dancers extending upright as they seemingly defy gravity. Whether classical or contemporary in presentation, technical body lines, impressive flexibility and range of motion within the back and hips, and a dynamic fluidity reveal both strength and grace simultaneously and equally within performance.

A Codified Technique

Ballet is a **codified technique**, meaning that it is guided by a delineated system of body and arm positions, defined movement vocabulary and terminology, and a methodical approach to movement execution. During the seventeenth century, under the reign of King Louis XIV in France, names were assigned to the steps utilized within court ballet. Pierre Beauchamp, dancing master to the king, devised the classical body positions and the five standard positions of the feet from which all classical ballet movement begins and ends. Regardless of where a class occurs or who is teaching, ballet continues to utilize these French terms today as well as the body and foot positions.

[margin note: Historic France started it]

Additionally, the idea of turnout was implemented into the ballet dancer's training and performance. Turnout is the active engagement of the muscles of the hips and legs to rotate the legs outward so that the knees and toes point away from the midline of the body. Initially, this act coincided with the increased use of the proscenium stage at the end of the 1600s and enabled dancers to travel sideways more effectively. Added benefits of the use of turnout within dance include the enhanced aesthetics of body lines, improved balance, and increased flexibility and range of motion of the legs, resulting in the leg's high extensions into the air. While stylistic nuances have been added to the movements throughout the various historical eras, the fundamentals of classical ballet technique have remained seemingly unchanged.

[margin note: why we turnout in ballet]

The Ballet Class

A ballet class often follows a standard structure. Regardless of where one takes a class or from whom, one can expect the class to begin with either a slow *tendu* (the sliding of the foot along the floor to extend the leg in a specific direction) or a *plié* (the bending of the legs) exercise, then follow a progression of movement exercises at the ballet ***barre***, and then transition to a sequential series of movement combinations in the center. While the specifics of the exercises vary, the structure of the class remains consistent from teacher to teacher and from class to class: *barre* work then center work. This is often the case with

5.1
Students at
the University
of Oklahoma
School of Dance
with guest artist
Christopher Ruud.
Photo courtesy
of the OU School
of Dance and
Sarah Cermak

traditional art forms. Yet, ballet teachers do have freedom to vary the manner in which they devise their exercises and may take liberties in the sequencing of the exercises performed at the *barre* and those performed in the center. This class structure references the traditional ballet class, yet, similarly to sports, techniques and methods can be questioned and may evolve in pursuit of the health and safety of the performer.

Barre work is comprised of those exercises executed during the first portion of a ballet class and done while holding onto the ballet *barre*. This is done to provide support to the dancers so they can focus on body placement and alignment, coordination, flexibility, strength, and movement articulation. The *barre* serves as a tool to aid the dancers in balance while dancers continuously warm their bodies and prepare for the technical demands of the center work. Exercises performed during the center portion of the class consist of the movements utilized within classical choreography. These exercises routinely progress in a methodical structure, beginning with movement patterns focused on placement, balance, traveling, and turning, and build to elevated jumps and leaps that are brisk in tempo or grandiose in presentation.

BOX 5.1 THE BALLET *BARRE*

The precursor of the ballet *barre* appeared during the sixteenth and seventeenth centuries. As the steps included within the court spectacles increased in difficulty, dancing masters would have their pupil practice while holding onto the back of a chair for balance.[1] In time, this method became a standardized component of the ballet class.

The structure of ballet and the development of the vocabulary have evolved over the centuries. Four major historical eras within the history of ballet serve as markers, highlighting the development of ballet from an early entertainment form within the royal courts of the European Renaissance to the conceptual modern ballets of the early twentieth century.

The Pointe Shoe

The first *pointe* shoes appeared in the early 1800s; however, they were nothing like the shoes that dancers wear today. The original *pointe* shoes used light darning around the toes that permitted the dancers to rise only briefly onto the tips of the toes. Today's shoes are much more sophisticated and crafted in such a way as to fit a ballerina's unique foot shape and technical needs. While they are certainly designed with enhanced technology and increased durability, a pair of *pointe* shoes will only last a dancer so long. Depending on the dancer's degree of ability and amount of dancing, *pointe* shoes may last a season or only a single performance.

Pointe shoes are made of layers of fabric stiffened by glue and a slim strip of leather. There are three basic parts to a *pointe* shoe: the shank, the toe box, and the vamp. The shank is the leather sole that fits snugly against the bottom of the foot. The shank may extend the length of the foot or run only midway up the foot, allowing a greater range of flexibility. The toe box surrounds the toes and provides an oval-shaped platform upon which the dancer can stand. The toe box, which may be shallow or deep, comes in varying degrees of stiffness depending upon the dancer's preference and needs. The vamp is the fabric that connects to the back of the shoe, wraps around the toe box, and covers the top of the foot. The vamp helps to hold the foot in place against the shank. *Pointe* shoes do not have a right or left foot; they are generally made to fit either foot.

Dancing *en pointe* requires a considerable amount of strength in the feet, ankles, calves, and legs. Dancers must have good technique and dance with proper alignment. Training includes specific exercises designed for *pointe* work; the transitions between standing on a flat foot, rolling through a mid-position, or demi-*pointe*, and arriving on full *pointe* require great strength. *Pointe* work should not be attempted by a young dancer until proper technique has been acquired so as not to risk injury to developing bones. It is often advised that *pointe* work should not begin until at least age twelve. Dancers who accomplish the feat

5.2
Dancers *en pointe*.
Photo by Jeff
Smith, WKU

of performing *en pointe* display true dedication to the art, demonstrating their disciplined efforts of constant practice in order to fluidly and technically conquer this art.

Positions Within a Ballet Company

Dancers maintain a hierarchy within their position in a traditional ballet company. The basic positions include principals, soloists, demi-soloists, and *corps de ballet*. **Principal dancers** are given the most important roles within a ballet. At times, these can include character roles as well. Soloists perform solo or minor roles in a ballet, such as one of the fairies in *The Sleeping Beauty*. Demi-soloists are a step above the *corps de ballet*. These featured roles are often performed in pairs. The ***corps de ballet*** is the lowest rank in the company, and the level where most dancers enter the company. It is the large group of dancers who do not perform a featured role.

Additional roles to note are the ballet master or mistress and the répétiteur. The **ballet master** or **mistress** of the company is the individual with the responsibility of instructing daily class for the company and rehearsing the ballets that the company will be performing. For those companies that have been granted a license to reconstruct or restage a particular choreographer's work, a répétiteur may be sought to assist in setting the choreography. A **répétiteur** is someone who teaches and rehearses choreography on a company in the event that the choreographer is unavailable or no longer living.

THE HISTORICAL DEVELOPMENT OF BALLET

Court Ballet to Professional Ballet (Fifteenth–Eighteenth Centuries)

The precursor of this art form is found within the early court spectacles of the European Renaissance. Court dance began first in Italy, and it is from the Italian word *ballare* which means "to dance," that the word "ballet" is derived.[2] By the end of the fifteenth century, however, Catherine de' Medici brought court dance to France upon marrying into the French ruling family. As de' Medici's authority increased, she incorporated the court dances of the Italian culture within her new home of France. These lengthy and lavish productions were performed by noblemen for audiences of the ruling class and consisted of movements that related more to social dance steps of the time period than to ballet as we recognize it today. At that time, there was little distinction between social and theatrical dance. The court spectacles featured classical stories and legends and included drama, opera, and interludes of dance. Movements emphasized grace, elegance, and social decorum, and costumes resembled the attire of the time period. The conclusion of the event brought both performers and spectators together in dance, thus highlighting the social aspect of the evening.

Yet, behind these social functions also lay a political motive. The spectacles presented a carefully calculated mix of art, politics, and entertainment with the chief purpose of glorifying the state. These events were also a way for nobility

[handwritten margin note: Ballet started as a court dance]

5.3
Engraving of a
scene from court
Italian dancing
master Balthasar
de Beaujoyeux's *Le
Ballet Comique de
la Reine*.
Universal History
Archive/Universal
Images Group via
Getty Images

to impress one another; wealth and power were on display. Rulers could amaze or even outdo their counterparts with the grandeur of their spectacle and the quality of the art presented.

A prominent characteristic of **court ballets** was the geometric floor patterns in which the dancers would travel. Court ballets were created for venues in which the audience sat in galleries above the dance space and looked downward upon the dancers. Therefore, the dances were designed in such a way that the dancers traveled through geometric floor patterns. Given that the attire of the day included layers of fabric that extended to the floor, obscuring the lines of the body, movements consisted primarily of steps, glides, low brushes of the legs, and hops. As a result of the simplistic use of body movement and the more complex use of spatial movement within the choreography, the visual pathways became a focal feature.

It was during the Renaissance that the dancing master emerged. In order to coordinate, design, and instruct the spectacular court functions in which dance was the primary entertainment, it was essential that the profession of the dance master be employed within the courts. Their responsibilities included instructing the nobility on the precise steps to be performed during courtly balls and the exact manner in which they were to be executed.

The zenith of these court ballets, or *ballet de cour* as they had come to be called, occurred during the reign of King Louis XIV. In his quest to maintain power and authority over his court, Louis XIV also desired to control the dance.[3] He established institutions that eventually merged in 1672 to become the *Académie Royale de Musique et Danse*. Known today as the Paris Opera, this establishment was paramount in the history of ballet for several reasons.

It was during this period that the concept of _danse d'école_, or dance school, emerged within the constructs of the _Académie_. The _danse d'école_ provided strict training on how to dance ballet, integrating the five classical positions of the legs, the required use of turnout, and the codification of ballet steps. The academy also resulted in the transition of the dance from an amateur art to a professional art form. Noblemen were replaced by male professionals, and women were later granted the right to perform as well. The performances were relocated from casual locations within the courts to formal proscenium theaters.

The shift from venues within the court to the proscenium stage had numerous effects on ballet. First, the idea of an actual stage space forced dancing masters to consider choreography in new ways. Audiences were no longer seated in galleries above the performers looking down but were instead seated in front of the dancers, who now performed on an elevated stage framed by a structural "arch." Consideration had to be given to the design created by the dancers' bodies on the stage rather than strictly the geometric pathways in which they traveled. Additionally, the increased choreographic demands required greater levels of technique and skill by the dancers. Another noticeable change included the new distinction between "house" and stage. The action used to extend into the house of a traditional theater, or the area in which the audience was seated. Once the dance was moved into a proscenium theater space, the movement was confined to the stage. The proscenium arch separated the performers and the audience; the social connection was lost between audience and performer, and theatricality was emphasized.[4]

[handwritten margin note: transition from being a court dance]

5.4
King Louis XIV appears dressed in the role of Apollo from _Le Ballet de la Nuit_. His performance earned him the nickname of the Sun King.
API/Gamma-Rapho via Getty Images

As ballet transitioned from a social function within the court setting to a theatrical form, societal attitudes toward the dance also began to shift. The dance was no longer something to simply look at or in which to join. Society felt that the dance should mean something, and, as a result, emotion and expression slowly crept into its performance.

In 1760, Jean Georges Noverre wrote *Letters on Dancing and Ballets*. His theories called for a shift in the way that dancing masters approached ballets, which ultimately initiated a transformation of the art form and set the path for the development of ballet as we recognize it today. Plots became more logically developed, integrating all of the theatrical elements into the storyline and choreography. The use of masks, which were worn during court ballets, was eliminated and replaced with gestures and the dancer's individual expression to convey meaning and dramatic content. Costumes were changed; the length of skirts was shortened, and flat slippers replaced heeled shoes.

Classic stories we know originated here

These costume changes encouraged the development of a greater range of movement options along with an increased level of difficulty. The new ballet that emerged was referred to as **ballet d'action**, or dramatic ballet. Previously, the storyline in court ballets had been told through speech and song separated by various dancing interludes. *Ballet d'action* allowed the dramatic action to unfold through the use of mime and gestures incorporated into the dance itself, and the narrative could continue without the need of speech or individual song. Ultimately, the movement of the dance created a visual picture, while the *danse d'école* enabled the technique behind the movement, and the integration of pantomime and gesture provided emotional content within the performance.[5] With the development of the *ballet d'action*, ballet was now a vehicle in and of itself for dramatic expression and action. It no longer needed spoken word or song to relay storyline or message and, as a result, had secured its artistic independence.[6]

◆ Romantic Ballet (Nineteenth Century)

In history, the Romantic Era followed the French Revolution and occurred during the first half of the nineteenth century. Romanticism was both an artistic and an intellectual movement in Western civilization, which emphasized the individual and emotions over the inherent rationalism of the Enlightenment. The ballets choreographed between the years of approximately 1830 and 1870 are known as **Romantic ballets**, as they embrace the ideals of this era.

In the early 1800s, European society felt a divide between the life they lived and that which they desired. Art, music, and literature captured the combination of realism and escapism while underscoring emotion rather than logic.[7] A number of two-act ballets appeared in which the first act, or sunlit act, was rooted in reality and an earthly and human scenario, while the second act, or moonlit act, was set in a spiritual realm. There, a fantastical scene would unfold, where spiritual creatures, often sylphs or nymphs, would appear, and the

5.5
The ballerina Marie
Taglioni in the
ballet *La Sylphide*,
ca. 1830s.
DeAgostini/
Getty Images

[handwritten note: Classics now to be thought to be less creative, whats the relationship between creative and being New?]

unattainable would be revealed. Choreographers unleashed their imaginations and created scenarios in which characters could transcend the human condition. The poetic pursuit of love was the common theme among Romantic ballets, where the prominent male served as the Romantic hero, while the featured female became the unattainable, perfect Romantic ballerina. The emotional content of the Romantic ballets was quite appealing; the escape into a fantasy world was something with which the middle-class audiences could connect.

Romantic ballet storylines were female-centered, which led to the rise of the ballerina. Many women attempted to emulate the women they observed on stage, both idealizing and idolizing them. One such ballerina was Marie Taglioni. In 1832, she appeared in *La Sylphide* (*The Sylph*), which was choreographed by her father, Filippo Taglioni. Prior to her performance, few dancers had actually danced **en pointe**, meaning rising onto the tips of the toes, and no other females had artistically incorporated *pointe* work into their performance.[8] However, following Taglioni's performance in *La Sylphide*, all principal female dancers were then required to dance *en pointe*.

[handwritten note: Pointe started]

BOX 5.2 ROMANTIC BALLET HIGHLIGHT: *GISELLE*

Giselle is a ballet that has become synonymous with the Romantic Era. Choreographed by Jules Perrot and Jean Coralli, the ballet premiered in 1841 at the Paris Opera, marking a high point for Romantic ballet. Since its premiere, *Giselle* has been restaged by a vast number of ballet companies worldwide and continues to be performed in the twenty-first century.

Synopsis: The storyline of the ballet is rooted in gothic legend. Giselle, a young peasant woman, falls deeply in love with Albrecht, a handsome young man. Upon learning that he is betrothed to a noblewoman, she goes mad and commits suicide. The setting for the second act occurs at Giselle's tombstone, deep in the forest and lit by moonlight. It is here at night that the Wilis, who are the ghosts of women who have died unhappy in love, reveal themselves. When Albrecht comes to visit Giselle's grave, the Queen of the Wilis instructs Giselle to "dance him to death." Giselle, however, is unable to abide by her orders and protects Albrecht until the sun rises and forces the Wilis away.

Ballet continued to evolve in many ways during the early nineteenth century. The costumes changed once again, and the Romantic tutu was adopted. With her form-fitting bodice and bell-shaped skirt that extended toward the ankle, the ballerina appeared airy and light. And, without the layers of fabric that she had previously worn, she was able to move more freely. Movements could become trickier and more challenging, requiring an increase in technique and the further expansion of steps. *Pointe* work advanced as well. Modifications were made to the front of the slippers to increase support as more females began to dance *en pointe*. New theatrical elements were introduced, including the use of trap doors, flying machines, imbedded tracks to enable shifting scenes, the dimming of house lights and gas lighting, which helped in creating the moonlit scenes, and the lowering of the main curtain on stage between acts. These technical elements enhanced the mood and overall effect of the performance.

5.6
A scene from the second act of *Giselle*, performed by dancers from the Los Angeles Ballet. Earl Gibson III/ WireImage, Getty Images

The developments in ballet, along with focus of the era itself, brought society's attention to the ballerina. The female dancer now superseded the male dancer, marking the first time that the female presence on the European stage was more important than that of her male counterpart. Audiences clamored to see these superstars grace the stage. Yet despite this attraction, ballets slowly began to drift away from the ideals of Romanticism toward the end of the nineteenth century. Many of the great choreographers and ballerinas were no longer performing or living. New choreographers were shifting away from the expressive themes of the Romantic Era in favor of technical virtuosity.[9] Audiences were ready for a new visual and a new experience, which would soon be revealed on the Russian stage.

Imperial Russian Ballet (Late Nineteenth Century)

Peter the Great was a great admirer of Western culture and sought to develop and westernize Russia by importing European architects, engineers, scientists, and artists, including several of the prominent dancing masters from the Italian and French court ballets. By 1800, St. Petersburg had become the epicenter for the arts within Russia, and it was not long before the Russian government began to protect and support the ballet. While the *Académie* in France had guided the development of ballet throughout the 1700s, a counterpart was established in Imperial Russia. In 1738, the St. Petersburg Ballet School was founded, and in 1766, Catherine the Great founded the Directorate of the Imperial Theaters.[10] Under the watchful eye of the tsars, the arts, specifically ballet, profited, and by the end of the nineteenth century, the ballet in Russia had claimed the title of **Imperial Russian Ballet**.[11]

The most influential choreographer of this era of ballet was Marius Petipa. This French dancer became the ballet master of the Imperial Ballet of St. Petersburg (now the Kirov Ballet), and under his leadership, ballet choreography advanced both in technique and in presentation. Petipa made *pointe* work obligatory for all females, not just the soloists. Tutus were shortened to knee-length as a diverse range of movement rooted in the classical ballet vocabulary continually advanced. The use of pantomime remained as a choreographic tool to convey meaning and message, much like a sign language unique to ballet. To provide greater contrast and variety within his ballets, Petipa incorporated an increased use of national, or character, dances within his choreography.

During the years of the Imperial Russian Ballet, choreographic attention was given to the principals, groups of soloists, and the *corps de ballet* in such a manner that the principals were featured, soloists highlighted, and the *corps de ballet* provided accent. More focus was given to the *corps de ballet*, providing choreography that was individual for them rather than simply arranging the group as a backdrop around the soloists. Petipa emphasized individual variations for the principals and soloists, which allowed those dancers to perform movement that featured their particular strengths and qualities.[12]

5.7
The court scene from *The Sleeping Beauty* performed by the New York City Ballet, choreography by Peter Martins. Nikolay Vinokurov/ Alamy Stock Photo

BOX 5.3 IMPERIAL RUSSIAN BALLET HIGHLIGHT: *THE SLEEPING BEAUTY*

Petipa choreographed *The Sleeping Beauty*, based on the Brothers Grimm's version of the tale. The ballet, which premiered in St. Petersburg in 1890, included a prologue (the christening) and three acts (the spell, the vision, and the wedding), for which Tchaikovsky composed the score. The *Sleeping Beauty* provided quite a memorable and historical collaboration. Petipa had very specific ideas for the ballet, including the scenario, the choreography, and the music. Rather than engaging in a true collaboration with Tchaikovsky, he instead prescribed 101 detailed instructions to the musician for the musical composition. At times, he even specified what instrumentation should be played during a section of music.[13]

The ballet provides a clear example of ballets of the era of Imperial Russian Ballet. The scenery depicts the opulence of the palace, the principal ballerina is the focus as witnessed in "The Rose Adagio" variation, the grand *pas de deux* is performed by the prince and princess, and an array of *divertissements* are presented by characters during the wedding scene.

Petipa's grandiose ballets follow a standard choreographic structure. The narrative is drawn out over the course of three or four acts. Toward the end of the production, a series of dances, referred to as *divertissements*, are performed. These are not directly connected to the storyline but included simply to divert the audiences' attention. At their most fundamental level, these series of dances are a sparkling collection of entertaining choreography. The grand ***pas de deux*** can also be found toward the end of the ballet. This duet between the ballerina and her male partner follows a codified format. The pair first perform an *adagio*, or slow dance, together. This section is very stately and presents fluid and controlled movements. Next, the dancers perform their individual variations, or solos. The male dances first, followed by the female's variation. The two reunite in a dazzling and fast-paced coda that completes the *pas de deux*.

During the years of the Imperial Russian Ballet, the government controlled the training and education of the art form. The tsar subsidized training for students at the ballet school in St. Petersburg. Hundreds of young pupils would apply, yet only handfuls would be chosen, based on qualities such as physicality, aptitude, and musicality.[14] Enrollment within the ballet school was considered equal to that of a military academy and was a highly desirable career pathway for young individuals. Control of ballet did not end within the schools; only those within the aristocracy and higher-ranking governmental and military positions were permitted into the audience of the two imperial theaters within St. Petersburg. This in turn influenced the performance itself. The costumes and the scenery were opulent and lavish, an intentional effort to reflect and please the royalty within the audience. At the end of a performance, the ballerina would not bow to the audience but, rather, first to the tsar, then to the theater director, which was a position appointed by the government. Only after the tsar and director were acknowledged would the ballerina bow to the general audience.[15] The choreographic productions of this era offered a reflection of Imperial Russia and served to glorify the monarchy. The costumes, the sets, the music, and the choreography each emulated that which society admired, including wealth, power, hierarchy, and technical virtuosity. These ballets mirror the aristocracy for whom they were designed, much as the court spectacles reflected the noblemen for whom they were created.[16]

Diaghilev's Ballets Russes (Early Twentieth Century)

Russians continued to lead the next phase of development in the history of ballet, yet they did not do so from inside the country of Russia. Sergei Diaghilev was neither a dancer nor a choreographer but, rather, an art critic and ballet impresario. Diaghilev maintained the perspective that ballet should reflect the twentieth century through "a more timely, natural, and unified style of movement, plot, music, and painting."[17] This theory diverged from the ballets of Petipa. Diaghilev formed the company the Ballets Russes, and the choreographers he employed brought his concept to life. The Ballets Russes unveiled an altogether new and modern form of ballet, and revitalized ballet in the West.

The Ballets Russes performed choreography by Michel Fokine, Vaslav Nijinsky, Léonide Massine, Bronislava Nijinska, and George Balanchine. While each choreographer had their own unique approach to choreography, some overarching themes remained visible throughout the repertoire of the company. Classical ballet steps, poses, and positions were adjusted to meet the specific needs of each work; rather than using strictly classical vocabulary,

Interesting that it was so govt. controlled

becoming even MORE different

5.8
Dancers of the
Kremlin Ballet
perform Michel
Fokine's *Le Spectre
de la Rose* at the
London Coliseum.
Robbie Jack/Corbis
via Getty Images

5.9
Dancers of the
Boston Ballet
Company perform
Vaslav Nijinsky's
*Afternoon of a
Faun* at The London
Coliseum.
Leo Mason/
Popperfoto/
Getty Images

the movement was shaped to suit the specific storyline of a given dance. Previously, emphasis had been given to the ballerina in performance; the choreography of the Ballets Russes increased the focus of the male dancer on stage, creating equal status between the male and female dancers. Support was given to the concept of total theater, which called for a complete collaboration of all of the designers – including the choreographer, musicians, and costume and set designers – engaged in a production to work democratically together in the creation of that production. The previously used program format of Petipa's three to four act ballets was revised. A performance by the Ballets Russes consisted of three or four single-act ballets that were separate yet complete works of differing styles. The ballets offered had dramatic storylines or were plotless.

The Ballets Russes altered the trajectory of ballet. Great feats had been achieved in technical skill, yet as a whole, the art was growing stale. The new dance that Diaghilev's company presented reinvigorated ballet and paved the way

always changing

for innovative approaches in both movement and choreography. The company, which remained based in Paris while touring throughout Europe and America, lasted until Diaghilev's death in 1929, yet its effects continued. The company generated many great artists who continued to advance ballet throughout the twentieth century, particularly in both England and America.

TWENTIETH CENTURY AND BEYOND ➜ *TODAY!*

In America, ballet is an imported art form. It originated in Europe, yet America has embraced the ballet and claimed its role within ballet's evolution. Although individual European ballerinas had visited and performed throughout North America during the 1800s, ballet's biggest influencers within the United States were Diaghilev's Ballets Russes and a later company known as the Ballet Russe de Monte Carlo. Their performances sparked an interest in ballet, created enthusiastic patrons across the country, and led many individuals to study the art form, paving the way for companies to emerge in America. Following the Ballets Russes' innovative approaches to ballet choreography, new styles of ballet – first neoclassical and then contemporary – gained momentum throughout the twentieth and into the twenty-first century. Ballet choreographers found inspiration not only in movements from other dance forms, such as modern, jazz, tap dance, and non-Western dance forms, but also from other genres of music, visual art, cultural events, and social and political issues. The following serve only as a sampling of the many influential dancers and companies that have advanced or continue to advance the art of ballet in America through the preservation of the historical classics, presentation of groundbreaking choreography, and carrying forward of ballet education.

American Ballet Companies

Ballet ensembles began to form in the United States as early as the 1930s. Catherine Littlefield founded the Littlefield Ballet, which later became known as the Philadelphia Ballet in 1935. Although this company only survived six years, it was the first company directed by an American and comprised of American dancers. It was also the first American ballet company to tour Europe. The 1930s also saw the formation of the San Francisco Ballet, the first American company to perform productions of *Swan Lake* and *The Nutcracker*.

George Balanchine, a former ballet master with the Ballets Russes, laid roots in America when he founded the New York City Ballet, along with Lincoln Kirstein, in 1948. A vast majority of the company's repertoire consists of work choreographed by Balanchine, whose work is modern yet classical in form and often regarded as **neoclassical** in style. In neoclassical ballet, traditional ballet vocabulary is used, and the *pointe* work is still emphasized, yet the narrative element is removed from the choreography and replaced with a modern, abstract approach. Balanchine's movement often incorporated turned-in leg positions, flexed hands, and positions of the body that shifted the body out of traditional alignment. His choreography focused on the dance itself, rather than the production aspects; therefore, costumes were often minimal, and many ballets were void of storyline or plot. In these instances, Balanchine highlighted the relationship between the movements and the music within the ballets. While the movements in his ballets were grounded in classical ballet vocabulary, he also blended new body lines and positions that fell outside the traditional ballet language. The New York City Ballet's website notes that Balanchine created 465 ballets throughout the course of his life. His legacy continues today, as a great number of companies are granted permission to perform his choreography, sharing his creative vision and voice with dancers and audiences worldwide. The School of American Ballet is the training academy officially associated with the New York City Ballet.

The American Ballet Theatre, established in New York City in 1939, thrives today as one of the world's leading ballet companies, presenting timeless classical ballets along with contemporary ballet works. In 2006, the United States Congress passed an act declaring it the American National Ballet Company. Various levels and divisions of education and training programs are formally connected with the ballet company.

[handwritten note in margin: Contemp. Ballet's sorta]

5.11
The simplistic look of Balanchine's later ballets as depicted in the Royal Ballet's production of *Agon*. Robbie Jack/Corbis via Getty Images

The latter half of the twentieth century witnessed the formation of two unique companies. Robert Joffrey founded the Joffrey Ballet in 1956. Joffrey first launched his ballet troupe and toured the United States with the goal of spreading classical ballet performance across the country. Today, this company continues to thrive in its home city of Chicago, presenting original works that blend ballet and modern dance as well as restaging many of the historical classical ballets. In 1969, Arthur Mitchell, the first African American to perform with a leading national ballet company (New York City Ballet), founded the Dance Theatre of Harlem in New York City, which is a predominantly African American ballet company. His company proved to the nation that ballet extended beyond race and was not a dance form suited for only European body types and structures.

Contemporary Ballet

Ballet choreography today can take on many shapes and styles. Some choreographers may utilize standard ballet vocabulary in its traditional formal style to comprise the movement for a ballet dance. In this sense, they are creating a **classical ballet**, as pictured in Figure 5.12. *Don Quixote* (1869, choreographed by Marius Petipa), *Cinderella* (1948, choreographed by Frederick Ashton), and *Onegin* (1965, choreographed by John Cranko) are all examples of classical ballets. Other choreographers may choose to take standard ballet vocabulary and manipulate it from its traditional form. For example, the dancers may execute a traditional movement but vary it in some way from its "textbook" definition. Perhaps, instead of executing a movement with turned-out legs, the dancers may turn the legs inward. In this instance, the choreographer

5.12
A classical ballet look is featured in this photo of Carlos Acosta and Marianela Nunez in Marius Petipa's *Don Quixote*.
Robbie Jack/Corbis via Getty Images

5.13
A scene featuring the Wilis in Akram Khan's version of *Giselle*.
©Bill Cooper/ ArenaPAL

is creating a ballet in a contemporary style. **Contemporary ballet** is rooted in classical ballet technique and vocabulary yet blended with modern dance technique, incorporating off-center positions, manipulations of the torso and body lines, and use of floorwork. *Pointe* shoes may or may not be worn.

Both classical and contemporary ballet companies exist throughout the modern world. While some companies choose to perform work solely in one style, many choose to perform a diverse range of material. Complexions Contemporary Ballet, Alonzo King's LINES Ballet, and Ballet X are examples of contemporary ballet companies within the United States.

Today, many companies often look for choreographers of other genres of dance to enhance and diversify their repertoire with work fused with differing styles and forms of dance. In 2016, choreographer Akram Khan created a reimagined version of the classical ballet *Giselle* for the English National Ballet. His work fuses ballet with *kathak*, a traditional Indian dance in which he is trained. In 2018, the American Ballet Theatre commissioned three works by tap dancer and choreographer Michelle Dorrance, which challenged the company's dancers to approach ballet vocabulary from a tap dancer mentality, with a new focus on movement approach rooted in the audible rhythmical sounds produced by the *pointe* shoes striking the floor during the execution of the dance.

Regardless of whether a ballet company is working in a classical or a contemporary approach, the delivery is highly technical, producing clean body lines and clearly articulated movement throughout the body. As more and more ballet companies present contemporary work, it can be hard for the novice audience member to determine whether or not the genre is ballet, as it is no longer mandated that the females must wear *pointe* shoes or the traditional tutu. While

Basics still don't change

the "Romantic" tutu or short "Classical" tutu may be utilized, a more contemporary costume choice could be selected, including a simple unitard, a sports bra with jogger pants, or even briefs with bare legs. Musical accompaniment could include live or recorded music in genres ranging from classical to popular, or a ballet could be performed in silence. Regardless of these performance selections, the classical ballet technique class lies at the root of every great ballet performance. While ballet dancers may incorporate other forms of dance training or focus primarily on contemporary ballet classwork, they most likely all have classical ballet study in their backgrounds.

Ballet Commercialized

As contemporary ballet increased in appearance, and choreography experimented with the fusion of ballet and other dance forms and the integration of other art forms and technology, the boundaries of ballet have been pushed beyond its traditional limits. Ballet no longer appears solely on the proscenium stage as part of an evening-length performance or theatrically in staged musicals. Frequent films featuring ballet have been produced in just the last two decades, including The Nutcracker and the Four Realms (2018), Center Stage: On Pointe (2016), Leap! (2016), and The Black Swan (2010). With the advancements in technology, ballet now appears in diverse facets of society that extend beyond the stage and big screen, including within digital apps, internet and streaming platforms, and reality television. *even more modernized*

CONTEMPORARY ISSUES WITHIN THE FIELD

The world of ballet today is rife with racial and gender issues, caused in part by the historical developments of the art form. From historical ballets that embrace old world viewpoints to increasing awareness of gender inequality, dancers and leaders within the ballet profession grapple with realigning a centuries-old art form with contemporary ideals and perspectives. Tradition is a characteristic that is cherished and respected within ballet, yet there is a fine line between upholding the legacy of great choreographers and their historical repertoire and acknowledging the grotesque treatment of humanity, the mischaracterization of cultures, or the insensitivities to one's fellow humankind. Several historical classical ballets include depictions of women as slaves or white ballet dancers appearing in blackface. Variations from the infamous ballet The Nutcracker are called into question for their racist stereotypes, as the second act depicts a series of short character dances from various cultures. The Chinese variation is performed by dancers wearing conical hats who execute a series of springing jumps while holding their hands in the air with the index fingers pointed upward – a hand gesture appropriating Chinese culture. The Bolshoi Ballet has been called out for its use of blackface in its productions of La Bayadère.

Racial barriers have permeated the ballet profession. These have ranged from decisions regarding casting within professional companies to the costuming of dancers of color. As we have learned, ballet began in Europe and was traditionally centered around the European physique and ideal. After centuries of European ballerinas and their male counterparts, a certain body type and physical aesthetic trickled down the lines of *corps de ballet* members of company dancers worldwide. The African American female in particular struggled first to maintain her place in the ranks of the *corps de ballet* and then to become a soloist and principal in national companies. Today, ballerinas of color are able to wear tights the color of their own skin tone as opposed to the traditional ballet pink tights. *Pointe* shoe manufacturers began to make shoes to better match

5.14
Misty Copeland is featured in the American Ballet Theatre performance of *Giselle* at the Metropolitan Opera House, 2015.
Hiroyuki Ito/ Getty Images

a dancer's skin tone in the late 2010s. Previously, *pointe* shoes were made primarily in a peachy pink tone, which best complemented a naturally white-skinned dancer and forced ballerinas with darker skin tones to use make-up to paint or "pancake" their shoes to match their skin, which is a time-consuming and annually costly process.

Still lots of change to come

BOX 5.5 MISTY COPELAND

Misty Copeland made history in 2015 when she became the first African American female principal with the American Ballet Theatre, one of the nation's leading ballet companies. She was featured in the 2015 documentary *A Ballerina's Tale*, has been showcased in a number of television programs and publications and endorsed by various companies and products, and is the recipient of numerous awards. In 2018, Copeland performed in the film *The Nutcracker and the Four Realms*.

Historically, ballet performance roles have reinforced conventional ideas of masculinity and femininity. Within classical ballets, the female is often perceived to be placed on a pedestal. Male dancers literally lift the female dancer above their heads; females rise onto the tips of *pointe* shoes in seemingly perfect balance. Within the traditional *pas de deux*, the male gingerly balances the female, carries and lifts her, and leads her across the stage. Many choreographers have challenged gender roles within ballets since the end of the twentieth century. Matthew Bourne's version of *Swan Lake*, which premiered in 1995, goes against the grain, taking a contemporary approach to a classical ballet and placing males in traditionally female roles. Many contemporary ballet choreographers encompass gender-neutral roles within their choreography today.

gender barriers coming down

Dancers are also now encouraged to practice vocabulary and aspects that were once reserved for certain genders. Females participate in men's classes, where tempos are often slower, and the focus is on gravity-defying jumps and multiple turns performed in the air while jumping. Males are engaging in *pointe* work to benefit from the increased foot and ankle strength that it can provide them. Yet, despite these advances, gender equity remains an issue. Research conducted by the Dance Data Project during 2016–2017 reveals that even though girls outnumber boys twenty to one within ballet classes, male choreographers and artistic directors strongly dominated the professional field. Looking at ballet companies within the United States, the Dance Data Project discovered that a male served as the artistic director for 72% of the companies. Just as other professions also grapple with gender inequality, the world of dance is no exception.

even in a majority female thing, there is an INSANE amount of sexism

BALLET AROUND THE GLOBE

Ballet originated as a European art form, yet today ballet training and pro-fessional companies exist across the world. Superb ballet artists can be found performing, choreographing, and/or directing companies in a variety of countries, including the United Kingdom, the Netherlands, Australia, Cuba, Canada, China, and Chile. For example, William Forsythe and Jiří Kylián are two leading choreographers who have pushed the boundaries of classical ballet, often blending the genre with modern and contemporary dance forms. William Forsythe directed the Frankfurt Ballet from 1984 to 2004 and then led The Forsythe Company from 2005 to 2015. His groundbreaking choreog-raphy tests the limits of ballet by deconstructing classical ballet vocabulary and preconceptions. He has incorporated spoken word, art installations, and technological elements into his ballets. Jiří Kylián served as the artistic dir-ector of the Nederlands Dans Theater from 1975 to 1999 and continued as a choreographer for the company until 2009. Born in Prague, he has become an internationally acclaimed choreographer known for his musically abstract ballets that blend the classical with the contemporary.

CHAPTER SUMMARY

Ballet is a highly technical art form that requires a great level of skill, prac-tice, and bodily facility before one can become competent in the genre. It is not easy to master; in fact, it takes years of serious training and a level of innate ability to reach a professional level. In America, children may begin the serious study of ballet around the age of seven. Dance studios across the country offer ballet classes for students of all ages, and pre-professional dance programs for more seriously focused ballet dancers annually accept a select number of students into their programs. Many regional and profes-sional ballet companies have summer intensives or trainee programs where younger dancers may study with the company or a school associated with the company. These companies often have an apprentice performance com-pany, which can serve as a stepping-stone for dancers to gain experience and continue their training.

As a profession, ballet is primarily a concert theatrical art form. National and regional ballet companies are located across the United States in both large and small cities. Depending upon budget, venues, and other resources, these companies present a variety of ballets each season for audiences of all ages. Many US cities are home to either pre-professional or youth companies, which may perform ballets as well as offer training classes. Yet, ballet can be found in venues aside from the concert stage. Theme parks, television shows and commercials, music videos, theatrical stage shows, and blockbuster hits have each featured or included ballet in many and various ways throughout recent decades.

Within its history and in modern society, ballet has served social, political, and theatrical purposes. Historically, the institutional structure associated with ballet training has inherently generated socioeconomic issues within the hierarchy of ballet. Gender roles within the art form have also been challenged throughout the decades. Contemporary choreography has presented thoughtful and often controversial themes, inciting conversation among society. It is undeniable that ballet today is a challenging art form that is enjoyed by the masses, appears in both popular and concert venues, and is performed in both classical and contemporary modes.

[handwritten: has changed a TON]

5.1 Notable Individuals in Ballet			
Early Ballet	**Catherine de' Medici** (1519–1589)		She produced *Le Ballet Comique de la Reine* (1581, *The Dramatic Ballet of the Queen*), which is considered the first authentic ballet.
	Pierre Beauchamps (1631–ca. 1705)		He is credited for devising the five classical positions of the legs, developing the use of the dancer's turnout, and codifying a number of ballet steps.
	Louis XIV (1638–1715)		His greatest performance role was as Apollo, for which he earned the nickname "*le Roi Soleil*," or "the Sun King," in *Le Ballet de la Nuit* (1653, *The Ballet of the Night*).
	Jean Georges Noverre (1727–1810)		He wrote *Les Lettres sur La Danse et Les Ballets* (1760, *Letters on Dancing and Ballets*) and produced over 100 examples of *ballet d'action*.
Romantic Ballet	**Filippo Taglioni** (1777–1871)		He choreographed *La Sylphide*, artistically presenting *pointe* work for the first time on the stage.
	Carlos Blasis (1797–1878)		His work led to the traditional structure of the three-part ballet class: *barre* work, center work, jumps and turns.
	Marie Taglioni (1804–1884)		She was the first and preeminent ballerina of this era, made famous by her leading role in the ballet *La Sylphide*.
	Jules Perrot (1810–1894)		He is considered as the greatest choreographer of the Romantic Era.

(continued)

Imperial Russian Ballet	Marius Petipa (1818–1910)	He created forty-six original ballets, revised seventeen ballets, and reshaped the art of ballet choreography.
	Lev Ivanov (1834–1901)	He shared with Petipa the choreographic responsibilities for *Swan Lake* (1898), creating the "white acts" of the ballet, which include the infamous "Dance of the Little Swans."
The Ballets Russes	Sergei Diaghilev (1872–1929)	He was the mastermind behind the Ballets Russes, which introduced a new and modern form of ballet, revitalizing ballet in the West.
	Michel Fokine (1889–1942)	He focused on the human form and depicted beautiful images rather than fanciful tricks. He emphasized the movement in storytelling rather than the use of pantomime. His ballets include *Firebird* (1910), *Petrushka* (1911), and *Le Spectre de la Rose* (1911).
	Vaslav Nijinsky (1889–1950)	He was a Russian-born ballet dancer referred to as one of the all-time greatest dancers and known for his gravity-defying leaps. His often controversial choreography sought to challenge how society viewed beauty upon the ballet stage. His ballets include *L'Après midi d'un Faune* (1912, *Afternoon of a Faun*) and *Le Sacre du Printemps* (1913, *Rite of Spring*).
	Léonide Massine (1895–1979)	He debuted as a choreographer with the Ballets Russes in 1915. The angular movements of his choreography are often highlighted with character dances and diverse styles. His ballets include *Parade* (1917) and *Le Tricorne* (1919, *The Three-Cornered Hat*).
	Bronislava Nijinska (1891–1972)	During the 1920s, she choreographed several ballets for the Ballets Russes. Her ballets included *Le Renaud* (1922, *The Fox*) and *Les Noces* (1923, *The Wedding*).
Twentieth and Twenty-First Centuries	George Balanchine (1904–1983)	He was a Russian-born dancer who took over as ballet master of Ballets Russes following Nijinsky until Diaghilev's death. He later helped create the New York City Ballet, for which he choreographed over 400 ballets. His neoclassical style often featured plotless ballets, minimal costuming, and attention to the relationship between movement and music over storyline. His ballets include *Apollo* (1928) and *Prodigal Son* (1929).

(continued)

5.1 Cont.		
	Robert Joffrey (1930–1988)	He founded the Joffrey Ballet in 1956 with the goal of spreading classical ballet performance across the country. The company continues to thrive in its home city of Chicago, presenting original works that blend ballet and modern dance as well as restaging many of the historical classical ballets.
	Arthur Mitchell (1934–2018)	He was the first African American to perform with a leading national ballet company (the New York City Ballet). He founded the Dance Theatre of Harlem, which is a predominantly African American ballet company, proving to the nation that ballet extends beyond race.
	William Forsythe (b. 1949)	He directed the Frankfurt Ballet from 1984 to 2004 and then led The Forsythe Company from 2005 to 2015. He tests the limits of ballet by deconstructing classical ballet vocabulary and preconceptions.
	Jiří Kylián (b. 1947)	He served as the artistic director of the Nederlands Dans Theater from 1975 to 1999 and continued as a choreographer for the company until 2009. He is known for his musically abstract ballets that blend the classical with the contemporary.

5.2 Notable Characteristics of Classical and Contemporary Ballet	**Classical Ballet**	**Contemporary Ballet**
	Erect torsos	Spiraling and/or off-center torsos
	Strictly adheres to traditional ballet technique	Incorporation of other dance techniques and movement vocabulary
	Utilizes traditional ballet vocabulary	Uses turned-in legs and other manipulations of the body that deviate from traditional ballet technique
	Utilizes turnout	May be performed barefoot, in soft slippers, or *en pointe*
	Incorporates *pointe* work	May focus on abstract themes rather than a storyline
	Often follows a narrative	

5.3 Historical Timeline of Ballet		
	1672	*L' Académie Royale de Danse* and *l' Académie Royale de Musique* merged to become *l' Académie Royale de Musique et Danse*, which remains today as the Paris Opera.
	1738	The St. Petersburg Ballet School was founded.
	1760	Jean Georges Noverre wrote *Letters on Dancing and Ballets*.

(continued)

1766	Catherine the Great founded the Directorate of the Imperial Theaters in Russia.
1832	Marie Taglioni performed *en pointe* in *La Sylphide*, choreographed by Filippo Taglioni.
1841	*Giselle* premiered at the Paris Opera, choreographed by Jean Coralli and Jules Perrot.
1847	Marius Petipa arrived in St. Petersburg to perform with the Imperial Ballet.
1862	Petipa became ballet master for the Imperial Ballet.
1890	Petipa choreographed *The Sleeping Beauty*.
1892	Petipa and Lev Ivanov choreographed *The Nutcracker*.
1898	Petipa and Ivanov choreographed *Swan Lake*.
1909	Sergei Diaghilev toured the Ballets Russes around Europe.
1929	Ballets Russes dissolved when Diaghilev passed away.
1933	The San Francisco Ballet, the first American company to perform productions of *Swan Lake* and *The Nutcracker*, was formed.
1935	Catherine Littlefield founded the Littlefield Ballet, which later became known as the Philadelphia Ballet, the first company directed by an American, comprised of American dancers, and the first American ballet company to tour Europe.
1939	The American Ballet Theatre (ABT) was established in New York City under the direction of Lucia Chase and Oliver Smith.
1948	George Balanchine and Lincoln Kirstein founded the New York City Ballet.
1956	Robert Joffrey founded the Joffrey Ballet in Chicago.
1969	Arthur Mitchell founded Dance Theatre of Harlem.
2006	The US Congress passed an Act declaring ABT the American National Ballet Company.
2015	Misty Copeland became the first African American female principal with ABT.

ballet d'action	contemporary ballet	neoclassical
ballet master/mistress	*corps de ballet*	*pas de deux*
barre	court ballet	principal dancer
classical ballet	*en pointe*	répétiteur
codified technique	Imperial Russian ballet	Romantic ballet

Reflective Prompts

1. What preconceived notions did you have about ballet or ballet dancers prior to this study? Have your ideas altered in any way? If so, how?
2. How did Imperial Russia control ballet and its development? What role does your government play in the control of art today? How is the development of art, specifically dance, affected or not affected?
3. Watch an excerpt from the second act of *Giselle* (Romantic ballet) and from the first act of *The Sleeping Beauty* (Imperial Russian ballet). Compare and contrast the two examples. How do the movement characteristics and theatrical elements differ between the two excerpts?
4. Do you prefer to watch classical or contemporary ballet? Explain your answer.
5. Can you recall any other films, television shows, or commercials in which ballet was featured or included? How was the dance integrated into the work? Was it effective? Why do you think it was selected rather than a different dance genre?
6. For centuries, ballet remained a strictly classical art form, appearing only on the proscenium stage in concert form. Why do you think ballet today has become more commercialized? What do you think might be the next step in ballet's evolution?

Movement Prompt

1. **Ballet Movement:** Learn the ballet movement on the companion website and try to execute the sequence.

NOTES

1 Jack Anderson, *Ballet & Modern Dance: A Concise History*, 2nd ed. (Princeton, New Jersey: Princeton Book Company, 1992), 34.
2 Jack Anderson, *Dance* (New York: Newsweek Books, 1974), 12.
3 Carol Lee, *Ballet in Western Culture: A History of Its Origins and Evolution* (New York and London: Routledge, 2002), 66.
4 Lee, 58–59.
5 Lee, 93.
6 Anderson, *Dance*, 34.
7 Anderson, *Dance*, 44.
8 Lee, 148.
9 Susan Au, *Ballet and Modern Dance*, 2nd ed. (London: Thames & Hudson Ltd, 2002), 58.
10 Lee, 184.
11 Lee, 202.
12 Lee, 211.
13 Lee, 213.
14 Lee, 208.
15 Anderson, *Dance*, 65.
16 Lee, 230.
17 Lee, 226.

CHAPTER 5 BIBLIOGRAPHY

Anderson, Jack. *Ballet & Modern Dance: A Concise History*. 2nd ed. New Jersey: Princeton Book Company, 1992.

_____. *Dance*. New York: Newsweek Books, 1974.

Au, Susan. *Ballet and Modern Dance*. 2nd ed. London: Thames & Hudson Ltd, 2002.

Clarke, Mary and Clement Crisp. *Ballet: An Illustrated History*. New York: Universe Books, 1973.

Lee, Carol. *Ballet in Western Culture: A History of Its Origins and Evolution*. New York and London: Routledge, 2002.

6 Modern Dance

A light breeze gently rustles the long flowing hair and white tunics adorning the dancers outside. Gracefully, they begin to skip through the grass like sprites in a forest. Their arms float gently around them as they bound through space, turning and hopping in the sunshine …

A figure shrouded in purple and sitting on a bench twists and writhes in angular shapes. The tension in the air is palpable as the figure repeatedly throws its head back and then slowly folds forward again …

Several dancers scattered about the stage perform seemingly independently of one another as they each kick, turn, reach, jump, and run at different times, while the music plays not a recognizable melody but eerily long drawn-out notes in dissonance with no recognizable meter …

The brightly lit stage reverberates with energy as eighteen dancers sway, point, and clap their hands to the lively gospel music. The women swish their skirts masterfully as their hats exaggerate their movement, while the men stretch the limits of their vests in this vigorous celebration …

Modern dance is anything but limited. Born with a spirit of freedom, this dance form explores the endless possibilities of movement, at times calling into question what dance is. From barefoot, gritty, aggressive movement to lighter-than-air buoyancy, modern dance experiments with movement in inventive and revolutionary ways.　　　　No bounds whatsoever

MODERN AS A DANCE FORM

Though the word "modern" means relating to present times, modern dance spans over a century of movement. The visual and visceral characteristics of modern dance are vast and diverse, but at the heart of the form is a spirit of curiosity. Modern dance evolved to include such disparate styles because each new chapter stemmed from modern dancers trying to find something new. These artists were searching for a way to express the spirit of their times. As times changed, so did the dancing. Modern dance is more easily described as an attitude toward dance rather than one specific way of dancing.

In the Western world, modern dance broke away from the formality of ballet, which some artists considered sterile, restrictive, or irrelevant. In this comparison, the modern movement explored freer use of the pelvis and torso, swinging momentum, a more three-dimensional use of the body in space, and bare feet. Often, modern dance choreographers placed emphasis on the importance of expressing emotions and ideas, and individuality was more emphasized than in ballet. The history of modern dance is easily observed and most often discussed as generations of dancers. In this text, we will instead be exploring modern dance by looking at various characteristics, meaning that the leading figures and movements discussed are not presented in chronological order. However, a timeline is provided at the end of the chapter, and Table 6.1 lists the generations of leaders. The characteristics discussed in this chapter are not a complete list of modern dance attributes, but they serve as an access point into this dance form.

BOX 6.1 A GLOBAL FORM

Modern dance has flourished all over the world, with Germany being another particularly influential country of development. At the same time as modern dance was forming in America, artists such as Rudolf Laban and Hanya Holm were developing their own modern dance practices in Germany. The popularity of modern dance spread gradually, and similarly to ballet, there are modern dance companies based in countries all around the globe.

6.1
Dancers of Alvin Ailey American Dance Theater in the opening section of Ailey's iconic work *Revelations*. Doug Gifford/ Getty Images

The Modern Dance Class

Just as the modern dance that is seen on stage varies, so do modern dance classes. Within the form of modern dance, there is a variety of different techniques developed by diverse individuals. Some of these techniques are codified, or guided by a delineated system of body and arm positions, defined movement vocabulary and terminology, and a methodical approach to movement execution, while other techniques are more loosely based on a guiding principle. Let us look at a few selected examples.

Codified Techniques

One of the most well-known modern dance techniques is Graham. Developed by Martha Graham in the early twentieth century, her technique is built on the principle of contraction and release. Contraction refers to the engagement of the muscles in the core, which in Graham technique is centered in the lower abdominals and pelvis, resulting in concave abdominals and chest and a rounded back. In the moment of release, the spine lengthens to return to an elongated neutral posture. The simple inspiration behind this technique was breathing, with the contraction as the exhale and the release as the inhale. After training at the Denishawn School in Los Angeles (which will be discussed later in this chapter) and then performing with the company for several years, Graham moved to New York in 1923. She presented her first dance concert in New York City in 1926, and in that same year, she opened her school, the Martha Graham School of Contemporary Dance. The school and the Martha Graham Dance Company have been operating in New York City ever since.

[handwritten: Graham's style is codified and contains specific attributes]

[handwritten: specific traits for a class of this]

A Graham class always begins seated on the floor, which allows students the time to build and understand the very specific technique of contraction and release before standing. After several floor exercises, there are standing exercises in the center, which include some standard ballet technique exercises, such as *plié* and *tendu*, but with modern dance principles layered on top of them. For example, a class may be asked to contract as they close the leg in from *tendu*. After this, the class then begins to work on traveling exercises across the floor and may end with learning a movement phrase in the center.

Graham's technique is referred to as being developed backwards. That is, rather than developing a movement technique to prepare dancers for the stage and using that as the foundation for choreography, Graham began by creating choreographic works and then developing a classroom technique to support her choreography. Graham's choreographic work was always guided by the criterion that the movement is based on the need to express the heart and mind. She believed in no extraneous movement but only in movement used to communicate, which meant that, for example, she never included an arm gesture to fill space or time. Every movement in her work contributed to the message or feeling. In addition to conveying the introspective, Graham also believed in America having a voice in dance. Because of this, she created works such as *Appalachian Spring* (1944), which focused on the pioneering spirit of the Wild

[handwritten: Nothing is ever just to fill time, —all intentional]

6.2
Modern dance
pioneer Martha
Graham.
UCLA Library/
Getty Images

West. Another common theme in Graham's work was Greek mythology, such as in her works *Cave of the Heart* (1945) and *Night Journey* (1947). Graham described her passion for choreographing in a letter:

> I refuse to admit that the dance has limitations that prevent its acceptance and understanding – or that the intrinsic purity of the art itself need be touched. The reality of the dance is its truth to our inner life. Therein lies its power to move and communicate experience. The reality of dance can be brought into focus – that is into the realm of human values – by simple, direct, objective means. We are a visually stimulated world today. The eye is not to be denied. Dance need not change – it has only to stand revealed.[1]

Pure Freedom

Another codified modern dance technique was developed by Lester Horton. Horton grew up in Indiana with interests in history, Native American culture, and snakes. He eventually moved to Los Angeles and in 1934 founded the Lester Horton Dance Group. Horton's company functioned as a total dance theater. He and the dancers conducted research on the subjects of their works and also made costumes, props, and sets for their productions. Horton's productions halted with the outbreak of World War II. After the war, he established the Lester Horton Dance Theater in 1946. If Horton's company was not the first, then it was at least one of the first to racially integrate its dancers. Horton also choreographed for Hollywood films, including *Phantom of the Opera* (1943).

Horton is most renowned for his technique, which he structured and developed to be streamlined, so that every part of it contributed to the big picture of the work. He wanted his technique to serve as corrective training. While the work in the technique builds strength and flexibility, it also develops performance quality and musicality. Horton's technique was developed with a drummer to accompany the exercises, which allowed him to have irregular count patterns – in other words, instead of steady counts of repeated eights, there would be four eights, two tens, and then a seven. Horton developed seventeen **fortifications**, or exercises, that are set with counts and specific movements. These very specific exercises were designed to build certain skills and tone the muscles. In addition to these fortifications are various studies and preludes that

6.3
Dancers performing Graham's *Appalachian Spring* in 1987. Originally choreographed in 1944, *Appalachian Spring* captures the pioneering spirit of the Wild West and is still performed today.
Robert R. McElroy/ Getty Images

6.4
Dancer of Alvin Ailey American Dance Theater performs a lateral T, one of the signature positions of Horton technique, onstage.
Desiree Navarro/ Getty Images

also focus on strengthening specific muscles and training distinct skills, such as a hinge or percussive quality in movement. All of these are codified and published in a book written by Marjorie B. Perces, Ana Marie Forsythe, and Cheryl Bell. The shapes that dancers move through in Horton technique are very linear (see Figure 6.4), yet the technique also includes small isolations that are layered to create complicated coordination studies.

Though Horton died unexpectedly in 1953, his former dancers were able to carry on his legacy. In particular, Alvin Ailey went on to have an extremely successful career in New York City, founding the Alvin Ailey American Dance Theater. Ailey made Horton technique a part of the school he founded and used Horton vocabulary extensively in his choreography. His contributions to modern dance are explored more thoroughly later in this chapter. There are many other modern dance techniques that are still taught and utilized today. Great influencers like Merce Cunningham and Katherine Dunham created their own distinct techniques. We will discuss some of these figures and explore other aspects of their careers later in this chapter.

Alvin Ailey does Horton's style →

Other Class Structures

While not all modern dance techniques are codified, other class structures are based on founding principles or guiding theories of movement. One of the schools that trained generations of future modern dancers was Denishawn. This Los Angeles-based school was founded by Ruth St. Denis and Ted Shawn, who are often considered the most influential pair in American modern dance, though their careers began separately. The two met in 1914 and got married shortly thereafter. The next year, in 1915, they founded their dance school and company Denishawn.

BOX 6.2 STAR-CROSSED DANCERS

Ruth St. Denis began dancing in vaudeville (discussed in Chapter 7) as a teenager. While she was a young woman, she was inspired by seeing an image of the Egyptian goddess Isis on a cigarette poster and became enthralled with Asian art and dance. She studied Hindu art and philosophy and created and performed dance work inspired by her Asian studies, which was met with success both in the United States and in Europe. On the other hand, Ted Shawn first encountered dance after a severe illness left him temporarily paralyzed. At his doctor's request, he took up dancing, ultimately changing the trajectory of his entire life.

Denishawn offered a diverse curriculum that included ballet, Asian dances, dance history, and dance philosophy. In other words, studying dance at Denishawn did not mean training strictly in one codified technique. Class structures varied to suit the specific dance form that was being taught. The curriculum was wholistic, and dancers here transformed the body, mind, and spirit. Multiple future modern dance leaders trained at Denishawn, including Martha Graham, Doris Humphrey, and Charles Weidman. In 1931, St. Denis and Shawn parted ways as both business and marriage partners (though they never divorced). St. Denis turned her focus to dance in religion and also continued

Every choreographer has unique aspects they bring to modern. Modern is like a genre of a billion different styles

6.5
Ruth St. Denis and Ted Shawn (right) with a group of their student dancers ca. 1920. APIC/Getty Images

teaching South Asian dance. Shawn went on to form a company of male dancers called Ted Shawn and His Men Dancers, which performed the first all-male dance concert in Boston in March 1933. That same year, Shawn founded the now famous dance festival Jacob's Pillow in Becket, Massachusetts. This festival still occurs every summer, with residency studies available in ballet, modern, tap dance, and flamenco and Spanish dance. Additionally, the Pillow now offers several year-round opportunities as well as production studies (dance photography, theater management, etc.).

BOX 6.3 WHO'S WHAT?

Jacob's Pillow is the name of the farm on which the festival takes place. It obtained this name because of the geographical features surrounding it. The road that leads up to the property contains a lot of zigzags, which resulted in it being referred to as Jacob's ladder, in reference to the Bible story. Additionally, there is a pillow-shaped rock on the property. Combining these two features, the property became known as Jacob's Pillow.

Doris Humphrey and Charles Weidman both trained at Denishawn. In 1928, they left Denishawn together to start their own dance school and company. The Humphrey–Weidman company toured across the United States for over a decade. Humphrey in particular rooted her practice of dance on her theory of fall and recovery, which utilized the breath's rhythm of an inhale and exhale. Her movements emphasized momentum, much like a pendulum swinging, and incorporated the concept of being off-balance and then returning to center or stability. A phrase Humphrey famously used to describe these ideas was "the arc between two deaths." Humphrey never codified this technique, but she and Weidman influenced many dancers who worked in their company.

José Limón studied with Humphrey and danced in the pair's company. When he eventually started his own company, he convinced Humphrey to become artistic director. Limón developed his own technique, which was strongly rooted in Humphrey's fall and recovery concept. Though his technique is not formally codified into strict exercises, it is distinctive and continues to be taught at the Limón Institute in New York City.

Modern dance classes vary greatly in style and structure. An experience in a modern dance class could mean mastering Graham contractions on the floor, lengthening the body into long lines and lateral Ts in Horton class, experiencing the influence of other cultures' movements, finding the freedom and release of harnessing gravity's momentum, grounding the body and undulating to African drums, or something else entirely. There are many exciting and unique principles of movement to explore within the modern dance form. The next portion of this chapter will explore some of these ideas and the individuals who influenced the movements.

PRINCIPLES OF MODERN DANCE

Although each phase, or generation, in modern dance's development is unique, there are some themes that reoccur through its history. At its core, modern dance embodies the spirit of curiosity, exploration, and innovation. In a stark contrast to ballet, modern dance explores natural movement and often surrenders to gravity, rather than working to defy gravity and lift one's weight away from the ground such as in *pointe* work. At different stages in modern dance's history, individuals explored organic movement, preservation of cultural traditions, advancements in production technology, and new possibilities of what dance may be.

Organic Movement

VERY RADICAL

Isadora Duncan stripped dance of all the artificial techniques and materials to perform freely. In a very radical move for the late nineteenth century, Duncan removed her corset, wore a loose and flowing white tunic with bare legs and bare feet, and allowed her hair to flow freely as she danced. Duncan's costuming along with her sense of abandonment in movement was considered by a majority to be scandalous. Additionally, she allowed herself to dance with abandon. Dance was highly spiritual to Duncan. She had a deep connection to nature, from which she drew great inspiration. Likewise, she used natural movements, such as walking, running, skipping, and jumping, to fuel her dancing. The subject of her dancing was the soul. She had no need to be inundated with complicated narratives or forced intentions in dance. Duncan equated dance with love, and thus saw no need for any "extra." Her dancing focused on the most natural, free-flowing way of moving, otherwise known as **organic** movement.

Duncan is often referred to as the "Mother of Modern Dance" for being one of the first artists to explore this new expressive dancing. Her performances abstractly expressed the human condition. She traveled across America from her home on the West Coast to Chicago and New York before moving to Europe, where her career took off. She founded a dance school in Berlin and trained students in her dance style; these students were adorned with the nickname "Isadorables." Duncan suffered a sudden death when she was only fifty years old, but her spirit of dancing impacted generations of dancers and continues to inspire artists; there are many books, drawings, paintings, documentaries, plays, and poems about Duncan and her life.

In more recent decades, Ohad Naharin developed his own organic movement. Naharin trained extensively in ballet and Graham modern dance technique. During his success as a choreographer, he was appointed as artistic director of Batsheva Dance Company in Israel in 1990. It was in Israel that he

6.6
Photograph of
Isadora Duncan in
her loose robes and
bare feet, as she
often performed her
dances.
ullstein bild Dtl./
Getty Images

developed his Gaga movement language after facing a serious injury. Naharin defines Gaga as "an innovative movement language based on research into heightening sensation and imagination, becoming aware of form, finding new movement habits, and going beyond familiar limits."[2] In 2003, he coined the term Gaga for the movement language he had been creating, and he still continues to research and develop the work. Dancers training in Gaga sense their bodies in unique new ways, such as trying to feel the friction between flesh and bones, the weight of body parts, or the heat of the floor. In an effort to make dancers aware of their bodies in new ways, emphasis in this movement language is on sensation instead of physical positions. The organic feel of the movement is explored in order for dancers to increase physical awareness, expand their movement possibilities, and enhance their energy and texture of moving. Naharin is also house choreographer of the Batsheva Dance Company, and his works are licensed to and performed by a variety of the top dance companies in the world. Some of his most notable works are *Minus 16* (1999), *MAX* (2007), *Field 21* (2011), and *Hole* (2013).

This sounds insanely cool to try

BOX 6.4 LABAN MOVEMENT ANALYSIS

Laban Movement Analysis (LMA) was developed by Rudolf Laban, creator of Labanotation, which was discussed in Chapter 3. LMA is a methodical approach and specific language used to describe movement of the human body. Broken into four categories – body, shape, space, and effort – with several subcategories each, this systematic approach guides the Labanotation system and trains dancers to gain a deeper understanding and stronger control of their movement and dynamics. For example, the eight efforts are float, wring, press, glide, dab, flick, slash, and punch.[3] These are each made up of different combinations of the elements of weight, space, time, and flow and produce distinct qualities of movement.

Developed by Irmgard Bartenieff throughout the mid-1900s, Bartenieff Fundamentals[SM] (BF) is an extension of Laban Movement Analysis (described in Box 6.4) that is based in the progression of motor skill development of babies and toddlers. Bartenieff trained with Rudolf Laban in Germany before emigrating to the United States in 1939 at the threat of war. She had had a dance company in Germany, and after coming to America, worked as a physical therapist in different capacities, eventually teaching Laban-based movement therapy at the Dance Notation Bureau, where the foundation for BF was laid. BF is a somatics technique with a specific approach to movement that utilizes deep muscles and breath support to train dancers to move in the ways similar to how they naturally developed movement skills in childhood. Concepts at the root of this technique include body connections, the center of weight, and initiation and follow through. These core principles are rooted in the natural movements and movement development of children, yet they require devoted training and great skill to master. Based in kinesiology, BF focuses on efficiency and functionality, therefore allowing artists to move more easily and expressively while also reducing the risk of injury.

6.7
Ohad Naharin's work *Minus 16* performed by Alvin Ailey American Dance Theater. Hiroyuki Ito/ Getty Images

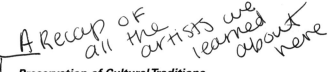
A Recap of all the artists we learned about here

Preservation of Cultural Traditions

Our culture helps shape us as individuals, and dance is one way in which to express our cultural DNA. Multiple modern dance artists infuse their own cultural experiences into their choreographic works and in doing so preserve their cultural heritages in their creations. For example, as mentioned earlier in this chapter, American modern dancer Martha Graham celebrated the spirit of Americans pioneering in the West in her choreographic work *Appalachian Spring*. Modern dance artists have used and continue to use this art form to preserve and celebrate diverse cultures.

Katherine Dunham, an educated anthropologist and social activist, researched black dance and its tradition as a means to educate audiences. She established one of the first African American dance companies, Ballet Nègre, in 1930 in Chicago. Later, after spending two years in the Caribbean – mostly Haiti – studying all aspects of dance, she returned to the United States and infused the Caribbean and African influences into her creative works and technique. Her work was influenced by modern dance, jazz dance, and Caribbean and African dance traditions, and she codified her own technique, known as the Dunham Technique. The movement of her technique fuses the long lines and turnout of her base in ballet technique with isolations, Afro-Caribbean movement vocabulary, and exciting rhythmic challenges.

Dunham relocated to New York City, where she founded the Dunham Company (later the Katherine Dunham Company) in 1940 and opened the Dunham school in 1945. In addition to training many modern dance masters, such as Alvin Ailey, Dunham had an extensive performance career dancing on Broadway and in Hollywood films. Today, teachers can become certified in Dunham's codified dance technique, and her movement practices are still taught to the next generation of dancers.

Alvin Ailey – modern dancer, choreographer, teacher, and master – was a voice and leader of African American dancers through some of the most racially polarized times in American history. Born in Texas, Ailey was forced to work in cotton fields and in white homes before the family relocated to Los Angeles. He was introduced to dance here and trained with Lester Horton. After one year directing Horton's company following his death, Ailey moved to New York City and performed on Broadway. A few years later, he founded the Alvin Ailey American Dance Theater in 1958 with the vision of a company "dedicated to enriching the American modern dance heritage and preserving the uniqueness of the African-American cultural experience."[4]

Ailey created many masterpieces of movement. However, his most famous ballet is undoubtedly *Revelations* (1960), which was mentioned in Chapter 3 of this text. Danced to a score of African American spirituals, gospel songs, and blues, the piece captures the human condition while based in Ailey's "blood memories" of growing up in Texas. *Revelations* is divided into three sections: the first expresses the weight of pain and sorrow that people carry while still reaching for hope, the second depicts a baptismal celebration and the desire to be ready

6.8
Dancers in the
section "Wade in
the Water," part
of Alvin Ailey's
Revelations.
Doug Gifford/
Getty Images

for death, and the final section reflects on Sunday church services and the eternal joy from hope and faith. Premiering in the midst of the tumultuous civil rights movement, this work is rooted in Ailey's experience growing up as an African American, but it speaks to audience members of all backgrounds and continues to be performed regularly by the company today.

In 1969, Ailey formed the Alvin Ailey American Dance Center, now the Ailey School, to offer classes and training for dancers. The school is now internationally renowned and offers several different programs for children, young adults, pre-professionals, Bachelor of Fine Arts (BFA) students, and professionals. Classes are taught in Horton, Dunham, and Graham techniques as well as ballet, jazz, hip-hop, and conditioning classes. Generations of dancers, dance teachers, patrons of the arts, and the general population have been affected by Ailey's career and continuing legacy.

Miss Kayla studied here!

BOX 6.5 CELEBRATING THE AFRICAN DIASPORA

The Alvin Ailey American Dance Theater and Ailey School are not restricted to modern dance. The company performs works, such as *Four Corners* depicted in Figure 6.9, and students at the school train, in dance styles across the African diaspora. Although it is identified as a modern dance company, jazz, hip-hop, traditional African dance, and fusions of these forms are all prominent in the Ailey company's history and repertoire.

Production Innovation

In addition to discovering new movement possibilities, modern dance artists also have been innovators of production technology. Loie Fuller was known for her dramatic effects with fabrics and lighting during the late nineteenth century. She wore huge skirts or draperies that she kept in constant motion with her arms and layered by shining inventive lights onto the fabric. She created dyes for her fabric, experimented with electrical lighting, colored gels, and projections, and even

6.9
Ronald K Brown's
Four Corners being
performed by Alvin
Ailey American
DanceTheater in
London.
Robbie Jack –
Corbis/Corbis via
Getty Images

patented special mirror arrangements to enhance the effects. She also invented underlighting in which she stood on frosted glass that was lit from underneath; this effect can be seen in her work *Fire Dance* (1895).

BOX 6.6 RADIOACTIVE DANCE

When Marie and Pierre Curie discovered radium in 1898, ever-curious Loie Fuller befriended them. She originally hoped to be able to use radium on her costuming for dramatic effect. However, when they rejected this idea because of cost (the deadly effects were still unknown), Fuller choreographed a dance that imitated the phosphorescence of the element through her innovative lighting and fabrics and titled it *Radium Dance*.

Like Horton, Alwin Nikolais operated his company, formed in 1951, as total dance theater, working as designer and composer in addition to choreographer. Nikolais wanted to step away from the internal focus on self with which modern dance was so infatuated. His view of the art form was a much wider, cosmic-sized picture. As such, he regularly dehumanized his performers by changing the form of their bodies, for example, encapsulating dancers in full-body length stretch bags or extending limbs with props. Nikolais wanted to transport his audience to an inhuman world and achieved this through costuming, set design, props, or lighting. He also asked his dancers to stop emoting through the movement and would frequently ask them for "motion, not emotion."[5] For example, his work

6.10
Dancers of Alwin Nikolais Dance Theatre performing *Imago* in elaborate costumes that abstract the human form. Manuel Litran/ Paris Match via Getty Images

Tensile Involvement (1953) includes long elastic ribbons hanging from above the stage to the stage floor, and his dancers constantly move these ribbons around the space, creating patterns and shapes independent of the dancers.

Experimentation

Modern dance is known for **avant-garde**, or unorthodox, works that push the boundaries of what might be called dance. During the 1960s, dancers, composers, and visual artists started gathering at the Judson Memorial Church in Manhattan to exchange ideas and art work. The group became known as the Judson Dance Theater. These individuals rejected conventional dance theater as it had been known up to this point. This collective met weekly for workshops in which they performed and critiqued each other. Judson Dance Theater was a breeding ground for new ideas and possibilities in dance and the arts, ultimately prompting the post-modern movement in dance. **Post-modern dance** is a concert dance form that rejected all previous dance constructs and considered all movement to be dance. Radical ideas led to innovative artists and pieces that looked to pedestrian movement more often than virtuosic dance steps and controversial practices for the concert stage, such as dancers performing nude.

Making Dance that is anything but traditional dance!

One tremendously influential figure who emerged from the post-modern movement was Merce Cunningham. Cunningham, as well as some other artists like Alwin Nikolais, decided to abandon the idea that dance had to communicate a narrative or emotion. This idea was not entirely revolutionary to Western dance, as Balanchine and others had explored it in ballet. However, Cunningham began original experiments pushing the art form. He collaborated often with John Cage, an American composer known for his unorthodox arrangements, which included sounds considered to be outside the realm of music. In Cunningham's works,

the sound happened to exist at the same time as the dance and the scenery happened to exist in the same place as the dance, but neither of them had anything to do with the dancing. In essence, Cunningham took all the rules of choreography about stage space, form, time, energy, order, and so on and creatively challenged them.

Furthermore, Cunningham developed what can be called **chance composition**. This idea of chance or uncertainty manifested itself in multiple ways in his works depending on the piece. In *Sixteen Dances for Soloist and Company of Three* (1951), the order in which the sections are performed may change. *Field Dances* (1963) allows the dancers to enter and exit the stage whenever they wish. For *Story* (1963), the dancers choose their costumes from a pile of second-hand items the designer brings each night, and the scenic designer remakes the set each night with items lying around the theater. *How to Pass, Kick, Fall and Run* (1965) has readers sitting in the corner of the stage reading short stories throughout the work in mostly whatever order they choose; each story must take one minute to read no matter the length of the story, resulting in some being read extremely quickly and others with long pauses between words. The methods through which these various chance elements were determined each night also varied and could include coin tosses, dancers' will, number drawing, and so on. Cunningham referred to this use of chance as an avenue through which to open his mind to new possibilities and avoid clichés of choreography.

Cunningham's works are now preserved by the Merce Cunningham Trust, which licenses out his choreography to both educational, or student, and professional productions. The trust also maintains the Cunningham technique, which is characterized by coordinated and opposing torso and legwork, spatial awareness, and rhythmical accuracy and creates dancers that are strong and flexible both physically and mentally. The trust offers classes in the Cunningham technique to keep the practice and legacy alive.

[handwritten margin note: So so diff- out of the box ideas]

BOX 6.7 EARLY USE OF TECHNOLOGY IN DANCE

Merce Cunningham embraced technology early on in his career. He experimented with television, video, computers, body sensors, and motion-capture technology. He was a pioneer in the use of computers for choreography in modeling and animating the human form. These topics are explored more in Chapter 10.

MODERN APPROACHES

Legacy companies are dance companies that carry on the tradition of an individual artist. Many of these legacy companies mentioned in this chapter are still performing today, including the Martha Graham Dance Company and Alvin Ailey American Dance Theater. Additionally, countless small regional modern dance companies have formed in the last several decades. These small companies' performance seasons vary anywhere between one annual performance and multiple performances, and explore the gamut of modern dance possibilities.

Other modern dance artists are still continuing their careers and influencing dance onstage in many capacities. Garth Fagan, originally from Jamaica, came to the United States in 1960. After growing up dancing in Jamaica, he trained with Alvin Ailey, Martha Graham, José Limón, and other modern masters. In 1970, he founded his dance company, eventually titled Garth Fagan Dance, in Rochester, New York. His choreography incorporates elements of modern, jazz, and African dance. Fagan has created works on esteemed companies like Alvin Ailey American Dance Theater and New York City Ballet, though he is perhaps best known for his legendary work on Disney's Broadway musical *The Lion King* (1997). He also developed Fagan Technique™, which fuses modern, Afro-Caribbean, ballet, and post-modern qualities into one dynamic technique.

In Germany, Pina Bausch's career as a choreographer left an indelible mark on modern dance. Bausch began her dance training under Kurt Jooss as a teenager and went on to study at the Julliard school in New York City. After a successful performance career, she returned to Germany, eventually becoming artistic director of Wuppertal Dance Theatre. Bausch took many radical risks during her career as a director. She changed the name of the company to Tanztheater (dance theater) Wuppertal and created explosive works of choreography. For example, her 1978 piece *Café Müller* was inspired by growing up in her parents' restaurant and involved many dancers performing with their eyes closed and stumbling into tables and chairs. Her rendition of *The Rite of Spring* (1975) requires the stage to be completely covered in soil, and the dancers become progressively dirtier as the piece

I LOVE this and I had no idea!

6.12
Dancers from
Garth Fagan Dance
perform his blended
movement style.
TIMOTHY
A. CLARY/AFP via
Getty Images

6.13
A dancer from
Tanztheater
Wuppertal Pina
Bausch performs
Bausch's work *Like
Moss on a Stone*.
Leo Mason/
Popperfoto/
Getty Images

continues. Her company, now called Tanztheater Wuppertal Pina Bausch, continues to present her repertoire and carry out her artistic vision.

Contemporary

More and more often nowadays, different dance genres are blending onstage. In a simple manner, dance companies are hiring choreographers from different genres to set works on that company (i.e. tap dance artist Michelle Dorrance was commissioned to set work on American Ballet Theatre). In a more complicated manner, the characteristics of the movement being presented by companies are blending. Moreover, the word "contemporary" dance has been thrown around before any clear definition was prescribed. This has led to widespread confusion about what the dance genre "contemporary" is.

On the other hand, modern dance has evolved for over a century. Artists and scholars must consider at what point the form has changed enough from its original that it is now a new form of dance, and perhaps that form

6.14
Dancers from
the premiere
contemporary
company Hubbard
Street Dance
Chicago perform in
Mexico.
Humberto Romero/
Getty Images

is contemporary, or contemporary modern. There is no governing body to determine what these definitions mean; rather, it is a now constant conversation between artists. Many dance companies exist that identify as contemporary dance companies, several of which were founded in the last forty or so years. Hubbard Street Dance Chicago refers to itself as a contemporary company on its website, while other companies, like Peridance Contemporary Dance Company, based in New York City, and Dayton Contemporary Dance Company, include the term in their names.

In an article published in 2012, *Dance Magazine* asked several leading modern/contemporary dance artists what the difference between these two words is in terms of dance. Among the ten individuals, no two had the same answer. One choreographer, Mia Michaels, even stated, "Contemporary is an easy way out – it's when you don't know what to call it, you call it contemporary."[6] For now, artists must be thoughtful about how they use the terms "modern" and "contemporary" and be deliberate in which they choose.

'okay,' take

CHAPTER SUMMARY

Over the course of time, the modern dance genre has evolved to encompass many different movement families. This twentieth-century dance formed most prominently in America and Germany and has since spread around the world. Modern dance classes will vary depending on the specific type of modern being studied. Some modern techniques are codified, or written down, and preserved, such as Graham and Horton. Yet, modern dance also includes artists who are or were focused on free-flowing, natural, organic movement. Some artists have focused on preserving cultural traditions such as the American pioneers, African American heritage, and Afro-Caribbean roots. Others were innovators of technical and production elements. All of these artists experimented with new movement ideas and principles of dance. Additionally, contemporary dance is a blending of forms with modern dance that still defies definition. The freedom of expression inherent in the root of modern dance has generated many influential figures in dance.

6.1 Notable Individuals in Modern Dance	**Forerunners**	**Isadora Duncan** (1877–1927)	She practiced dance as a spiritual activity. She drew inspiration from the nature around her. Duncan focused on the soul and danced freely in light and flowing robes with her hair down. She utilized natural human movement such as walking, running, skipping, and jumping to inspire her dancing.
		Loie Fuller (1862–1928)	She was known for her experimentation and invention of effects with fabric and lighting. With the limited technology at the turn of the century, she created unique and innovative methods to create luminous effects onstage.
		Ruth St. Denis (1879–1968) and **Ted Shawn** (1891–1972)	Together, St. Denis and Shawn co-founded the Denishawn school and company in Los Angeles, California. Their unique training program created a breeding ground for the future stars of American modern dance. Shawn later went on to form the first all-male dance company as well as the summer dance festival at Jacob's Pillow.
	Pioneers	**Martha Graham** (1894–1991)	She was an American icon for her contributions to modern dance, including her codified technique of contraction and release. She trained and performed at Denishawn in Los Angeles before moving to New York to begin her career as an independent artist. Her dance school and company opened in 1926 and continue to run today. She choreographed over 180 dances in her lifetime; a few highlights include *Lamentation* (1930), *Chronicle* (1936), *Appalachian Spring* (1944), *Cave of the Heart* (1946), *Errand into the Maze* (1947), and *Night Journey* (1947).
		Lester Horton (1906–1953)	He developed his own codified technique on the West Coast with a focus on stretching and strengthening the human body. He founded Lester Horton Dance Theater in 1946, from which his dancers were able to carry on his legacy after his untimely death a few years later.

(*continued*)

6.1
Cont.

	Doris Humphrey (1895–1958) and **Charles Weidman** (1901–1975)	Both trained at the Denishawn school before starting a dance company together. Humphrey taught her students her concept of fall and recovery, or "the arc between two deaths," as her guiding principle in movement.
Second Generation	**Alvin Ailey** (1931–1989)	He was a dancer, choreographer, teacher, and leader of the African American voice in modern dance. In New York City, he founded the Alvin Ailey American Dance Theater and Ailey School, which continue today to uphold his vision of preserving the African American cultural experience. His ballet *Revelations*, based on his "blood memories" of growing up, captures the essence of what it is to be human and is still regularly performed today.
	Merce Cunningham (1919–2009)	He began original experiments pushing the art form while often collaborating with musician John Cage. He utilized chance composition often in his work and developed his own technique, designed to build strong and flexible bodies and minds.
	Katherine Dunham (1909–2006)	She held a PhD in anthropology and spent two years studying black dance in the Caribbean. These studies informed her work as she developed her technique and creative work.
	Alwin Nikolais (1910–1993)	He worked on all elements of his dance productions, including lighting and scenic design. He dehumanized his dancers by taking the self out of their human forms and then using them as clay on stage to represent anything else. Notable works include *Tensile Involvement* (1953), *Kaleidoscope* (1955), and *Prism* (1956).

6.1 Cont.	Contemporaries	Garth Fagan (b. 1940)	Originally from Jamaica, he founded his dance company in Rochester, New York, and creates choreography that incorporates elements of modern, jazz, and African dance. He is perhaps best known for his legendary work in Disney's Broadway musical *The Lion King* (1997). He also developed Fagan Technique™, which fuses modern, Afro-Caribbean, ballet, and post-modern qualities into one dynamic technique.
		Ohad Naharin (b. 1952)	He is Artistic Director of Batsheva Dance Company in Israel and creator of Gaga. This modern movement language focuses on sensation instead of physical shapes and helps dancers become more aware of their bodies.
6.2 Notable Modern Dance Choreography	*Fire Dance*	1895 Chor. Loie Fuller	An innovative work utilizing Fuller's technical creativity with fabric and lights, including underlighting
	Lamentation	1930 Chor. Martha Graham	Portrays the embodiment of grief
	Appalachian Spring	1944 Chor. Martha Graham	A celebration of the spirit of Americans pioneering in the West
	Tensile Involvement	1953 Chor. Alwin Nikolais	A work utilizing long elastic ribbons hanging from above the stage to the stage floor, which dancers constantly move around the space, creating patterns and shapes independent of themselves
	Stormy Weather (film)	1943	A Hollywood movie musical that features Katherine Dunham and her dancers in a dream sequence performing her blend of ballet and modern movement with Haitian influence.
	Revelations	1960 Chor. Alvin Ailey	A work danced to a score of African American spirituals, gospel songs, and blues, capturing the human condition while based in Ailey's "blood memories" of growing up in Texas

(continued)

6.2
Cont.

How to Pass, Kick, Fall and Run	1965 Chor. Merce Cunningham	A work utilizing chance composition, as it has readers sitting in the corner of the stage reading short stories throughout the work in mostly whatever order they choose; each story must take one minute to read no matter the length of the story
The Rite of Spring	1975 Chor. Pina Bausch	German choreographer Bausch's reimaging of the ballet in an avant-garde production that requires the stage floor to be covered in soil
Minus 16	1999 Chor. Ohad Naharin	One of Naharin's signature works utilizing his Gaga movement language with a diverse score of music full of surprises

6.3
Historical Timeline of
Modern Dance

1892	Loie Fuller presented her work *Serpentine Dance*, debuting her work with skirts and lighting effects.
1904	Isadora Duncan opened her school in Berlin, Germany.
1915	Ruth St. Denis and Ted Shawn founded their dance school and company Denishawn.
1926	Martha Graham presented her first dance concert in New York City and opened her school, the Martha Graham School of Contemporary Dance.
1933	Ted Shawn founded the now famous dance festival Jacob's Pillow in Becket, Massachusetts.
1935–1936	Katherine Dunham studied black dance in the Caribbean, mostly Haiti.
1945	Katherine Dunham opened the Dunham School in New York City.
1946	Lester Horton established the Lester Horton Dance Theater, one of, if not the, first racially integrated dance companies in America.
1951	Alwin Nikolais formed his total dance theater company, which came to be known as Nikolais Dance Theater.
1953	Lester Horton died suddenly.
1953	Merce Cunningham formed his company, Merce Cunningham Dance Company.
mid-1900s	Irmgard Bartenieff developed her Bartenieff Fundamentals[SM] technique.
1958	Alvin Ailey founded the Alvin Ailey American Dance Theater in New York City.
early 1960s	Judson Dance Theater began to meet, ushering in the age of post-modern dance.
1969	Alvin Ailey formed the Alvin Ailey American Dance Center, now the Ailey School, in New York City to offer classes and training for dancers.

6.3 Cont.	1973	Pina Bausch became artistic director of Tanztheater Wuppertal, later to be renamed Tanztheater Wuppertal Pina Bausch.
	1977	Hubbard Street Dance Chicago, a self-identified contemporary dance company, was founded by Lou Conte.
	1984	Igal Perry founded Peridance Contemporary Dance Company in New York City.
	1997	Garth Fagan choreographed the Disney Broadway musical *The Lion King*.
	2003	Ohad Naharin coined the term Gaga for the movement language he had been creating.

| 6.4
Chapter 6 Vocabulary | avant-garde | fortification | organic movement |
| | chance composition | legacy company | post-modern dance |

Reflective Prompts

1. Do you think having codified dance techniques is important? Why or why not?
2. How would you describe modern dance to someone unfamiliar with the form?
3. View videos of classic modern dance and modern dance today online. Do you think these should share the title of "modern dance?" Or has it evolved so much that one should have a different name? Why?
4. How would you define contemporary dance? Explain your answer.
5. Have you been to a modern dance performance? Was the performance what you expected it would be? Why or why not?

Movement Prompts

1. **Modern Dance Movement:** Learn the modern dance movement on the companion website and try to execute the sequence.
2. **Movement Efforts:** Revisit the efforts described in Box 6.4. Try performing an arm gesture that to you embodies each effort. Can you describe the difference in weight, space, or time for each?
3. **Group Phrase:** Get into groups of four. Design your own chance composition parameters. Use these parameters to create ten to twenty seconds of performance.

NOTES

1 Martha Graham, *The Vision of Modern Dance*, ed. Jean Morrison Brown, Naomi Mindlin, and Charles H. Woodford (New Jersey: Princeton Book Company, 1998), 52–53.
2 "Ohad Naharin," Batsheva Dance Company, accessed September 29, 2019, https://batsheva.co.il/en/about?open=ohas_naharin.

3   Cecily Dell, *A Primer for Movement Description: Using Effort-Shape and Supplementary Concepts* (New York: Dance Notation Bureau Press, 1970), 37.
4   "Alvin Ailey," Alvin Ailey American Dance Theater, accessed September 27, 2019, www.alvinailey.org/alvin-ailey-american-dance-theater/alvin-ailey.
5   Susan Au, *Ballet and Modern Dance*, 2nd ed. (London: Thames & Hudson Ltd, 2012), 160.
6   Victoria Looseleaf, "Modern vs. Contemporary," *Dance Magazine*, December 1, 2012, www.dancemagazine.com/modern_vs_contemporary-2306900829.html.

CHAPTER 6 BIBLIOGRAPHY

"Alvin Ailey." Alvin Ailey American Dance Theater. Accessed September 27, 2019. www.alvinailey.org/alvin-ailey-american-dance-theater/alvin-ailey.

Au, Susan. *Ballet and Modern Dance*, 2nd ed. London: Thames & Hudson Ltd, 2012.

Dell, Cecily. *A Primer for Movement Description: Using Effort-Shape and Supplementary Concepts*. New York: Dance Notation Bureau Press, 1970.

Forsythe, Ana Marie, Cheryl Ball and Marjorie Perce. *The Dance Technique of Lester Horton*. New Jersey: Princeton Book Company, 1992.

Graham, Martha. *The Vision of Modern Dance*. Edited by Jean Morrison Brown, Naomi Mindlin, and Charles H. Woodford. New Jersey: Princeton Book Company, 1998.

Looseleaf, Victoria. "Modern vs. Contemporary." *Dance Magazine*, December 1, 2012. www.dancemagazine.com/modern_vs_contemporary-2306900829.html.

"Ohad Naharin." Batsheva Dance Company. Accessed September 29, 2019. https://batsheva.co.il/en/about?open=ohas_naharin.

7 Tap Dance

The theater darkens, and the curtain partially rises to reveal only the knees, lower legs, and feet of forty dancers in gold shoes rapidly moving their feet in time with the music. The audience is mesmerized even by this limited view of the stage, as the dancers are so in sync that their 160 metal taps sound as if they are controlled by one foot ...

The upbeat swinging rhythms of the big band fill the movie theater as the audience gasps in amazement, watching the two brothers leap effortlessly from music stand to music stand over musicians' heads and sliding trombones, tapping out a quick intricate tap step on each stand as they go ...

Young children in their first dance class excitedly jump up and down in their new shiny black shoes, delighting in their raucous sound echoing off the walls and mirrors around them ...

Three dancers are lit in a soft spotlight as they balance on one leg and delicately approach the wooden floor with one of their shoes. They scrape metal across wood before lightly stepping in place. Unexpectedly, they break out into a fury of complex footwork with heavy stamping, and the rich tones reverberate through the theater ...

Audiences have enjoyed tap dance in a variety of venues for over a century. From the Broadway stage to the silver screen to some of the most renowned concert halls in the country, tap dance has awed countless individuals. Young children starting dance lessons more often than not are thrilled to be making noise with their feet. Through the years, students learn a variety of steps as well as music principles. Today, young adults can study tap dance at colleges and universities. However, tap dance did not begin in an institutional setting. This art form has a vibrant story with prevailing African American roots that still echoes in its rhythms today. This chapter will explore the many stages of tap dance, both in performance and in its development, as we explore the dynamic landscape of American dance.

TAP AS A DANCE FORM

Tap dance is a versatile form of American dance unique in its percussive and auditory elements. Born from the colliding of cultures on North American soil, tap dance reflects the blending of cultures that formed the United States. As

7.1
Tap dance shoes on
wooden floor.
Serkan Zanager/
Shutterstock

such, this dance form mirrors American history and appears on a wide variety of stages performed by diverse artists. Tap dance began as, and remains today, a dance of the people. Unlike ballet, it was not developed by aristocrats and remains uncodified. Training in tap dance also continued informally for decades. However, tap dancers have always maintained a strong sense of community that spans generations, continents, and abilities. Part of the tap dance culture is jamming, in which artists gather together and take turns performing improvised solos. Nowadays, in these jam sessions, anyone, regardless of the language they speak or years of training, is welcome to join the circle and share their passion for tap dance.

Dancing Musicians

All dancers must be musical, but not all dancers are in fact musicians. Tap dancers, however, truly are equal parts dancer and musician. In other words, tap dancers are musicians who just happen to have their instruments strapped to their feet. While performing any style of tap dance – from high-heeled and presentational Broadway tap to flat-footed and loose hoofing – the dancers are ultimately responsible for the sounds they are making with their feet, hands, and body. A highly trained ear and advanced understanding of rhythm are imperative for any professional tap dancer. While dancers can choose to move their bodies in any style, the sounds are either in time with the music or "off," no matter the chosen visual aesthetic. Thus, it is widely believed and taught that the greatest "sin" in tap dance is to be off the music. While the movements of other dance genres like ballet, modern, and jazz must still be accurate, they usually can only accomplish up to three movements in one count, but most often take a few counts to complete one movement. On the other hand, tap dancers often squeeze six or more sounds within one count, or beat, of music. This requires extraordinary precision, whether the dancer uses all six or more of those sounds or decides to hit one exact spot in that note.

(handwritten note: Musicality IS SUPER important)

Tap dance developed alongside the exciting rhythms of jazz music. Both instrumental musicians and tap dancers informed each other's developments, from ragtime to swing to bebop. Early jazz music and tap dance both appeared on the minstrel and vaudeville stages, two early American performance venues that we will discuss later in this chapter. Most tap dance acts at this time were

7.1
Selected Jazz
Music Eras

Ragtime and Stride – 1890s to 1920s
- Syncopation
- Duple meter
*Listen to: "Maple Leaf Rag" and "The Entertainer" by Scott Joplin, and "Black Bottom Stomp" by Jelly Roll Morton

Early Big Band – 1920s to mid-1930s
- Sections of instruments: brass, reeds, and rhythm
- Homophonic (playing the same tune)
- Upbeat, faster tempo
- Swing rhythm in a faster "2/4" feel
*Listen to: "Sweet Georgia Brown" by Ben Bernie, "Old Man Blues" by Duke Ellington's Cotton Club Band, and "Shanahi Shuffle" by Fletcher Henderson & His Orchestra

Swing – mid-1930s to mid-1940s
- Sections of instruments – each section larger than in early big band
- Swinging rhythm in a 4/4 tempo
- Popularity of jazz vocalists
*Listen to: "One O'Clock Jump" by Count Basie and His Orchestra, "In the Mood" by Glenn Miller & His Orchestra, and "Jumpin Jive" by Cab Calloway

Bebop – late 1940s
- Small group of horns and rhythm instruments rather than large groups of instruments
- Individualism emphasized
- Intricate melodies
- Fast tempo
- Busy solos with a lot of notes
- Virtuosic
*Listen to: "Shaw Nuff" by Charlie Parker and Dizzy Gillespie, "Confirmation" by Charlie Parker, and "Tempus Fugit" by Bud Powell

soloists or small ensembles of duets, trios, or quartets, and these tap dance artists could perform as part of the jazz music. Later, it was common for a tap dancer to perform as a featured visual component with big name bands such as Duke Ellington, particularly during the early big band and swing eras of jazz music in the 1930s and 1940s. Just as in jazz music, syncopation, or accenting or emphasizing a normally unaccented beat, was a key element of tap dance. The exchange of ideas between jazz musicians and tap dancers helped to formulate the sound and rhythms of each.

Throughout the first half of the twentieth century, jazz musicians and tap dancers alike gathered in popular clubs and dance halls to enjoy the intoxicating rhythms and excitement of their shared music. Some of the most prominent clubs were in the Harlem district in New York City. Harlem was a predominantly African American neighborhood in which these jazz and tap artists flourished. The Cotton Club was a hot jazz social club designed for music and

7.2
Tap dancers The
Three Brown Jacks
perform with
Jimmie Lunceford
and His Orchestra
in 1936 during the
Swing Era.
Archive Photos/
Stringer via
Getty Images

dancing, though notably segregated. African Americans were only allowed to perform, not dine, while white patrons were allowed to dine but never perform. The Apollo Theatre was also located in Harlem and presented stage shows throughout the week. Opening nights at the Apollo were just as highly anticipated as any opening on Broadway. Two amateur nights were included in the weekly lineup. Audience members were notoriously tough on amateur performers, and it was not uncommon for an act to end only to be met with silence from the audience.

New York clubs had a big influence (tho not racially okay now)

As the swing scene of jazz music became saturated with many bands, jazz musicians gradually became bored with the swing style and began exploring their own virtuosity as artists. This shift of focus led to the creation of bebop music in the 1940s, in which the musicians pushed their limits with intricate melodies and essentially played as many notes as possible. The dense music of bebop left no room for tap dancers to lay down their own rhythms. While World War II helped to maintain the popularity of swing music into the mid-1940s as a symbol of the freedom in America, by the 1950s, tap dance became much less prominent in the popular scene. Between bebop and the popular rock 'n' roll music, there was no room for the sounds of tap dance. Additionally, ballet and jazz dance began taking over the Broadway stage, and clubs were hit with high taxes, causing some of them to close their doors, which left fewer opportunities for tap dancers to perform. Tap dance declined but never "died," as some historians claim, and in the 1970s and 1980s, the Tap Renaissance brought tap dance back to the public eye.

7.3
Tap dancer Savion
Glover interacts
with the other
musicians while
performing during
Wycliffe Gordon's
Jazz A La Carte at
the Apollo Theatre.
Shahar Azran/
Wirelmage/
Getty Images

Training and Mentorship: Tradition in Tap

Tap dancing was originally learned not in formal lessons but on street corners, in vaudeville family acts, and in jazz clubs. Eager tap dancers carefully watched soloists perform and then worked on steps they saw and added their own styles or variations. Performers were always trying to best each other on the dance floor with more intricate rhythms, unique flair, or fancy footwork. It was very important never to steal someone else's step outright; simply repeating a step someone else had done would result in being kicked off the dance floor and perhaps out of the establishment. This custom led to rapid development of virtuosity in the form as well as a lack of codified terms. Steps were often named based on the type of sound they made (i.e. *shuffle*), who invented them (i.e. *Maxie Ford*), or where they were created (i.e. *Cincinnati*).

this is why there can be so many names and variations of the same step

BOX 7.1 TAP DANCE VOCABULARY

A general tap dance vocabulary is widely used throughout the dance community; however, it is not uncommon for one step to have two or more different names. For example, one three-sound step is commonly referred to by three different names: *third*, *closed third*, or *slurp*. Another step that travels side to side with alternating patters of brushes, steps, and heel drops is called both a *Broadway* and a *Shirley Temple*.

Up until the mid-twentieth century, rather than learning a regimen of steps in a classroom setting, aspiring tap dancers often had mentors who helped train

7.4
Brenda Bufalino
tap dancing with
mentor Charles
"Honi" Coles.
Photo by Ray
Abbott, courtesy of
Brenda Bufalino

them. The next generation of tap dancers would learn from the "old masters" of the form. Not only did mentors pass on technique and performance practices, but they also shared stories of their experiences and the values of tap dance. This tradition of mentorship contributes greatly to the strong sense of community among tap dancers. Routines and steps can be traced through a lineage of teachers (i.e. Sally learned this step from Brenda Bufalino, who learned it from Honi Coles, who created it in 1937). Often, dancers find themselves only a few generations away from some of the most historical figures in tap dance. This close-knit community creates a unique feeling of ownership in the form and helps to continuously inspire artists to pass their knowledge on to the next dancers in line.

During the Tap Renaissance, many tap dance masters from the first half of the twentieth century mentored the next generation of great dancers. Often, the younger dancers sought out these masters for training. Many tap dancers of this next generation had trained in modern and/or ballet and had a background in concert dance, which would eventually help move tap dance to the concert stage. In 1986, a historic tap dance festival, Fascinating Rhythms, took place in Colorado. Following the model from three festivals earlier in the 1980s, tap dancers from all over the country gathered for two weeks to teach or take classes, attend lectures and film screenings, participate in panel discussions, perform, and exchange ideas and teaching practices.[1] Many more festivals were soon to follow, and now there are annual tap dance festivals in New York City, Los Angeles, Washington DC, Chicago, Boston, Stockholm, Tokyo, Sydney, Oslo, Odessa, and several more cities worldwide.

TAP DANCE ROOTS

Tap dance is the result of a cross-pollination of cultures. Influences came from Africans, who were brought against their will and forced into slavery, and Irish and English, who came to North America in search of a new beginning.

Though the role that the barbaric practice of the slave trade played in the creation of this art form is devastating, tap dance is a uniquely American art form that came to be because of the specific circumstances that took place on American soil.

The African influence came from their refined and rich dance traditions. Although the different societies in Africa each have unique dance practices, there are a few general characteristics vastly different from western European cultural dances. Movement characteristics of African dance emphasize a connection to the earth with a grounded quality. Dancing is often performed with bent knees and shoulders slightly leaned forward and includes gliding, shuffling, or stomping steps with flat feet. While most often accompanied by drums, African dance features complex **polyrhythms** in which multiple rhythms are being performed at once. At times, African dance involves improvisation, in which the dancer is making the movement in the moment rather than performing set movements. Dance in the African culture most often focuses on the community. Unlike the removed theatrical performances and set folk dances of Western culture, African peoples developed dances believed to be essential for their survival, whether the dance supplied plentiful crops, victory in battle, or the passage of a deceased soul to the rest of their ancestors. Spectators often are involved in these rituals by singing, chanting, or clapping, and the entire community – with the occasional exceptions for religious beliefs – attends or is involved in the performance of dance.

The most prominent European influence in tap dance came from the Irish. The Irish jig is a lively folk dance performed in a triple meter in which the upper body remains rigid as the lower body performs rapid and percussive footwork. This dance is most commonly performed solo but can also be done by a couple. Like many Europeans, Irish immigrants came to America in search of a better life with new opportunities; however, many were also forced into labor as indentured servants under British rule in the Caribbean, where the cultural exchange between the Irish and West Africans also contributed to the development of tap dance. Many Irish immigrated in particular during the Great Potato Famine of 1845 to 1849, as many were dying of starvation and disease in Ireland. Most Irish were poor upon their arrival on North American soil and settled among the lower class.

These dance cultures clashed and met on southern plantations and in northern cities. This exchange of movement continued on plantations, resulting in new dances blending idiosyncrasies from each culture. Over time, the term "jigging" came to be associated with African American dancers. African and European cultures also blended in urban areas, both before and after the Civil War. One of the most infamous of these neighborhoods was the Five Points District in New York City. The name was derived from the five-pointed intersection in the neighborhood. This neighborhood housed many free African Americans and poor Irish immigrants, providing a breeding ground for cross-cultural exchange of ideas and the development of new movement.

7.5
Painting of the Five
Points District titled
"The Five Points"
ca. 1827 by an
unknown artist.
Metropolitan
Museum of Art,
2016.797.17. Bequest
of Mrs. Screven
Lorillard (Alice
Whitney), from the
collection of Mrs.
J. Insley Blair, 2016

AMERICAN DANCE ONSTAGE

Authentic American dance has graced a variety of stages throughout history.
Each stage featured unique aspects of American dance and was instrumental
in the development of tap dance. Together, they reveal the versatile artistry and
powerful impact of tap dance.

Minstrelsy

Minstrel shows were first performed in the 1830s by white men dressed in blackface – the use of burnt cork applied to the face in order to appear dark-skinned.
A gross appropriation of an entire race of human beings, performing in blackface
was common practice in this era. These performances consisted of song, dance,
variety acts, jokes, and banter mimicking the white men's perception of African
Americans. Black men were mischaracterized as lazy, ignorant, hypersexual, and
cowardly, among other negative qualities. This portrayal helped the white population
of America justify, in their minds, their horrendous treatment of blacks in America.
To the white men, it validated the conditions of slavery. In essence, this performance venue was the appropriation of African American culture for the benefit of
entertainment. As this was the oppressive culture of the time, **minstrelsy** rose to
be the most popular form of entertainment in the United States by 1840.

The format of the show was divided into two parts. In the first, the
performers sat onstage in a semicircle. The interlocutor, who was the only performer not wearing blackface, sat at the center and more or less hosted the
show. Two co-hosts, Mr. Tambo and Mr. Bones, sat at either end of the semicircle
and played their respective instruments – the tambourine and the bones, a pair
of clappers. The show opened with a group song, often with a grand entrance at
the end of which the interlocutor instructed the other men to have a seat. Then
a collection of jokes, songs, and instrumental music ensued. The second part of
the show, called the olio, featured individual variety acts that included singing
and dancing before concluding with a hoedown or walkaround performance such
as the Cakewalk (an African American dance discussed in Chapter 8). Audiences
were made up of white men, as these shows included distasteful humor that
was not suitable for women or children. These minstrel show dances included
early forms of tap dance, most notably **buck dancing**, a flat-footed dance in
which the feet remained close to the floor.

[handwritten annotations:]
AH! It's terrible this history exists!!! an
Shocking & scary
like the buck one-step

140 □

BOX 7.2 DECOLONIZING CURRICULA

Dance scholars and educators are pushing to decolonize dance curricula in higher education. The historically African American dance forms of jazz, tap, and hip-hop are included in very few degree programs. Often, when they are included at a college, they only count as elective credits and may or may not count towards a dance degree. Furthermore, classes labeled as Dance History usually only cover white dance history. Currently, there are no advanced degree programs (MA, MFA, or PhD) that allow a student to focus solely on these forms.

Professionals in the field are calling on schools to include equal opportunities for students to experience and research African American dance. This requires institutions to offer technique courses in jazz, tap, hip-hop, and/or other diverse genres of dance at multiple levels, allow these credits to count towards a dance degree, hire specialists and support research and creative activity in these forms, include African American artists, work, and scholarship within individual coursework, and provide equitable credit requirements across genres.

It was during the minstrel age that William Henry Lane, nicknamed "Master Juba," rose to fame. An African American born free in Rhode Island in 1825, Lane grew up in New York City, where he learned to dance from "Uncle" Jim Lowe, an African American jig-and-reel dancer of exceptional skill.[2] He lived in the Five Points District, where he honed his skills in various social clubs and dance halls. Lane began performing himself as young as ten years old and was immediately recognized for his talent. His performances featured Lane imitating all the other notable dancers of the day and ended with his own style of dancing, which was renowned for being unique and impressive. Because of his genuinely original dancing, he was advertised as the best dancer in America before he turned twenty. As such, most scholars credit Lane as the first American tap dancer.

BOX 7.3 EARLY DANCE CHALLENGES

In early percussive dance challenges, there were three judges to determine the winner. These judges stood on the side of the stage, under the stage, and out in the audience, so that they could assess a competitor's sound, precision, speed, and presentation or style. Together, they determined the champion.

After the Civil War, African Americans began forming their own minstrel troupes. As free or escaped slaves moved north to evade the oppression of the South, many had little or no means of providing a living due to the still overwhelming racism in the country. African Americans ended up in poor urban areas and looked for work with few options available to them; some found work performing in minstrelsy. Groups of blackface minstrels formed troupes and began traveling on performing circuits, while other troupes performed on Broadway for several years. At first, they followed the traditions of the white minstrel shows and therefore wore blackface and portrayed the same characters. However, over time, as minstrelsy waned in popularity, African American performers began to shift the oversimplified characters to more accurate portrayals of their people. For example, these African American performers stopped wearing blackface and toned down the insulting characters. Though the popularity of minstrel shows died out during the turn of the century, blackface continued to occasionally appear in movies, as film stars such as Fred Astaire, Judy Garland, and Shirley Temple can be seen donning the make-up into the 1930s.

Vaudeville

As the performance circuit became overcrowded with minstrel troupes, the minstrel structure fell away. Ragtime music began to take over, and more women joined the men on stage. Theater owners looked to grow a wider audience base. They maintained a variety show structure with acts that included song, dance, comedy, acrobatics, and other unique skills. However, the term "variety show" at that time insinuated that alcohol and immorality were involved. Instead, New York City theater owner Tony Pastor started calling his performances **vaudeville** shows in the late 1880s.[3] This new style of show permitted women and children to attend, thus increasing ticket sales.

Vaudeville theaters were in every town and city in America, and all of them featured tap dance acts among the other talents showcased. Shows with such variety created a sense of competition among performers. In order to be granted time onstage, their acts had to be extremely impressive, unique, or include a gimmick or novelty such as dancing around eggshells, playing instruments while dancing, or changing costumes on stage (without ever being naked). The dancers in these shows typically either wore hard-soled shoes to perform percussive buck dances or clog dances, or wore soft shoes to perform graceful song and dance. Dance challenges also became popular on the vaudeville stage. Two talented performers would dance back and forth until one was declared victorious, an early form of cutting contests later held between tap dancers. The vaudeville stage is where tap dance started to take form into what we recognize it as today.

BOX 7.4 "BREAK A LEG"

Did you know that the good luck wish used among actors, "break a leg," has nothing to do with breaking bones? Theater owners commonly booked more performers than would be able to appear in a show, allowing the crowd favorites more time on stage. Performers who were booked but never went on stage did not get paid. In the theater, the term "legs" refers to the three or four curtains running perpendicular on either side of the stage creating the wings through which performers appear and disappear. The call "break a leg" was a goodwill wish that the performer would get past the leg and onto the stage to perform that night in order to receive a paycheck.

Broadway to Hollywood *⟹ evolved throughout*

Throughout the decades, tap dance has evolved in jazz clubs and vaudeville, as noted earlier, and alongside popular Broadway shows and Hollywood films. The development of tap dance took place in these various performance venues simultaneously, resulting in a wide variety of tap dance styles being represented on the stage and in film. A selection of tap dance styles is discussed later in this chapter.

Broadway

The exceptionally successful 1921 Broadway show *Shuffle Along* featured the buck and wing dancing that predated tap. This production was a true showcase of African American song, dance, and comedy entirely produced by African Americans. It housed one of the first integrated audiences and will be discussed more in Chapter 8.

BOX 7.5 METAL TAPS

Metal taps did not appear on shoes until the mid-1920s. Until then, tap dance (and its predecessors) was performed in hard-soled shoes, thick leather-soled shoes, clogs, or boots on wooden floors, which provided rich and resonant tones. A man named Haney is credited with providing the first metal taps for the Broadway show *No, No, Nanette* in 1925. Several other metal tap designs began appearing after this. Metal taps were not widely used until the early 1930s.[4]

7.6
Ruby Keeler during a dress rehearsal for the 1971 production of *No, No, Nanette*.
Phillip Harrington/ Alamy Stock Photo

The swing music trend of the 1930s and 1940s increased the presence of tap dance on the Broadway stage. Multiple productions from this era featured tap dance, including *Best Foot Forward* (1941) with choreography by Gene Kelly, *On the Town* (1944), *Kiss Me Kate* (1948), and *Anything Goes* (1933), which has been revived several times and won the 1987 Tony Awards for Best Revival of a Musical and Best Choreography. However, by the 1950s ballet and jazz were becoming the popular Broadway dance forms, and tap dance began to fade from the stage.

In 1971, the Broadway revival of *No, No, Nanette* initiated a resurgence in tap. By 1980, Broadway producer David Merrick decided to adapt the 1933 movie musical *42nd Street* to live theater. Although adaptations usually went in the reverse direction, the stage show was a huge success. Set in 1933, this show brought back the classic charm of the movie musicals in the Swing Era and won the 1981 Tony Awards for Best Musical and Best Choreography. Nine years later, the production *Black and Blue* opened at the Minskoff Theatre. The entire show was rooted in jazz rhythms featuring renowned blues singers, a jazz orchestra, and three generations of rhythm tap dancers. (**Rhythm tap dance** is a style of tap characterized by intricate footwork with extended musical phrasing, complex patterns, and syncopated heel drops.) Choreographed by four of the old tap masters, *Black and Blue* showcased the versatile possibilities of tap dance, incorporating numerous styles and different rhythms. This production took home three Tony Awards, including Best Choreography. Tap dance was growing in popularity again in the beginning of the Tap Renaissance.

[handwritten annotation: probs where the faster, syncopation comes into play]

7.7
Artists perform the famous number "We're in the Money" in the musical *42nd Street*. Photo by China Photos/ Getty Images

7.8
Savion Glover
performs his
hip-hop style of
tap dance.
Paul Zimmerman/
WireImage/
Getty Images

Fun fact:

BOX 7.6 THE TONY AWARDS

A Tony Award is the highest honor a Broadway show can receive, and it is actually named after a woman. Antoinette Perry (1888–1946) carried a lifelong passion for theater. Throughout her career she was an actress, investor, director, and co-founder of what became the American Theatre Wing. After her death, her longtime business partner, the successful producer Brock Pemberton, suggested that a theater award be given in her honor. The first Antoinette Perry Awards ceremony took place in 1947, and as Pemberton handed out one of the awards, he called it a Tony. The name has stuck ever since that first evening.[5]

The Broadway stage served as a platform for passing the traditions of tap from one generation to the next. In 1984, an eleven-year-old named Savion Glover made his Broadway debut in the production *The Tap Dance Kid* (1983) and was the fourth dancer to take on the lead role. This led to his role as the youngest actor in *Black and Blue*, which lasted eight months and awarded Glover the opportunity to learn from the tap elders in the show. Glover went on to choreograph the innovative musical *Bring in 'da Noise, Bring in 'da Funk*, which opened on Broadway in 1996 showcasing his hip-hop style of tap dance. Glover successfully modernized tap to fit the popular hip-hop scene. Vastly different from the Broadway shows up to this point, Glover choreographed to the rap score with heavy, flat-footed tap steps that were pounded out in a fury of passion. Dressed in baggy pants and T-shirts, the cast portrayed the journey of African Americans

You've met him!

in North America with the ever-present African beat that accompanied them. This inventive production was awarded six Tony Awards, including Best Musical, Best Original Score, and Best Choreography.

BOX 7.7 *HAPPY FEET*

Savion Glover provided the movement and sound for the tap-dancing penguin Mumble in the Warner Brothers animated hit *Happy Feet* (2006). Glover choreographed the tap dance numbers, wore a motion-capture suit for animation, and performed the tap sounds recorded for the lovable penguin.

Hollywood Film

The predecessor of tap dance, buck dancing, was recorded on film as early as 1894 in a film titled *The Passing Show*, which featured three African American dancers. Several silent films made around the turn of the century and into the 1920s included scenes of African American dance, sometimes performed by white men in blackface.[6] However, it was the development of film with recorded sound in 1927 that propelled tap dance to the silver screen in theaters across the nation, and studios began producing more musical films. Tap dance's premier in "the talkies" occurred in MGM's film *Hollywood Revue* in 1929. That same year marked a significant leap forward in the portrayal of African American characters. The film *Black and Tan* featured the tap dance group The Five Hot Shots – five African American men dressed in suits who danced in impressive synchronicity – and centered around a tender love story between African Americans. It was the first film of its kind to step away from the stereotype of blackface minstrels and slaves and portray a loving and meaningful character of African Americans.

[handwritten margin note: Hollywood film boosted popularity even more]

Movie musicals were wildly successful in the box offices during the Swing Era as studios produced one after the other through the 1930s and 1940s. Consequently, the tap dance stars of the age became household names across America. The most famous tap dancer, Bill "Bojangles" Robinson, appeared in several films in this era; he is thoroughly discussed later in this chapter. One pair of household names was the Nicholas Brothers, Fayard and Harold. Growing up in Pennsylvania with parents who were musicians, the two brothers began performing locally at a young age before being whisked off to New York City by a show manager. While in New York, the brothers both opened at the Cotton Club and appeared in their first film in 1932. Their success only continued to skyrocket with regular jaw-dropping acts at the Cotton Club, performances on Broadway, and appearing in over fifty films. The Nicholas Brothers were among the first and most prominent African Americans to break racial boundaries by performing in films with white actors. Known for their high-energy performances with astounding flash steps and acrobatics, the brothers' routines were often the highlights of their films. One of their most celebrated Hollywood performances was in *Stormy Weather* (1943) in a number with Cab Calloway and his band

7.9
The Nicholas Brothers performing an acrobatic feat for the camera as commonly seen in their flash acts.
Keystone-France/ Gamma-Rapho via Getty Images

Even the name is so energetic

performing "Jumpin Jive." Their performance began with vigorous tap steps and jumping between musicians' stands, the stage, and the piano, before rushing over to their grand finale on an oversized dual staircase, where they leapfrogged into splits over one another down the stairs, only to return to the top and slide down ramps in their splits. Remarkably, the entire number was filmed in one take.

Two other men, Fred Astaire and Gene Kelly, also overtook the Hollywood musical scene. With their own signature styles and outstanding talent, Astaire and Kelly starred separately in at least thirty films each. Astaire was known for his incredible grace and impeccable taps in *Holiday Inn* (1942), *Easter Parade* (1948), *Royal Wedding* (1951), and *The Band Wagon* (1953), as well as his partnering with Ginger Rogers in *Top Hat* (1935), *Swing Time* (1936), and *Shall We Dance* (1937). Kelly, known for his athleticism, boyish charm, and insistence on perfection, headlined films such as *Anchors Aweigh* (1945), *On the Town* (1949), *Summer Stock* (1950), *An American in Paris* (1951), and *Singin' in the Rain* (1952) – a musical about the development of sound in film.

Love him Yessss

The claim to fame was not only for men; numerous female dancers rose to stardom in Hollywood musicals as well. Eleanor Powell emerged as a female tap soloist first in New York performing in dance halls, at private parties, and on Broadway and then in her prolific, albeit unintended, Hollywood career. Her first film, *Broadway Melody of 1936* (1935), received such rave reviews that she was immediately awarded a long-term contract with MGM Studios. She went on to star in several films, including *Born to Dance* (1936), *Broadway Melody of 1938* (1937), and *Broadway Melody of 1940* (1940). Powell's fierce tapping paired with her ballet training and acrobatic abilities formed routines with dizzying turn sequences, backbends, and innovative rhythms in her taps. She choreographed all her own routines and was known to rehearse for up to twelve hours at a time.

7.10
Fred Astaire and
Cyd Charisse on
set for the movie
musical *The Band
Wagon* (1953).
Sunset Boulevard/
Getty Images

Powell was not simply a pretty face for the screen; she was a powerful dancer with incredible creative abilities and determination. Fellow female Hollywood tap stars included Ann Miller, Jeni LeGon, Ruby Keeler, and Vera-Ellen.

BOX 7.8 QUIET ON THE SET, PLEASE

Starting in the mid-1930s, the sounds of the tap shoes in movie musicals were recorded separately for clarity and because of all the noise that the heavy film equipment made while shooting. After filming the visual dance number on set, dancers would return to the sound studio to record just their tap sounds to be dubbed into the film.

7.11
Gene Kelly in the
iconic rain dance
sequence in the
movie musical
Singin' in the Rain
(1952).
MGM Studios/
Hulton Archive/
Getty Images

So cool how tap was casually incorporated into every movie and film for entertainment

7.12
"Queen of Tap
Dance" Eleanor
Powell in the movie
Born to Dance
(1936).
Donaldson
Collection/
Getty Images

By the mid-1950s, studios stopped producing these lavish movie musicals for a variety of reasons. These films were extremely expensive to make, with grand sets, big bands, and numerous dancers. Pop culture was changing from the swing time and jazz frenzy to rock 'n' roll and television. Plus, racial tensions were beginning to rise again, with riots breaking out in several cities, influencing a growing lack of interest in fantasy tap dance musicals that did not reflect the realities of American life.

During the tap dance resurgence of the 1970s and 1980s, the form also returned to Hollywood in several high-energy tap dance films with the next generation of stars. While several of the old masters were still around and performing in film, this was a period of transition and passing the torch to the next tap dance stars. Perhaps the most influential disciple of the early tap gods was Gregory Hines. Born in New York City, Hines began his performance career in 1951 at the ripe young age of five with his older brother Maurice as the Hines Kids. He learned from the tap masters backstage at the Apollo Theatre during and between shows. After several years of performance and a brief hiatus, Hines made his Broadway debut alongside his brother in *Eubie!* (1978). Six years later, he booked his first starring role in a film called *The Cotton Club* (1984), based on the real club in New York City during the 1930s. In the following year, 1985, Hines starred opposite Russian ballet star Mikhail Baryshnikov in the film *White Nights*. Hines portrayed an exiled American who moves to Soviet Russia to escape the rampant racism in America and encounters a Russian ballet dancer attempting to defect. The climax of the film features a dance challenge between Hines and Baryshnikov, with their dueling steps in tap rhythms and ballet feats. Hines starred once again in the 1989 film simply titled *Tap*, in which he plays an ex-con and talented tap dancer who, after being released from prison, must choose between his life in crime and the opportunity to dance. Several old masters are featured in the thrilling challenge scene in this film showcasing each of their famed tap styles.

Hines was not only a brilliant tap artist and performer; he was also an incredible promoter and ambassador for the art form. In 1988, Hines played host for an episode of the PBS *Great Performances* series titled *Tap Dance in America*. The great tap elders made appearances during the show, but most attention was given to the new and current tap dance artists. Hines used this opportunity to feature the modern-day tap dancers and showcase the variety of styles in tap dance. In 2019, Hines was celebrated by the United States Postal Service

T-5
It's a "challenge" when Max Washington (GREGORY HINES) proves
he's better than ever making a surprise return to the tap dance studio
where he grew up. (ARTHUR DUNCAN, PAT RICO, HAROLD NICHOLAS,
TAP   STEVE CONDOS, SANDMAN SIMS, HENRY LeTANG, and SAMMY DAVIS, JR.)

7.13
Gregory Hines in the center of a semicircle surrounded by tap masters in the challenge scene of the movie *Tap* (1989).
Michael Ochs Archives/ Getty Images

when he was inducted as the forty-second honoree in the Black Heritage Stamp series for his contributions to the American art of tap dance. The stamp features a picture of Hines in his tap shoes and went on sale in February 2019. Other tap dance documentaries include Brenda Bufalino's *Great Feats of Feet* (1977), *No Maps on My Taps* (1979), *Tap World* (2015), and *American Tap* (2018).

Tap in Concert

As tap dance was enjoying a resurgence on Broadway and in movies, numerous concert tap companies were formed during the Tap Renaissance in the 1970s and 1980s. These companies featured tap dancers performing as an ensemble rather than the traditional solos and duets of early tap dance. The length of pieces varied from a short three to four minutes up to an entire evening length's work. One of the women leading the charge was Brenda Bufalino in New York City. Bufalino, with her modern dance background in addition to tap, took an avant-garde approach to her tap choreography. Her tap dance mentor was Charles 'Honi' Coles, a renowned rhythm tap dancer during the Golden Age of tap. She broke with traditional gender roles to perform in flat Oxford style (or men's) shoes rather than high-heeled taps and wore a white tuxedo onstage instead of a form-fitting costume accentuating the female body. This helped successfully earn her respect for her brilliant tap rhythms and compositions instead of as a female figure to be ogled by men.

In 1986, Bufalino formed the American Tap Dance Orchestra (ATDO). Her dancers wore white ties and coat tails and performed as a dancing symphony, creating music with their feet. At its height, there were thirty dancers in the orchestra. The ATDO performed extensively throughout the United States – including at the prestigious Joyce Theatre and Apollo Theatre in New York City and the Kennedy Center in Washington DC – and abroad. The organization was renamed the American Tap Dance Foundation (ATDF) in 2001 under the artistic direction of Tony Waag. Housed in New York City, the ATDF hosts several programs, including weekly classes and annual tap dance festivals, teacher

7.14
Brenda Bufalino (right) with her company the American Tap Dance Orchestra.
Courtesy of Brenda Bufalino

AYY y they'll be visiting Clemson coming this spring!

7.15
Syncopated Ladies performing at the Dizzy Feet Foundation's *Celebration of Dance Gala.* Angela Weiss/Getty Images for Dizzy Feet Foundation

7.16
Dorrance Dance in *ETM: The Initial Approach,* created by Michelle Dorrance and Nicholas Van Young. Permission Granted by Dorrance Dance, photo by Christopher Duggan

trainings, and awards, all in an effort to fulfill its mission of "establishing and legitimizing Tap Dance as a vital component of American Dance."[7]

In 1985, Heather Cornell co-founded Manhattan Tap, a combination dancer and musician ensemble that performed for over two decades and commissioned works from masters such as Gregory Hines. On the West Coast, Lynn Dally formed the Jazz Tap Percussion Ensemble in 1979. Other companies founded during the Tap Renaissance include Anita Feldman Tap, Changing Times Tap Dance Company, DancEllington, Balletap, and Rhythm Anonymous, to name a few.

Many tap companies thrive across the country today. In 1989, Acia Gray co-founded Tapestry, a company of mixed dance forms still performing and based in Austin, Texas. Mark Yonally formed the Chicago Tap Theatre Company in 2002. His company presents unique story shows in which tap dance drives the narrative. Chloe Arnold founded the Los Angeles female tap dance band the Syncopated Ladies in the early 2000s. After releasing their first video in 2012, the Syncopated Ladies have become iconic for their original flavor of tap dance performed to pop music, including hip-hop and rap. Blending tap dance with film and technology, the Syncopated Ladies are known for going viral. In 2016, Beyoncé made the Syncopated Ladies' video performing to the beat of her hit "Formation" the homepage of her own website. In 2011, Michelle Dorrance founded her company Dorrance Dance, which is based out of New York City. Dorrance Dance is renowned for pushing the boundaries of tap dance while honoring the form's history. In 2015, Dorrance received the MacArthur Fellowship, which is also known as the "MacArthur genius grant," for her innovative and passionate work in tap dance artistry and education.

BOX 7.9 REIMAGINING A CLASSIC

In 2019, Dorrance Dance premiered a tap and vernacular dance spin on the holiday classic *The Nutcracker*, titling their work *The Nutcracker Suite*. This project was a collaboration between Michelle Dorrance, Hannah Heller, and Josette Wiggan-Freund set to the Duke Ellington and Billy Strayhorn jazz album of three suites exploring some of Tchaikovsky's score. The artists took liberties with the familiar classical ballet version of the story to suit their tap and jazz dance tone. For example, the Sugar Plum Fairy is renamed the Sugar Rum Cherry, reflective of Ellington's score.

SELECTED TAP DANCE STYLES — all 50 000 diff, yet sooo similar still

Multiple tap dance styles have been discussed throughout this chapter. This section reviews the styles that have been discussed, but this is not meant to be an exhaustive list of tap dance styles. Rather, it serves as a sampling of the many styles of tap dance that exist.

Buck Dancing

Buck dancing, a predecessor of tap dance, was popular in the nineteenth century and consisted of flat-footed stomping, shuffling, and swinging steps. Hard-soled shoes amplified the percussive nature of the dance as the upper body remained relatively still. This type of dancing was almost always performed by men as a solo act.

Soft Shoe

more like irish

The **soft shoe** is characterized by elegant style, graceful movements, and light tap sounds usually performed at a slower tempo. In this style, the heels barely touch the ground as the dancer performs gliding, sweeping, and brushing steps. Emphasis is placed on grace and poise of the dancer as well as the tap sounds.

Buck and Wing

Buck and wing is a term for an early style that developed into tap dance. Buck and wing dancing featured on-the-toes footwork, energetic jumping maneuvers of wings, and traditional phrasing of "three-and-a-break."

Flash Act

The high-energy, upbeat **flash act** combines tap dance with daring acrobatics, including flips, splits, specialty moves called "over-the-tops" and "trenches," and dancing on small, raised platforms. This style was most popular during the early to mid-twentieth century and was usually performed as a solo, duet, or small group.

Broadway Tap Dance

looking at the world through Rose colored glasses

Broadway tap dance is not one distinguishable style. It is any style of tap that happens on the Broadway stage – styles that have changed with the evolution of American music and theater. Traditionally, it places more emphasis on the visual and theatrical aesthetic of tap dance than many other styles. At times, the rhythms of the feet can be simpler while the upper body is more dynamic. While other tap dance styles allow freedom in the torso, **Broadway tap dance** often includes very specific choreographed arm and head movements that enhance the visual spectacle of the dance and can be utilized to highlight the rhythms of the music or feet.

Rhythm Tap Dance

In contrast to the time step structures and on-the-toes, buck and wing style prominent in early forms of tap dance, rhythm tap dance features accented heel drops and steps that punch into the floor. Complex musical phrasing and rhythms are central in this style, with sharp syncopation and accents as well as what is known as dancing over the four-bar phrase, or dancing in longer musical phrases. The primary focus in rhythm tap is the sound and composition, rather than any visual components. John W. Bubbles is considered the Father of Rhythm Tap. Famous from the 1930s through the 1950s for his ad lib or improvisational dancing, he influenced later generations of tap dancers.

Concert Tap Dance

Bang Bang

Concert tap dance can consist of any style of tap dance, but is specifically composed to be presented in a theatrical production in front of an audience with emphasis on the pure artistry of the form, without the dramatic story of a musical. In general, concert tap dance pieces are longer works that range from about five minutes to twenty minutes or more. These works may convey a narrative or simply focus on the music and dancing. While early tap dance routines and pieces were aimed at simply entertaining the audience, concert tap dance purposefully utilizes the choreographic elements of space, time, and energy to communicate with audience members through both movement and sound.

TAP HIGHLIGHTS

Bill "Bojangles" Robinson

The most iconic figure in tap dance, Bill "Bojangles" Robinson, led a phenomenal career that spanned seventy years and transcended racial barriers of the day. Born in 1878, Robinson danced on street corners before making his way onto the vaudeville stage. Around 1915, Robinson became the first African American allowed to break the vaudeville "two-colored" rule requiring African Americans to perform in at least pairs, and he began performing solo on white vaudeville stages.

BOX 7.10 MR. BOJANGLES

The nickname Mr. Bojangles originated from Bill's mischievous nature. The story goes that there was a man named Lion J. Boujasson in Robinson's town who owned a hat shop. Since the children could not pronounce this foreign name, they referred to Mr. Boujasson as Mr. Bojangles. One day, Bill and a friend swiped a hat from his shop, and without being able to sell it, Bill began wearing the hat. The kids began to joke, asking, "Who took Mr. Bojangles' hat?" and then pointing to Bill and replying, "Why, Bojangles took it!" After that, the name stuck.[8]

A few years later, Robinson developed his iconic stair dance. Though he did not originate dancing on stairs, he certainly perfected it. By applying a different thickness of wood on each step, he created a variety of tones and effectively a new musical instrument. Robinson was also known for his

7.17
Bill "Bojangles" Robinson in a promotional photo for the film *The Little Colonel* (1935). George Rinhart/ Corbis via Getty Images

crystal-clear sounds and dancing on the balls of his feet. This slight shift of weight gave him a different tone from the heavy flat-footed dancers of the age. Robinson was credited for always being ready to help the next generation of dancers in learning a step. He went on to perform in films and once again broke barriers by performing on screen with a white partner, none other than child star Shirley Temple. They appeared in their first film together in 1935 and went on to co-star in three more films. Although he was able to perform with a white cast, Robinson was forced to play the enslaved butler who was degraded on screen; this, coupled with the age difference, is probably part of the equation that allowed the duet to happen. Robinson claims several more film credits, including the hit *Stormy Weather*, which also featured the Nicholas Brothers.

After a lifelong career of bringing joy to countless people through his dancing, Robinson passed away in a New York City hospital in November 1949. Over 30,000 people came to see him at his wake, and 13,000 people attended his funeral the next day (although only 3,000 could fit in the church), including Duke Ellington, Jackie Robinson, Danny Kaye, the New York City mayor, and many other notable celebrities and people of power and influence. Ed Sullivan presided over the funeral and professed, "despite the softness of his taps, no performer

7.18
Bill "Bojangles" Robinson performing with child star Shirley Temple.
Afro American Newspapers/Gado/ Getty Images

and very few Americans ever touched the heart of this city, and this nation, with greater impact than Bojangles."[9]

Bill Robinson had his own catch phrase, "Everything's copasetic," simply meaning everything is fine or good. Upon his death, a group of twenty-one artists formed a social club that they decided to call the Copasetics. This group devoted themselves to preserving Robinson's legacy and promoting goodwill and character, while also frequently performing together in Robinson's honor.

Shim Sham Shimmy

Recognized as the national anthem of tap dance, the **Shim Sham Shimmy**, also referred to as the *Shim Sham*, is a fairly short tap dance routine known throughout the tap dance community. It was choreographed in the late 1920s or early 1930s; the original choreographer remains unknown. Leonard Reed is often credited by historians; however, he claimed ownership very late in his life, and there are disagreements as to whether or not his performance partner or a sister act helped.

This routine is comprised of four sections, or steps: the shim sham, the crossover step, the tack Annie, and the half break. After being passed down for a century, slight variations in the specifics of the steps have occurred, yet the structure and rhythmic integrity remain constant. Originally performed as a finale, the *Shim Sham* is often still performed at the conclusion of a tap dance performance. This tradition of tap dance is carried on worldwide and practiced in multiple countries, including Austria, Mexico, Brazil, and Australia.

National Tap Dance Day

In 1989, three women of the Tap America Project presented a resolution to the United States Congress to create a National Tap Dance Day. Nine months later, on November 8, President H.W. Bush signed the bill into law, declaring May 25th to be National Tap Dance Day in the United States. Why May 25th? Although he had no birth certificate, this is believed to be Bill Robinson's birthday.

The bill read:

To designate May 25, 1989, as "National Tap Dance Day":

Whereas the multi-faceted art form of tap dancing is a manifestation of the cultural heritage of our Nation, reflecting the fusion of African and European cultures into an exemplification of the American spirit, that should be, through documentation, and archival and performance support, transmitted to succeeding generations;

Whereas tap dancing has had a historic and continuing influence on other genres of American art, including music, vaudeville, Broadway musical theater, and film, as well as other dance forms;

Whereas tap dancing is perceived by the world as a uniquely American art form;

Whereas tap dancing is a joyful and powerful aesthetic force providing a source of enjoyment and an outlet for creativity and self-expression for Americans on both the professional and amateur level;

Whereas it is in the best interest of the people of our Nation to preserve, promote, and celebrate this uniquely American art form;

Whereas Bill "Bojangles" Robinson made an outstanding contribution to the art of tap dancing on both stage and film through the unification of diverse stylistic and racial elements; and

Whereas May 25, as the anniversary of the birth of Bill "Bojangles" Robinson is an appropriate day on which to refocus the attention of the Nation on American tap dancing: Now, therefore, be it

Resolved by the Senate and House of Representatives of the United States of America in Congress assembled, That May 25, 1989, is designated "National Tap Dance Day". The President is authorized and requested to issue a proclamation calling upon the people of the United States to observe such a day with appropriate ceremonies and activities.[10]

CHAPTER SUMMARY

purely american!

Tap dance is one of the few original American art forms. Its rhythms echo the story of how this nation was formed. Born from the polyrhythms, groundedness, and propulsive movements of the Africans forced to North America and the percussive dances of the European immigrants, tap dance's unique characteristics capture the spirit of America.

The form of tap dance has evolved alongside the American culture, resulting in a vibrant and versatile art form. After the early years of blackface minstrel shows, tap dance transitioned to the vaudeville stage, where demand for variety continued to push the boundaries of the artists. The upbeat Swing Era of the 1930s and 1940s, with big band music and movie musicals, presented a golden era for tap dance. During this time, tap dance appeared frequently on Broadway and in Hollywood films; tap dance stars became household names. African Americans such as Bill "Bojangles" Robinson and the Nicholas Brothers were able to break through racial barriers, performing solo and in white films. Expense and the onset of bebop and rock 'n' roll culture drove tap dance out of the mainstream during the 1950s and 1960s, though the art form never "died" as some historians claim. Tap dance was still happening but was less prominent. The Tap Renaissance of the 1970s and 1980s brought tap dance back to the Broadway stage and on film and television, including several documentaries. The next generation of tap dancers sought out old masters for training, inheriting by the oral tradition this uncodified technique and repertoire. Tap dance entered the concert stage, and several companies have been formed that perform and tour extensively. In recent decades, artists such as Savion Glover and Chloe Arnold have helped transfer tap dance to the hip-hop and pop music culture and blended it with technology.

No matter the era or stage, tap dance is tied to tradition. Even as artists of today continue to develop the form, tap dancers have a strong bond with the form's history. Tap dance artists practice paying homage to the elders that came before them as they continue to create new rhythms, steps, styles, and works. Tap dance is an exciting, versatile, original, musical form of art. Recognized worldwide as an American art form, tap dance tells the story of this nation's past while artists today continue to innovate the form, shaping the future of American dance and art.

7.2 Notable Individuals in Tap Dance		
Chloe Arnold	She is the director, choreographer, and founder of the L.A.-based all-female tap band the Syncopated Ladies. She and her company are known for their viral and fully produced performance videos to pop music and in tribute to pop artists including Beyoncé, Justin Timberlake, and Prince as well as their appearances on television shows such as *So You Think You Can Dance*, *Good Morning America*, and *Ellen* and at New York Fashion Week.	
Fred Astaire (1899–1987)	He was known for his incredible grace and impeccable taps in Hollywood movie musicals like *Holiday Inn* (1942), *Easter Parade* (1948), *Royal Wedding* (1951), and *The Band Wagon* (1953), as well as his partnering with Ginger Rogers in *Top Hat* (1935), *Swing Time* (1936), and *Shall We Dance* (1937).	
Brenda Bufalino (b. 1937)	She studied under Charles "Honi" Coles and is known for her avant-garde performance career, which began during the Tap Renaissance. Bufalino performed as an equal with the men, and in 1986, she founded her tap company, the American Tap Dance Orchestra, which performed her concert tap compositions extensively throughout the United States and abroad. Bufalino continues to work as a mentor and teacher at the American Tap Dance Foundation, which formed out of her company. She has published three books, including her autobiography *Tapping the Source* (2004).	
Charles "Honi" Coles (1911–1992)	He learned to tap dance on the street before beginning a performance career in New York City in 1931. Throughout his career, he was a part of various tap dance groups, including the Three Millers and the Lucky Seven Trio, and performed extensively as a soloist. He combined talents with fellow tap dancer Charles "Cholly" Atkins in 1940, which was the beginning of a nineteen-year partnership as the class act Coles and Atkins. Later in his career, Coles made his film debut in *The Cotton Club* (1984) and mentored and performed with tap dance artist Brenda Bufalino.	

(continued)

7.2
Cont.

Michelle Dorrance (b. 1979)	She is a prominent tap dance performer, choreographer, teacher, and artistic director. She trained with some of the great tap masters, and her performance credits include *STOMP*, *Imagine Tap!*, and *Rhumba Tap*. She is founder and artistic director of the tap dance company Dorrance Dance, which presents full-length concert works. With her company, Dorrance honors the tap elders who came before her while also creating innovative works that push the boundaries of tap dance, and in 2015, she became a MacArthur Fellow.
Savion Glover (b. 1973)	He is a renowned tap artist known for developing his own hard-hitting style of tap dance. He began as a child prodigy with Broadway credits as a kid including *The Tap Dance Kid* (1983) and *Black and Blue* (1989). In 1996, he starred in, as well as choreographed, the hit musical *Bring in 'da Noise, Bring in 'da Funk*, blending tap dance with the hip-hop music of the day.
Gregory Hines (1946–2003)	He was beloved throughout the tap dance community as a performer, choreographer, "improvographer," and advocate of the form. Hines called his performance improvisation "improvography." His Broadway credits include *Eubie!* (1978), *Sophisticated Ladies* (1981), and both performer and choreographer for *Jelly's Last Jam* (1992). Hines' extensive film credits include starring in *White Nights* (1986) and *Tap* (1989). He also appeared in several television series, including *Sesame Street* (1992–1993), *The Gregory Hines Show* (1997–1999), *Will and Grace* (1999–2000), and *Law and Order* (2003), and hosted the PBS documentary special *Tap Dance in America*. In 2019, Hines was honored with his own stamp by the United States Postal Service as part of the Black Heritage Forever Stamps Series.
Gene Kelly (1912–1996)	He was a dancer, actor, choreographer, director, and producer. Known for his boyish charm and athletic dancing, Kelly rose to fame during the Golden Age of tap dance in the 1930s and 1940s. His movie credits include *For Me and My Gal* (1942), *Anchors Aweigh* (1945), *Summer Stock* (1950), and *An American in Paris* (1951), which won six Academy Awards, including Best Picture. He both starred in and co-directed the films *On the Town* (1949) and *Singin' in the Rain* (1952). Kelly's choreography credits include Broadway's *Best Foot Forward* (1941) and *Singin' in the Rain* (1985, stage show).
William Henry Lane (1825–1852)	A free African American in the early nineteenth century, he was nicknamed "Master Juba" and named the best dancer in America for his unique buck dancing. His genuinely original style of dancing has earned him the title of the first American tap dancer by most historians.

7.2 Cont.	**Fayard** (1914–2006) **and Harold** (1921–2000) **Nicholas**		The Nicholas Brothers remain unparalleled in their hypnotic and thrilling blend of flips, splits, vernacular dance, and hot-footed tap dancing. As the epitome of a flash act, the brothers transcended racial barriers as two of the few African American artists performing in the movie musicals of the Golden Age. Their performance of "Jumpin Jive" in *Stormy Weather* (1943) has been deemed the "greatest dance sequence ever filmed." The Nicholas Brothers performed at the Cotton Club, on Broadway, and in other films, including *Tin Pan Alley* (1940) and *Down Argentine Way* (1940).
	Eleanor Powell (1912–1982)		She was a dancer and actress with performances both on Broadway and in Hollywood. She was known for being just as skilled in tap dance as the men in the industry, earning her the title "Queen of Taps." Her unique blend of acrobatics, ballet, and tap dancing catapulted her to fame in the Golden Age of tap dance, with films including *Broadway Melody of 1936* (1935), *Born to Dance* (1936), *Broadway Melody of 1938* (1937), and *Broadway Melody of 1940* (1940).
	Bill "Bojangles" Robinson (1878–1949)		He was the most famous tap dancer in history. Known for bringing tap dance up on the toes, he was a true entertainer who was always ready to pass his knowledge on to the next generation. He was the first African American dancer to perform solo on a white vaudeville stage and with a white partner on film in his movies with Shirley Temple. His vaudeville act included his iconic stair dance. After his death, a group of artists used his catch phrase "everything's copasetic" to form a social group called the Copasetics with the mission of honoring Robinson's memory.
7.3 Notable Tap Dance Choreography	***No, No, Nanette***	1925 (stage)	This Broadway show was the first time that metal taps were used in a production.
	Anything Goes	1933 (stage) 1987 (revival)	A hit Broadway musical that has been revived several times. The 1987 revival received Tony Awards for Best Revival of a Musical and Best Choreography.
	42nd Street	1933 (film) 1980 (stage)	Originally a film, the transition of this show to the stage nearly fifty years later was wildly successful and brought back nostalgia for the classic charm of the movie musicals of the Swing Era.
	Stormy Weather	1943 (film)	A Hollywood movie musical that featured many talents of the era in both tap and jazz dance. In this film, the Nicholas Brothers perform their famous routine "Jumpin Jive."

(continued)

Singin' in the Rain	1952 (film)	A movie musical starring Gene Kelly with a plot centering around the invention of film with sound.	7.3 Cont.
Black and Blue	1989 (stage)	This entire show was rooted in jazz rhythms featuring renowned blues singers, a jazz orchestra, and three generations of rhythm tap dancers. It showcased the versatile possibilities of tap dance, incorporating numerous styles and different rhythms.	
Bring in 'da Noise, Bring in 'da Funk	1996 (stage)	Choreographed by Savion Glover, this Broadway production showcased his hip-hop style of tap dance and helped contemporize tap dance at the end of the twentieth century.	
ETM: Double Down	2016 (stage)	This Dorrance Dance concert tap dance work features the Dorrance Dance company of tap dancers, live musicians, vocalists, and revolutionary electronic tap dance boards that serve as instruments as well.	

1825	William Henry Lane, nicknamed "Master Juba," was born.	7.4 Historical Timeline of Tap Dance
1830s	Minstrel shows were first performed during this time period by white men dressed in blackface and featured buck dancing.	
1845–1849	Many Irish immigrated to North America during the Great Potato Famine.	
1865	Civil War ended.	
1878	Bill "Bojangles" Robinson was born.	
1880s	Vaudeville shows began to replace minstrelsy.	
1890s	Ragtime Era.	
1915	Bill Robinson became the first African American to perform solo on the white vaudeville stages.	
1920s–mid-1930s	Early Big Band Era.	
1921	Premier of the Broadway show *Shuffle Along*, featuring buck and wing dancing.	
1923	The Cotton Club opened.	
1925	Metal taps were used for the first time in the Broadway show *No, No, Nanette*.	
1927	Film with sound was developed.	
1929	Tap dance premiered in "the talkies" in MGM's *Hollywood Revue*.	
mid-1930s–mid-1940s	Swing Era.	

7.4 Cont.		
	1932	The Nicholas Brothers opened at the Cotton Club and premiered in their first film.
	1933	The Broadway musical *Anything Goes* premiered and was later revived several times.
	1935	Bill Robinson and Shirley Temple starred in their first film together.
	1936	Eleanor Powell starred in her first film, *Broadway Melody of 1936*.
	1937	Fred Astaire and Ginger Rogers starred in *Shall We Dance*.
	late 1940s	Bebop Era.
	1943	The Nicholas Brothers filmed their iconic routine "Jumpin Jive" in one take for *Stormy Weather*.
	1949	Bill "Bojangles" Robinson passed away, and the Copasetics formed.
	1952	Gene Kelly starred in *Singin' in the Rain*.
	1977	Brenda Bufalino produced her documentary *Great Feats of Feet* with several old tap dance masters.
	1980	The 1933 movie musical *42nd Street* was adapted to live theater.
	1985	Gregory Hines starred opposite Russian ballet star Mikhail Baryshnikov in the film *White Nights*.
	1986	Tap dance festival Fascinating Rhythms took place in Colorado.
	1986	Brenda Bufalino formed the American Tap Dance Orchestra.
	1988	Gregory Hines hosted an episode of the PBS *Great Performances* series titled *Tap Dance in America*.
	1989	May 25th was established as National Tap Dance Day.
	1996	Savion Glover choreographed *Bring in 'da Noise, Bring in 'da Funk* showcasing his hip-hop style of tap dance.
	2011	Michelle Dorrance founded Dorrance Dance.
	2012	Chloe Arnold's Syncopated Ladies released their first video.
	2015	Dorrance received the MacArthur Fellowship.
	2019	Gregory Hines was inducted as the forty-second honoree in the Black Heritage Stamp series for his contributions to tap dance.

7.5 Chapter 7 Vocabulary		
Broadway tap dance	minstrelsy	soft shoe
buck dancing	polyrhythm	vaudeville
concert tap dance	rhythm tap dance	
flash act	*Shim Sham Shimmy*	

Reflective Prompts

1. How would you describe tap dance to someone who has never seen it before?

2. In your own words, what makes tap dance an American art form?

3. For many decades, tap dance was considered "low brow" art, in other words a less valuable art form than ballet and modern dance. Today there are still people who view dance in a hierarchical structure, with ballet and modern dance clearly and significantly ranked above tap, jazz, and hip-hop dance. Why do you think this is? Do you agree? Why or why not?

4. Many people today still say that tap dance is a "dying" art form. Why do you think they say this? Based on what you learned in this chapter, do you believe this is true? Why or why not?

5. Tap dance began as a predominantly African American art form and was challenged by racism in its development. What barriers did this art form and the artists face throughout the eighteenth, nineteenth, and twentieth centuries?

6. Do you believe it is important to preserve American tap dance? How is it being preserved? What else could be done to help preserve this form of American art?

Movement Prompts

1. **Tap Dance Movement:** Learn the tap dance movement on the companion website and try to execute the sequence.

2. **Polyrhythm:** Gather into groups of three or four. Working together, create your own one bar (four-count) polyrhythm. Each of you (or pairs of you) should have a different rhythm that you clap/stomp/snap and that layers with the rest of your group.

NOTES

1 Constance Valis Hill, *Tap Dancing America: A Cultural History* (New York: Oxford University Press, 2010), 272–273.
2 Valis Hill, 12.
3 Mark Knowles, *Tap Roots: The Early History of Tap Dancing* (North Carolina: McFarland & Company, 2002), 135.
4 Valis Hill, 83–84.
5 "Antoinette Perry," The American Theatre Wing's Tony Awards®, accessed September 27, 2019, www.tonyawards.com/history/antoinette-perry/.
6 Valis Hill, 23–25.
7 "About the ATDF," American Tap Dance Foundation, accessed September 29, 2019, http://atdf.org/ATDFBIO.html.
8 Jim Haskins and N.R. Mitgang, *Mr. Bojangles: The Biography of Bill Robinson* (New York: Linus Multimedia, 2014), 37.
9 Haskins and Mitgang, 15–18.
10 "S.J.Res.53 – 101st Congress (1989-1990)," Congress.gov, Library of Congress, October 27, 1989. www.congress.gov/bill/101st-congress/senate-joint-resolution/53/text?q=%7B%22search%22%3A%5B%22national+tap+dance+day%22%5D%7D&r=10&s=2.

CHAPTER 7 BIBLIOGRAPHY

"About the ATDF." American Tap Dance Foundation. Accessed September 29, 2019. http://atdf.org/ATDFBIO.html.

"Antoinette Perry." The American Theatre Wing's Tony Awards®. Accessed September 27, 2019. www.tonyawards.com/history/antoinette-perry/.

Haskins, Jim and N.R. Mitgang. *Mr. Bojangles: The Biography of Bill Robinson*. New York: Linus Multimedia, 2014.

Knowles, Mark. *Tap Roots: The Early History of Tap Dancing*. North Carolina: McFarland & Company, 2002.

"S.J.Res.53 – 101st Congress (1989–1990)." Congress.gov. Library of Congress, October 27, 1989. www.congress.gov/bill/101st-congress/senate-joint-resolution/53/text?q=%7B%22search%22%3A%5B%22national+tap+dance+day%22%5D%7D&r=10&s=2.

Valis Hill, Constance. *Tap Dancing America: A Cultural History*. New York: Oxford University Press, 2010.

8 Jazz Dance

So many diff. vastly scenes

In the middle of the dance floor, a pair of dancers move with a fierce purpose. They bounce and turn around one another as their legs kick wildly. Abruptly, one dancer quickly propels their partner's body through the air at a pace so quick you don't dare blink your eyes while watching …

The dancers slink across the stage with jutting hips, limp wrists, inverted knees, and shrugged shoulders in a rhythmic and smoothly stylized fashion that is simultaneously subtle and dynamic …

Energetically vocalized scats that reflect the reaches and accented pauses and hits of the dancers' movements ring out through the theater. The result is both a visual and an aural representation of the rhythm that is driving their every move …

On a street corner, a group of teenagers have formed a circle. The sounds of a hit R&B song float around them as their bodies groove independently to the rhythm of the music. Yet, they remain engaged as a community, with a competitive spirit, playfully attempting to outdance one another by way of movement and style …

During a performance on Beyoncé's national tour, the crowd cheers as Queen B and her army of backup dancers rhythmically dance in unison, isolating their torsos, dropping their bodies through various levels, and then slithering to encircle B before returning to the high-energy hits of previous movement …

What do all these scenarios have in common? The pulse and beat of jazz dance! Jazz dance is a multi-faceted art form. It is a vibrant genre of dance that can be difficult to discuss because it has morphed into many opposing shapes and styles. The question "What is jazz dance?" has been a point of contention among dancers and scholars for decades but has been called into question most critically in recent years. The original jazz dance that emerged in the early twentieth century has been influenced throughout the past century by a myriad of stylistic factors, both musical and cultural. As a result, a variety of forms have emerged, many of which seem far removed from the original jazz dance of the early 1900s. Author Wendy Oliver compares jazz dance and its many styles to the root of a great tree, and the many branches that grow and flourish from that firmly planted root represent the styles that have evolved.[1] The roots of the tree are planted in African dance, and the trunk developed within the unique setting of the US.

Jazz dance is America's dance! Jazz dance was developed on American soil, and American culture and music have propelled this original art form forward ever since.

JAZZ AS A DANCE FORM

There are a vast number of shared similarities in the development and evolution of jazz and tap dance. The seeds of both dance genres lie in African American vernacular dance. Vernacular dances emerge and evolve naturally within a given community and are learned without formal training or instruction. During the fifteenth to nineteenth centuries, the transatlantic slave trade forced nearly 481,000 African people to North America.[2] During the tragic and horrific period of slavery within America's history, people of diverse nationalities made a home in North America as their various cultures melted, blended, and mixed together. Despite the fact that neither they nor their culture were respected, the dances of the enslaved Africans prevailed in many ways. Their movement and rhythms were shared on plantations and later transplanted to the theatrical stages of minstrel and vaudeville shows, as highlighted in Chapter 7. Jazz music, a genre rooted in the bouncy and syncopated rhythms of ragtime music combined with the soulfulness of blues, was born in New Orleans around the turn of the twentieth century. The vernacular dances performed to this new music genre also came to be known as jazz, and from there the two genres – jazz music and jazz dance – developed along parallel lines, quickly leading America to become dance crazy. As a number of artists found joy in creating percussive rhythms in response to the sounds of jazz music, such as tap dance, other artists focused on an equally rhythmic genre of dance that also utilized improvisation, social and communal aspects, and personal expression. In the 1920s, the name "jazz dance" was coined for this form of dance.

8.1
Photo of a jazz
dancer jumping.
Photo by
Noor Eemaan

What Makes Jazz Dance Jazz?

Jazz dance can take on many shapes and forms. Jazz dance can be the care-free dances of the 1920s Jazz Age or the swinging Lindy Hop of the 1930s; it can be the vernacular social dances theatricalized on the Broadway stage, or concert dances that have been infused with traces of ballet and modern dance vocabulary and technique. Therefore, it can become difficult for individuals to discern, or even agree, on what true jazz dance is or is not. Yet, before acknow-ledging the outgrowth of styles that are prevalent today, it is important to recog-nize jazz dance in its authentic form. **Authentic jazz dance** developed parallel to the music of the Jazz Age (1920s) and Swing Era (mid-1930s–mid-40s). The movement features a grounded quality, often coupled with fast footwork, poly-rhythmic movements, and a high use of syncopation. Rather than an upright torso, dancers move with their torsos often inclined forward. The emphasis is on the personal freedom of the dancer and expression in the movement rather than a high degree of technique or an exactness of body positions. It is from this original form that the key elements of jazz dance – rhythm, isolation, a swinging quality, individual expression, and a social connectedness – distinguished jazz from other dance genres.

In today's world, dance forms are continuously fusing together and blending to create innovative movement, styles, and choreography. Without an understanding of what truly makes jazz dance jazz, it can be difficult to decipher exactly what genre one is seeing in performance. Further, as scholars, educators, choreographers, and dancers work to preserve one of America's great dance forms, it is imperative to distinguish the origin of jazz dance from the many styles that have since evolved, in the same manner as the clas-sical forms of other arts are upheld despite their contemporary developments. Additionally, authentic jazz dance is used at times within the performance world in various modes, making it necessary for the professional dancer to under-stand the movement and become proficient in its execution and performance. Knowledge of authentic jazz dance then becomes an important component of the jazz dancer's education and training, as it helps to build a foundation of creative ability and skill in preparation for more contemporary movement techniques and styles.

styles are CONSTANTLY evolving

Influence of Jazz Music

Jazz dance shares two distinct characteristics with jazz music: improvisation and a swing feeling. In Chapter 3, we learned that dancers improvise to spontan-eously create movement; musicians will also improvise or "jam" to instinctively generate music. There is a freedom of expression and individuality in jazz music and jazz dance that is revealed within improvisation. It is the act of improvisa-tion that has aided in the continuous development and evolution of both art forms. The other aspect, the swing feeling, is produced by syncopation within the music or movement. Syncopation occurs when accents do not coincide with the regular beat of the tempo, but rather, the accent falls right before or right

Big in Tap

168 □

after the down beat. The combination of off-beat accents leads to the swing feeling within the music or the movement itself, or both.

Early jazz dance did not begin as a dance form merely set to jazz music. Rather, the two evolved together in conversation with one another. Jazz dancers listened to the story and pulse of the music and responded in rhythm and movement. Instead of mimicking the rhythms played within the music, the dancer executed movement that complemented the rhythms. Improvisation became a key element of this exchange, in which musical riffs played by musicians were countered with instinctive rhythmical articulations of the human body.[3] Authentic jazz dance was traditionally performed to live music, whereas today jazz dance is most often performed to recorded music. As a result, it is more difficult for jazz dancers to maintain the same conversational relationship with the music; however, the swinging feeling and attention to rhythm remain as essential characteristics of jazz dance regardless of the style performed.

BOX 8.1 THE PARALLEL BETWEEN SOCIAL DANCE AND MUSIC TRENDS

Huge influence on dance

As jazz music evolved, so did the social dance trends that paralleled the music and cultural shifts. In the 1930s and 1940s, the Camel Walk, Flea Hop, Shorty George, Suzie Q, and Trucking emerged alongside the bounce of swing and big band music. With the advent of rock 'n' roll in the 1950s came dances called the Bunny Hop, the Locomotion, and the Stroll. Motown music of the 1960s led to the evolution of the Frug, the Hand Jive, the Mashed Potato, and the Twist. The pattern continued as disco music of the 1970s coincided with the disco walk, line dances, and the Hustle. The 1980s incorporated influences from Michael Jackson, rap, and MTV as breakdancing evolved as well as the Moon Walk. Throughout the 1990s and 2000s, dance fads, such as the Running Man, Vogue, Electric Slide, Cupid Shuffle, Macarena, Dougie, and Whip and Nae Nae, have come and gone, often aligning themselves with individual songs or styles of music.

As the style of jazz music evolved from decade to decade throughout the twentieth century, so did jazz dance. The most noticeable shift happened within the vernacular jazz dances. The social dance trends, which are rooted in elements of jazz dance, tend to reflect the musical quality and style of the time period and also demonstrate shifting cultural attitudes and behaviors. For example, the Black Bottom, a vernacular dance of the 1920s, patterned the syncopated bounce and lightness of ragtime music and mirrored the youth's rebellious attitude, as individuals would lean and reach forward and then slap their backsides before moving their hips around in a circle. The Lindy Hop dance matched the swing and energy of the Swing Era's big band music during the mid-1930s to mid-1940s. A feature of many dances during this period was the breakaway, where couples would step away from one another for a brief period to improvise individually before returning to a closed position with their partner. This movement pattern imitated the musical structure, which gave the opportunity for certain instruments to improvise a chorus of music and also provided the expressive outlet that individuals craved. Both of these examples, the Black Bottom and the Lindy Hop, began as social dances yet were also theatricalized on stage and in film.

Influence of Popular Culture — *aka. Trends!*

A synergy exists between culture, music, and dance. Throughout the twentieth and twenty-first centuries, the interplay between the two art forms and America's popular culture has created some of the most recognizable decades and eras in the nation's history. For example, while we may not have lived through them, we are familiar with the jazz craze of the Roaring Twenties, the infamous big bands and swing dance of the 1930s Swing Era, the exhilarating sounds and attitudes of rock 'n' roll during the 1950s, or the sensual grooves of the 1970s Disco Era. Within each cultural era, societal attitudes and behaviors contributed to the

8.2
Performance of the
Cakewalk by African
American dancers
in the early 1900s.
Hulton Archive/
Getty Images

fresh approaches in instrumentation, musical rhythms and melodies, and the innovative movement ideas that reflected the rhythms and energy of the music. The Cakewalk and the Charleston serve as two examples that demonstrate this inherent connection within jazz dance between culture, music, and dance.

The Cakewalk

With ties to festive African dance, the **Cakewalk** was born from African parody of the European minuets and other couples' dances that they saw the white men and women perform at parties. The Africans mocked their masters and mistresses by putting on their Sunday best and dancing in couples as they promenaded and improvised fancy steps. "In this couple dance, dancers stood side by side, linked arms at the elbows, leaned back and pranced about high-stepping and putting on airs."[4] The white onlookers were flattered by the imitation, either unaware or not caring that the aim of the entire spectacle was to deride them. The masters and mistresses would attend the display and award the best couple a cake. This African American dance, a leader of the ragtime dances, was the first to be widely accepted and celebrated – and appropriated – by white performers, as it was performed by white men in blackface minstrel shows.

The Cakewalk contests harked back to its African aesthetics in several ways. For example, the activity was performed in a circle, a staple formation of African dance, which also supported the theme of community. Improvisation was incorporated throughout the contests, which provided an outlet for the invention of new steps and dances that would also rise in popularity. Further, individual expression was highly valued and encouraged. The bouncing quality and rhythms of the dance and ragtime music went hand in hand. For African Americans, the dance provided an outlet of expression in otherwise dire circumstances. For white Americans, who were unaware of the dance's original intent or perhaps intentionally ignoring it, the Cakewalk was an entertaining form of social dance and performance. The results of this dance were lasting and paved the way for the great number of vernacular dances that would carry their jazz roots from the social dance scene to theatrical performance.

The Charleston

During the 1920s, the **Charleston** reflected the spirit of the Jazz Age and emerged as both a dance that one could watch (as it was performed on the theatrical stage) and a dance that one could do (a social dance form). The Charleston was an early jazz dance that demonstrated the swinging feel and syncopation of jazz music discussed earlier in this chapter.

Following the end of World War I in 1918, American society had shed its innocence while enjoying a period of prosperity and optimism. Youth rebelled in many ways against the older generations. Women shortened their skirts and bobbed their hair. Speakeasies, or illegal nightclubs, were frequented, where the sounds of jazz music filled the air. When mixed with the syncopated sounds of jazz music, this carefree, rebellious nature produced the great jazz-based social

8.3
Photo of Bee
Jackson, world
Charleston dance
champion.
General
Photographic
Agency/
Getty Images

dances of the 1920s, including the Black Bottom. Yet, the most recognizable, even roughly a century later, remains the Charleston. The Charleston has many variations and versions, but at its core lies the quick movement of the legs as the feet pivot and the knees flap inward and outward, while the leg may swing forward and backward and the arms move wildly and freely.

Characteristics of Jazz Dance

Throughout the history of jazz dance, we are able to pinpoint traces of Africanist aesthetics within the dance. The fundamental elements common to West African culture and art and adapted into the African American vernacular include freedom of expression, a low center of gravity, bends at the hip, knee, and ankle joints, flat-footed movement, isolations within body parts, a confrontational presentation, an interaction between dancers and musicians, and a social aspect among performer and spectator. Art historian Robert Farris Thompson also refers to what he calls "an aesthetic of the cool."[5] This phrase reflects the ease and control with which the dancer performs.

In its many forms, jazz dance expresses individuality, which may be achieved through improvisation or the dancer's own sense of personal style. The focus is on the energy behind the movement as well as the look of the movement; the swing feeling or the groove of the dance becomes the emphasis as opposed to the pure creation of body line or shape. Jazz dance exhibits polyrhythmic movement, in which one part of the body may move in one rhythm while another body part simultaneously executes a separate rhythm. Legs are often parallel (distinct from the turned-out rotation of the legs utilized in classical ballet), and movements may be done flat-footed or with flexed feet. The torso may incline forward at the hips with the knees bent, giving way to shortened or fractured body lines. Jazz dance may be a social or participatory form of dance but can also appear on the theatrical stage.

Huge Part!

In its purest form, jazz dance features the use of body isolations and a grounded sense of weight, is driven by rhythm, and is infused with style or individual expression. As jazz dance has evolved, other styles may emerge, adapting or embracing characteristics of the dance genres with which they are blended, but these four components are always inherent.

Education of the Jazz Dancer

The education of the jazz dancer has taken quite a different path from the concert dance forms of ballet and modern dance. Jazz dance was not an institutionalized art form; it was not governed by the upper echelons of society. Rather, jazz dance developed first on plantations, then in jook joints, night clubs, street corners, dance halls, and the theatrical stage, before dance studios, professional schools, and then higher education became sources of training for the jazz dance student. There were no studios, schools, or government-led institutions that provided training in the dance form. Individual mentorship, coaching from dance directors, the exchanging and borrowing of ideas, competitions, and the real-life practice and performance of these dances provided the means by which the genre both emerged and developed throughout the nineteenth and early twentieth centuries. During the middle of the twentieth century, local dance schools emerged offering classes in jazz dance, and by the turn of the twenty-first century, jazz dance entered institutions of higher education as course offerings within dance curricula. Select universities today now focus their degree programs on the genre of jazz dance, while others include the form as a component of study in technique, choreography, and performance.

diff from say, Ballet

The Jazz Dance Class

The style of jazz dance will dictate the approach to the class structure. An authentic jazz dance class will contain a greater amount of improvisation and components that focus on community within the class. Rather than detailing technique and body lines, attention will be given to the feeling and attitude behind the movement and the rhythm and quality in which the movements are executed. A jazz class that embraces a more concert- or theatrical-based form of jazz dance may more closely resemble the format of a ballet or modern dance class. In this instance, a three-part structure may be followed, including a warm-up, progressions, and center combination. The warm-up will include isolations, stretches, and strengthening movements intended to increase circulation and prepare the body for the demands of the class. The progression portion includes locomotor movements done across the floor, which enables students to focus on specific technical skills or the assimilation of movements in short, specific sequences. The center combination is comprised of a lengthier combination designed to allow the dancer to focus on artistry while executing longer, more complex movement sequences and increasing stamina.

bc each style can be so so so different

JAZZ DANCE IN SHOW BUSINESS

Vaudeville

Throughout the twentieth century, show business was the place for performers to market and disseminate popular dances. Chapter 7 discusses the emergence and historical context of minstrel (primarily nineteenth-century) and vaudeville shows. Vaudeville in particular became a source of theatrical innovation in a variety of forms, from acrobatics, to jazz and tap dancing, to juggling, to singing, while boasting family-friendly entertainment. Vaudeville produced a great number of stars, yet this performance format met its match as the cinema appeared. Once films integrated sound, there was no way the touring show format of vaudeville theaters could financially compete. Following the decline of vaudeville, Broadway became the primary source for the live performance of jazz and tap dancing. The Palace Theatre, which closed in 1932, had been the theater to which all vaudeville acts aspired "to make it"; however, it is no surprise that it later reopened in 1966 as a Broadway theater. Many great American vernacular dances have been featured in Broadway productions, enhancing the presence of vernacular jazz dance on the performance stage.

BOX 8.2 GOLDEN AGE OF MOVIE MUSICALS

In 1927, *The Jazz Singer* became the first motion picture to feature sound, ending the era of silent films. Shortly afterwards, *Broadway Melody of 1929* became the first film to fully integrate singing and dancing into the plot. Movie musicals – shows in which the narrative is delivered through modes of acting, singing, and dancing – quickly became the rage, ushering in the Golden Age of Movie Musicals from the 1930s through the early 1950s. Coinciding with the years of the Great Depression, these movies served as an escape for Americans from the bleakness of everyday life. They became a great outlet for jazz and tap dancers, encouraged the popularity of jazz and tap dance among Americans, and brought recognition to many great dancers.

In today's society, the production of movie musicals is rare. A number of films that feature jazz dance have been produced in recent years, such as *La La Land* (2016), *The Greatest Showman* (2017), and *Mary Poppins Returns* (2018). A remake of the film *West Side Story*, directed by Stephen Spielberg, was released in 2020. Made-for-television musicals have included *Hairspray Live!* (2016), *Rent: Live* (2019), and the Disney series for teens and tweens, including *Descendants 3* (2019) and *Zombies 2* (2020). Yet, the quantity does not compare to that which appeared during the mid-twentieth century.

8.4
Street view of
the intersection
of New York's
Broadway and 47th
Street in early 1920.
The tall building
on the left is B.F.
Keith's Vaudeville,
which later became
known as the Palace
Theatre.
PhotoQuest/
Getty Images

True across all dance styles and performances

The politics of American life were reflected within the world of early show business. African American performers faced numerous obstacles in seeking their spot in show business during the years of vaudeville, despite the fact that they were the influencers of the creation of jazz dance. Throughout its early years of development, jazz dance performers were challenged by segregation, and this was especially present during the period of vaudeville. Vaudeville theaters were divided into white and black circuits. A limited number of African American performers were featured within white-only circuits by complying with the "two-colored" rule, which meant that they must perform in pairs or larger groups. However, most of the African American dancers appeared in the black-only circuits. In the 1920s, Sherman Dudley, an African American performer and entrepreneur, created the Theater Owners Booking Association (TOBA) vaudeville circuit for African American entertainers, which provided them with added opportunities. Additionally, at the turn of the century, African American entrepreneurs brought African American dance styles to the Broadway stage.

Broadway Stage

Many of the great American vernacular dances were theatricalized and featured on the Broadway stage, while racial barriers within show business were challenged. In 1889, *Clorindy, The Origin of the Cakewalk* premiered as the first musical on Broadway to feature an all-African American cast. In 1903, *In Dahomey* also featured the Cakewalk and starred George Walker and Bert Williams, two iconic figures in vaudeville history. This show became the first African American musical to perform on the main stage of a Broadway theater. In 1921, *Shuffle Along* opened on Broadway, embodying all things jazz and making history. This revue featured jazz music and dance. It made stars out of Florence Mills and Josephine Baker and showcased the music and lyrics of Noble Sissle and Eubie Blake. *Shuffle Along* was produced, directed, and performed by African Americans, which had not occurred in several years, and depicted onstage the story of romantic love between African Americans; this was something that had never been done before. *Shuffle Along* legitimatized African American performance on Broadway. African Americans were permitted to sit within the orchestra seats rather than the balcony, which helped lead toward the dismantling of racial segregation within Broadway theaters. Today, Broadway is the premier level of stage show for performers of all backgrounds and is comprised of approximately forty theaters located in the Theater District of Manhattan. Shows produced on Broadway have regularly integrated jazz dancing in its various styles.

Important Shift for all of dance

BOX 8.3 DANCE DIRECTOR TO CHOREOGRAPHER

In 1936, ballet dancer George Balanchine choreographed the Broadway musical *On Your Toes*, which features the famous jazz ballet sequence "Slaughter on Tenth Avenue." This was the first musical to introduce a modern ballet within the show. Choreographers, such as Busby Berkeley and Ned Wayburn, had previously been listed as "dance director" within the musical theater setting; however, this was the first show to recognize the individual as "choreographer." Following this musical production, other shows also included the credit of choreographer within their program notes.

The innovations occurring on the concert dance stage during the twentieth century influenced the jazz dance presented in musicals, both on stage and in film. In 1943, modern dance choreographer Agnes de Mille choreographed the musical *Oklahoma!* on Broadway. In this show, de Mille presented a balletic dream sequence in the musical. Rather than characters randomly breaking out into song and dance, the dance sequences in *Oklahoma!* developed out of the storyline and advanced the action of the show, thus producing a more integrated musical between storyline and dance. In 1957, ballet dancer Jerome Robbins directed and choreographed the Broadway musical *West Side Story*. This production was significant to musical theater performance in that it was a "concept musical" in which all aspects of the production were integrated to advance the central concept of the show. The show also lacked a chorus; each dancer portrayed a specific character within the musical and was required to be a **triple threat**, demonstrating the ability to sing, act, and dance. Robbins emphasized the role of the director-choreographer within the effectiveness of an overall production.

Individuals such as Michael Bennett and Bob Fosse also served as director-choreographers during this time period, further solidifying the importance of one individual using dance as a means to further character development. Michael Bennett is best known for his work as director and co-choreographer of *A Chorus Line*, which opened on Broadway at the Shubert Theatre in 1975 and ran until 1990. It is one of the longest-running musicals of all time. The original production was nominated for twelve Tony Awards, of which it won nine, including Best Musical and Best Choreography. Bennett's work often focused on the plot and individual characters. While he did not have a distinct movement style, he was a master at staging musicals, using engaging visual designs and intricate

8.5
A 1961 publicity photo for the film *West Side Story* choreographed by American dancer, choreographer, and director Jerome Robbins.
Silver Screen Collection/ Getty Images

use of props within his choreography. His contemporary, Bob Fosse, is known for his signature movement style, which includes elbows dropped down and tucked in, raised shoulders and limp wrists, disjointed steps, jutting hips, body isolations, and sexual suggestiveness. Influenced by Jack Cole, Fosse's work remains one of the most distinctive styles of dance today. His choreography was both provocative and entertaining. Iconic choreographic works include the dance sequences "Steam Heat" in *The Pajama Game* (1957), "The Rich Man's Frug" in *Sweet Charity* (1966), and "All That Jazz" in *Chicago* (1975), which is billed as Broadway's "longest running American musical." His groundbreaking direction and choreography on stage and screen paved the way for many to follow.

As choreographers continued to infuse the technical forms of ballet and modern dance into the jazz dance appearing within musical theater productions, the choreography's level of difficulty continued to rise. One such choreographer who continued to challenge the demands of jazz dance choreography was Jack Cole. Cole was a heavily trained modern dancer who eventually established a career for himself in musicals, both on stage and screen as a performer and later as a choreographer. He became the preferred choreographer for many great talents in Hollywood, including Marilyn Monroe, for whom he choreographed the "Diamonds are a Girl's Best Friend" sequence from *Gentlemen Prefer Blondes* (1953). The complexities of Cole's choreography initiated a need for musical theater dancers to be classically trained. He developed a personal movement style, influenced by modern, East Indian, and African dance forms, that focused on rhythm and body isolation and was controlled in nature yet physically and

177 □

8.6
Scene of the "Steam Heat" sequence from Bob Fosse's *The Pajama Game*. Photo by Gjon Mili/ The LIFE Picture Collection via Getty Images

8.7
Photo of Jack Cole teaching his technique at the Harkness House for Ballet Arts in New York, 1966. Jack Mitchell/ Getty Images

mentally demanding. He is <u>known as the "father of theatrical jazz dance</u>," and his work has influenced generations of dancers and choreographers.

Agnes de Mille and Jack Cole, along with the efforts of ballet choreographers and directors George Balanchine and Jerome Robbins, were the pioneer choreographers of musical theater dance, who "propelled musical theater out of the vernacular/vaudeville styles and into the musical theater style we know of today."[6] Prior to their efforts, the dance routines had emerged within the plots of shows as a theatrical moment of song and dance that did not necessarily further the storyline. After the innovations of these choreographers and others, dance began to advance as a conceptual and integrated component of the narrative. Through their choreographic endeavors on the musical theater stage, they established a standard that allowed theatrical jazz dance to be regarded as a serious art form, requiring quality choreography to be an important component of the musicals produced.

Contemporary Approaches — Example of getting dance blended

Throughout the twentieth century, the majority of Broadway shows encompassed choreography rooted in vernacular dance. At the turn of the twenty-first century, contemporary dance began to infiltrate the musical scene. More than at any other point in history, dance forms fused together on the theatrical stage, further blurring the lines between genres. Two early examples of this succession of

8.8
The company
of *Hamilton*
performing at
Seattle's Paramount
Theatre.
TCD/Prod.DB/
Alamy Stock Photo

shows include *The Lion King* and *Movin' Out*. *The Lion King*, choreographed by Garth Fagan, premiered on Broadway in 1997. *The Lion King* is an awe-inspiring spectacle where dancers emerge as puppets and the human world becomes the animal world through expertly crafted movement that fuses elements of ballet, modern, and Afro-Caribbean jazz dance. In 2002, Twyla Tharp conceived and choreographed the musical *Movin' Out*, set to the music of Billy Joel. Tharp's choreography displays her distinct choreographic voice while blending classical ballet, modern, and jazz dance forms in a creative, dynamic, and theatrical manner. Both of these dance-heavy musicals focused on movement that intricately fused classical and contemporary genres of theatrical dance, and both were awarded a Tony Award for Best Choreography.

In 2015, the musical *Hamilton* opened on Broadway with choreography by Andy Blankenbuehler, quickly becoming a hit. The following year, the show received a record sixteen Tony Award nominations, ultimately winning eleven awards, including Best Musical and Best Choreography. This production tells the story of Alexander Hamilton, one of America's Founding Fathers, yet it does so in an innovative and contemporary fashion. Set to rap, R&B, and pop tunes, contemporary movement incorporates jazz, street, and hip-hop dance forms. Casting intentionally utilizes racially diverse performers as the Founding Fathers and other historical characters. The production clearly tells an aged story in contemporary terms. Since its inception, productions have been presented on Broadway, in Chicago, London's West End, Toronto, and on multiple US national tours.

Jazz dance continues to be integrated within the musicals that appear on Broadway, in the West End, in national US and UK tours, and in collegiate and community theaters. With the advent of the television and internet, along with the booming commercialization of dance, jazz dance performance has maintained a continued presence in the mainstream.

CODIFICATION OF JAZZ DANCE

During the late 1930s and 1940s, musicals on the stage and in film became infused with the forms of ballet and modern dance. The integration of the **concept musical**, a show in which the dance was fully integrated into the storyline or overall concept, required greater depth in dance choreography within the musical. As a result, a higher level of technical skill was required of dancers to meet the new demands placed upon them by the choreography in these shows. Individuals such as Luigi, Matt Mattox, and Gus Giordano each codified their forms of jazz dance technique, enabling individuals to train specifically in the genre of jazz dance. They recognized the popularity of jazz dance within the musical theater venues, the need for disciplined training within the dance form, and the opportunity to expand the dance beyond social and theatrical entertainment. Their individual endeavors helped to increase the status of jazz dance beyond that of a purely entertainment form of art to one that requires education and training in a codified technique and performance if one desires a professional career in the field of dance. Jazz dance evolved to become a dance genre that could extend beyond social dance patterns and convey conceptualized means of expression and narrative in a concert dance format.

Eugene Louis Faccuito, nicknamed Luigi by dancer Gene Kelly, was left paralyzed in the right side of his body and the left side of his face following a car accident as an adult. Refusing physical therapy, he created his own set of movement exercises and eventually recovered from his paralysis while maintaining his motto "Never Stop Moving." At the request of fellow actors and dancers, Luigi began to informally lead his system of exercises on stage sets before formally teaching his methods in studios in the late 1940s. Luigi's technique, while based on classical ballet, features movements that are all performed in the center of the room. Rather than using an actual ballet *barre*, he makes use of an imaginary *barre* that encourages dancers to appropriately engage the muscles of the body in order to achieve balance and proper placement. Luigi's technique never asks the human body to do more than it can. Its smooth, connected movement quality blends with focused isolations that portray a fluid strength. In 1956, Luigi founded his own school in New York City, the First World Jazz Centre, which was one of the first jazz dance schools in the world.

BOX 8.4 "5, 6, 7, 8"

When dancers attach counts to the movements in exercises, combinations, and choreography, they often group movements into counts of eight, unless the meter of the music is in triple form, such as a 3/4 time signature. When teaching, Luigi had a habit of leading his dancers into the movement by counting them in with "ah 5, 6, 7, 8." He would begin each exercise with this vocal command, which cued the dancers as to when to start moving. This phrase is commonly used by dance teachers today when cueing in their dancers!

[handwritten note: each with various emphasizes and focuses]

[handwritten note: All personal styles of jazz that are each so different → like modern]

Note: Tap dancers are an exception to this commonality. Because tap dancers are also considered musicians, they follow the musical format of counting in fours rather than eights. Therefore, the lead-in cue words for tap dancers often remain "ah 1, 2, 3, 4" (when working in a 4/4 time signature).

Dancer, teacher, and choreographer Matt Mattox developed a personal style of training that influenced the evolution of jazz dance in America and emphasized a freedom of expression in movement. He was influenced by the style of Jack Cole, along with modern dance, Eastern dance forms, flamenco, tap dance, and even ballet. With the intention of training the jazz dancer, Mattox created a system of exercises that are very intricate and clearly integrate the concepts of isolation and propulsive rhythm. His technique requires strength, concentration, and control; exercises are intensified by arm movements and quick tempos designed to make the dancer work not only physically but also mentally. In his later years, Mattox moved to Europe, where he formed Jazzart, a concert jazz dance company.

Gus Giordano influenced the world of jazz dance as a dancer, teacher, choreographer, author, and company founder. In 1953, he established the Giordano Dance Center in the Chicago suburb of Evanston, Illinois, which provided training for dancers, and ten years later he founded Gus Giordano Jazz Dance Chicago, now known as the oldest international dance touring company in the Midwest. His company, still in existence today under the artistic leadership of his daughter Nan, embraces the Giordano movement style throughout its diverse repertoire, presenting clean body lines, use of the deep *plié*, and muscular strength. Within the Giordano technique, movements are initiated from the pelvis and flow outward to the limbs, creating movement that is fluid yet powerful. Giordano further cemented his stamp on the jazz dance world in 1990 when he established the Jazz Dance World Congress as an annual jazz dance event that brought together master teachers, choreographers, and professional jazz dance companies worldwide for five days of classes, performances, and panel discussions. This event endured through the turn of the twenty-first century, with its final event occurring in Pittsburgh, Pennsylvania, in 2012. His school continues today as the Gus Giordano Dance School under the direction of his daughter, Amy Giordano.

The technique and movement of Luigi, Mattox, and Giordano each became referred to as classic jazz dance (discussed later in this chapter). Although the techniques of these individuals were established nearly a half century ago, their legacies remain today. Remnants of their exercises, movement techniques, and stylistic approaches appear in some fashion in a majority of jazz dance classes taught today. As a result of the efforts of Luigi, Mattox, and Giordano, jazz dance has become a formal dance technique that requires specific and focused training equal to that of ballet and modern dance. While still rooted in American vernacular dance and grounded in the aspects of authentic jazz dance, the technique of jazz has blended with other forms of dance and as a result has taken

8.9
Giordano Dance
Chicago founder,
Gus Giordano.
Photo courtesy of
Giordano Dance
Chicago

on additional characteristics. The metaphorical tree of jazz dance has grown, developing new branches over the years that extend from its strong trunk and authentic roots.

Concert Jazz Dance Companies

Giordano Dance Chicago, founded in 1963, is recognized as America's original jazz dance company. Gus Giordano, one of the founding fathers of jazz dance discussed earlier, established this company in an effort to legitimatize jazz dance as an art form. By the mid-twentieth century, ballet and modern dance were both appearing professionally as concert art forms on stages throughout the United States, yet the performance of jazz dance had not yet transitioned from social dance settings and theatrical musicals to the concert stage. Giordano sought to even the playing field between the dance forms, raise awareness of the art of jazz dance, and increase its prominence as a concert dance form.

Giordano Dance Chicago has presented work by a great number of choreographers, yet many of Giordano's signature works, including his famous classic jazz dance choreography entitled *Sing, Sing, Sing* (1983), remain a part of the company's repertoire.[7] Today, the company continues under the artistic direction of his daughter, Nan Giordano. The regal, grounded, and dynamic Giordano technique and style remain visible within the company, yet Nan Giordano continually stretches the definition of jazz dance through the diverse choreographers who create work for the company.

In 1990, Billy Siegenfeld, an actor-dancer-singer and a creator of what he calls "vocal-rhythmic theatre-movement," founded Jump Rhythm® Jazz Project in New York City and later relocated it to Chicago. Being a former drummer in jazz and rock bands as well as having loved to dance socially since boyhood, he instinctively sensed that the core of jazz dance is jazz rhythm. Three of his essays, "If Jazz Dance, Then Jazz Music," "Performing Energy," and "Democracy's

8.10
Giordano
Dance Chicago
in "Flickers,"
choreographed by
Marinda Davis.
Photo by Anderson
Photography

Energy," address this point of view. In his teaching as well as his writings, he also emphasizes that the roots of jazz dance lie in African American-originated, vernacular-bodied (i.e., non-balletic) rhythmic movement. That tradition, in turn, traces its own origins to the communally sung-and-danced rituals of West Africa. Thus, audiences watching Siegenfeld's work often see people working in tight, hand-held partnerships with each other to express strongly percussive rhythms with both their bodies and their voices. He has codified these Africanist elements into a system of vocally accompanied, full-bodied rhythm-making called Jump Rhythm® Technique (JRT). Classes in JRT can be enjoyed by persons of all ages and skill levels as well as by actors and singers who love to dance, since they focus on moving both rhythmically and communally over a base of body-friendly relaxation. This grounding of the body earthward is guided by a holistic philosophy of living as well as performing that Siegenfeld calls Standing Down Straight® (SDS). SDS is an ecologically informed, injury-preventive approach to performing arts training that uses gravity-directed relaxation as the source of postural, motional, vocal, and spiritual health. Since 2015, Siegenfeld has rebranded his company. It is now known simply as Jump Rhythm®. He and his collaborators continue to tour nationally and internationally to perform the musical plays he writes and the workshops in JRT and SDS he leads to entertain and educate audiences and learners of all ages, levels, and disciplines.

A variety of concert jazz dance companies have established themselves throughout the latter decades of the twentieth century and into the twenty-first century. Many of these companies have been unique to a specific genre of dance, whereas others market themselves as a fusion of dance genres, including the jazz idiom. For example, Decidedly Jazz Danceworks (DJD), founded by Vicki Willis, Hannah Stilwell, and Michèle Moss, was created in 1984 in Calgary, Canada. The movement of the DJD looks directly to authentic jazz aesthetics, including vernacular movement, as inspiration for their work. The company maintains a close connection to jazz music in its development of movement and choreography.

Odyssey Dance Theatre (ODT), based in Salt Lake City, was founded by Derryl Yeager in 1994. His company strives to present concert dance in a way that becomes accessible to all, not just the elite. According to ODT's website, the company blends "the classical virtues of ballet with the attack of jazz; the freedom of modern dance; the raw energy of hip-hop; the syncopated rhythms of tap; the fluid partnering of ballroom; and the spirit of Broadway and Vaudeville to create a fresh dance vocabulary and entertainment genre."[8] ODT serves as an example of a concert dance company that is rooted in jazz dance yet often blends other dance genres within its choreography.

STYLES OF JAZZ DANCE

Since its inception, jazz dance has shifted, morphed, evolved, and advanced, running parallel to the ever-changing culture in which it lives and matching the pulse of the progressing music in which it breathes. Jazz dance is the direct product of individual artists, eras in time, musical genres, and transitioning cultures. With each passing decade, societal attitudes and cultural styles have shifted alongside the progressing world around us. Technological advancements and changing political and economic environments all became factors that also influenced the development of jazz dance in nearly every decade throughout the 1900s and into the twenty-first century. The following list, while not all-inclusive, offers an overview of select styles of jazz dance that are found in historical and contemporary performance contexts.

It is important to note that style can be applied to dance in two distinct manners. In one sense, the use of the term "style" applies to a generalized mode in which a genre of dance is performed as a whole. Latin jazz, Broadway tap, and post-modern dance are all styles of dance. However, choreographers also have a personal movement style within which they dance and create dances. For instance, Bob Fosse was a theater jazz dance choreographer, yet he created a very unique style that is notably distinct from that of other theater jazz choreographers such as Jack Cole or Andy Blankenbuehler.

Authentic Jazz Dance → Jazz music, one of the OG's
Authentic jazz dance is social and community-based. It values individual expression and improvisation, incorporates body isolation, polyrhythms, and a grounded sense of weight, and makes use of the flat foot and bent joints, specifically in the hips, knees, and ankles. Authentic jazz dance is performed to jazz music, and the focus is often on the rhythm and the feeling of the movement rather than the specific look of a movement. Encompassed within this category are the vernacular dances of the early 1900s, such as the Cakewalk, Charleston, Black Bottom, Texas Tommy, and Lindy Hop. (The Lindy Hop is discussed in detail in Chapter 2.)

BOX 8.5 "PEPSI" BETHEL: AN AUTHENTIC JAZZ DANCER

Dance historian Sally Sommer has described Alfred "Pepsi" Bethel (1918–2002) as "one of the best of the authentic jazz dancers that America produced."[9] Bethel was an African American dancer, choreographer, and teacher who worked to preserve authentic jazz dance during the latter half of the 1900s when concert jazz dance was emerging, and jazz dance was blending with ballet and modern dance. In 1972, he founded the American Authentic Jazz Dance Company.

Theater Jazz Dance

As other dance forms fused with the authentic jazz dances presented on stage in the 1940s, the style of dance that emerged became known as **theater jazz**, or **Broadway jazz**.[10] Theater jazz dance blends jazz dance elements with the movement vocabulary and stylistic aspects of other dance forms, such as ballet, modern, tap, and other dance genres. For example, theater jazz may incorporate the rhythmical footwork of tap dance, the extending body lines and positions of ballet, or the deep and wide stances of *capoeira*. Individuality is often reduced as specific characters emerge or group work focuses on precision movement in unison. Theater jazz supplements the story line of the production, and the design of the choreography enhances the overall shape, form, and intent of the performance. What remains is a form of jazz dance that is clean and powerful. A choreographer may personally stylize the dance in a variety of manners to meet the needs of the production, the characters who perform it, or the choreography itself. Movement may appear graceful and as though lengthening through space. Or, movement may be executed with the body hunched over and feet seemingly dragging across the floor. Regardless of the personal stylistic approach, the jazz dance elements of rhythm and body isolations are ever-present.

8.11
Example of authentic jazz dance. Steps from the Lindy Hop are demonstrated by Leon James and Willa Mae Ricker, dancers of Whitey's Lindy Hoppers. Gjon Mili/The LIFE Picture Collection via Getty Images

8.12
Example of
theater jazz dance.
Performance
of the dance
sequence "One"
from the musical
A Chorus Line,
choreographed by
Michael Bennett.
Kevin Mazur/
WireImage for
PMK/HBH

Classic Jazz Dance

Classic jazz dance is similar to theater jazz dance in that it is a blended form of jazz dance as well. Classic jazz dance emerged during the middle of the 1900s as artists such as Luigi, Matt Mattox, and Gus Giordano codified jazz dance as a technique. As they blended the classroom structures, technical aspects, and even movement vocabulary of ballet and modern and other dance forms with jazz dance, they altered jazz dance from its authentic form, shifting their style to a new branch of the metaphorical tree of jazz dance. Classic jazz dance formed the basis of studio training during the latter twentieth century and was a component of the original movement of many early jazz dance companies. It may be performed to music genres other than strictly jazz.

Concert Jazz Dance

Concert jazz dance is also rooted in elements of jazz dance and fused with other dance forms. It is theatricalized, but unlike theater jazz, the purpose is not for musical productions. **Concert jazz dance** is created for performance by concert-based companies with the intent to produce conceptualized choreography on the concert stage. Singular works of choreography are crafted with individual concepts that may be narrative, thematic, or abstract. An evening concert may be produced by a single company or could be comprised of several different companies. The choreography performed could be created by a single choreographer or several distinct choreographers; most often, the pieces are unrelated to one another.

Commercial Jazz Dance

Commercial jazz dance is performed for the purpose of marketing a product or for venues in which a profit may be acquired. This style of jazz dance can include

8.13
Example of
classic jazz dance.
Giordano Dance
Chicago in "SOUL,"
choreographed by
Ray Leeper.
Photo by Gorman
Cook Photography

the dance that one sees performed during television shows or advertisements, at theme parks, in music videos, or during music concerts. Meant to entertain, this style is generally upbeat and energetic, showcases an array of impressive tricks, often incorporates elements of hip-hop or street jazz dance, and is often performed to pop music.

BOX 8.6 MUSIC TELEVISION

The MTV channel first aired in 1981, "introducing music, fashion, and dance trends to the masses."[11] MTV had a great impact on the development of jazz dance during the 1980s, as much of its material was focused on contemporary forms, which included jazz dance. The new format of presentation for jazz dance thus enabled audiences to view stylistic movements regularly and repeatedly from the comfort of their own homes. Michael Jackson was an artist synonymous with the beginnings of MTV. The sequences for his videos were choreographed by Michael Peters, who integrated a style of street jazz dance into the movement. However, this was not the only style choreographers would fuse within music videos. A host of big screen films, such as *Flashdance* (1983), and television series, like *Fame* (1982–1987), soon appeared, borrowing the music video style of dance and methods of filming.

Contemporary Jazz Dance —Blended a little

While the word "contemporary" has often served to describe art of the day, contemporary jazz dance emerged at the turn of the twenty-first century as its own unique style. **Contemporary jazz dance** is rooted in jazz dance vocabulary, incorporates movement from other dance genres, and often mixes in various jazz dance styles as well. This style of dance is certainly influenced by elements of jazz dance, yet it can appear far removed from the movement found within authentic jazz dance. While contemporary jazz dance integrates body isolations, emphasizes rhythm, incorporates a grounded quality, and expresses the individuality of the choreographer, it can be hard to decipher whether or not it is jazz or

8.14
Contemporary choreographer Mia Michaels' work is performed on the season fourteen finale of the reality television series *So You Think You Can Dance.* FOX Image Collection via Getty Images

perhaps another genre of dance. Contemporary dance could be considered as balletic lines merged with hip-hop elements along with traces of modern dance aesthetics, all stylistically fused together in a choreographic dance set to popular music, or even classical music. Movement often features broken lines, quick shifts of weight, and the incorporation of pedestrian movement. Contemporary dance is often featured on the reality television shows *So You Think You Can Dance* and *World of Dance*.

to help you identify this style think about this

This discussion of jazz dance styles is not meant to be exhaustive but, rather, to provide the reader with a foundational understanding of the primary categories of jazz dance prevalent within the dance scene today. Other styles not included in this chapter, such as Latin jazz (social or theatrical jazz dance that conveys South American influence within the movement that is executed along with the music to which it is danced and the costumes that are worn), afro-jazz (technical jazz dance emphasizing African influences), and street jazz (discussed in detail in Chapter 9), are also prevalent and valid within the dance scene.

CHAPTER SUMMARY

Jazz dance is one of America's greatest art forms. This genre evolved from the dances of Africans forced into slavery and developed parallel to jazz music during the twentieth century. As we have seen with the other dance forms, culture, specifically popular culture, can and does have a direct effect on dance. This has especially been the case for many styles of jazz dance.

Jazz dance performance is as diverse as its history. Movement may appear soft and fluid or punchy and athletic. Jazz dance may be participatory in nature or may occur on the stage with the intent to entertain or be conceptualized to make a social or political statement. It may be presented in any of its array of stylistic forms in a diverse range of venues. Today, concert companies perform work dedicated to the jazz dance genre in evening-length productions on the proscenium stage. Some companies feature jazz dance in a more authentic form on the concert stage, yet many companies also present jazz dance elements infused with other dance genres. Broadway shows and regional theaters regularly feature jazz dance within staged musicals. Styles of jazz dance on Broadway may range from classical to contemporary. Jazz dance has continued to find its way into Hollywood films since the late 1920s. Forms of jazz dance may be showcased in performances at theme parks, on cruise ships, and in music videos, television series and reality shows, and streaming programs. Finally, night clubs and social establishments scattered throughout the country, along with living rooms and other informal settings, provide venues for society at large to join together to engage in the latest social dance trends that have at their hearts jazz dance. The characteristics of jazz dance may vary depending upon the style of jazz dance or how it is blended with other dance genres, but the elements of isolation, rhythm, groundedness, and individual expression will be present.

8.1 Notable Individuals in Jazz Dance	**Andy Blankenbuehler** (b. 1970)	He is best known as the choreographer of the Broadway hit *Hamilton* (2015), which displays high-energy movement, full of propulsion and isolations and rich with jazz dance vocabulary. Other Broadway choreography credits include *In the Heights* (2008) and *Bandstand* (2017).
	Jack Cole (1911–1974)	He is known as the "father of theatrical dance," and his work has influenced generations of dancers and choreographers. Stage credits include *Magdalena* (1948), *Kismet* (1953), and *A Funny Thing Happened on the Way to the Forum* (1962). Film credits include *The Merry Widow* (1952), *Gentlemen Prefer Blondes* (1953), and *Les Girls* (1957).
	Bob Fosse (1927–1987)	He was a musical theater choreographer of the late twentieth century. Influenced by Jack Cole, Fosse's provocative and entertaining work remains one of the most distinctive dance styles today. His signature style includes elbows dropped down and tucked in, raised shoulders and limp wrists, disjointed steps, jutting hips, body isolations, and sexual suggestiveness. Stage choreography credits include *Damn Yankees* (1955), *Sweet Charity* (1966), and *Chicago* (1975). Film choreography credits include *The Pajama Game* (1957) and *All That Jazz* (1979).
	Gus Giordano (1923–2008)	He established the Giordano Dance Center in the Chicago suburbs and, in 1963, founded Gus Giordano Jazz Dance Chicago as the oldest international jazz dance touring company in the Midwest. His company embraces the Giordano movement style throughout its diverse repertoire, presenting clean body lines, use of the deep *plié*, and muscular strength.

(continued)

8.1
Cont.

Matt Mattox (1921–2013)	He created a system of exercises that are very intricate and clearly integrate the concepts of isolation and propulsive rhythm. His technique requires strength, concentration, and control; exercises are intensified by arm movements and quick tempos designed to make the dancer work not only physically but also mentally. In his later years, Mattox moved to Europe, where he formed Jazzart, a concert jazz dance company.
Mia Michaels (b. 1966)	She is an American choreographer and author who has worked with a number of famous celebrities. She was the founder and artistic director of her own contemporary dance company R.A.W. in the late 1990s, and, in 2005, choreographed Cirque du Soleil's world tour *Delirium*. She is perhaps best known for her work as a contemporary choreographer and judge on the reality television series *So You Think You Can Dance*, for which she has won two separate Emmy awards for choreography.
Billy Siegenfeld	Siegenfeld, an actor-dancer-singer and a creator of what he calls "vocal-rhythmic theatre-movement," founded Jump Rhythm® Jazz Project, now known simply as Jump Rhythm®. He has codified his teaching methods into a system of vocally accompanied, full-bodied rhythm-making called Jump Rhythm® Technique (JRT), which is guided by a holistic philosophy of living and performing that he terms Standing Down Straight® (SDS).
Sonya Tayeh (b. 1977)	She is an American contemporary choreographer based in New York City. She has choreographed a number of tours and live performances for celebrities including Florence and the Machine and Miley Cyrus. She has won Emmys for her choreographic work on the television series *So You Think You Can Dance*.
Travis Wall (b. 1987)	He earned his fame as a dancer on *So You Think You Can Dance*. He has continued to choreograph for the show and teaches for national touring conventions. He also appeared in *All The Right Moves*, a reality show on the Oxygen channel.

8.2
Notable Jazz Dance
Choreography

Shuffle Along	1921 (stage)	This show was produced, directed, and performed by African Americans. It legitimized African American performance on Broadway and helped dismantle racial segregation within Broadway theaters.
Oklahoma!	1943 (stage)	Agnes de Mille choreographed this Broadway musical and started the trend of including a dream sequence within musicals. Her choreography effectively integrated dance into the storyline.

8.2 Cont.	*West Side Story*	1957 (stage) 1961 (film) 2020 (film)	Both the 1957 and 1961 versions were choreographed by Jerome Robbins. *West Side Story* has been revived on Broadway multiple times. This musical was significant to musical theater performance in that it was a "concept musical."
	A Chorus Line	1975 (stage) 1985 (film)	Opened on Broadway at the Shubert Theatre in 1975 and ran until 1990, making it one of the longest-running musicals of all time. The musical was directed by Michael Bennett and co-choreographed by Bennett and Bob Avian. The original production was nominated for twelve Tony Awards, of which it won nine, including Best Musical and Best Choreography.
	Chicago	1976 (stage) 1996 (revival) 2002 (film)	Although *Chicago* originally premiered in 1976 with choreography by Bob Fosse, it is most known for its revival in 1996 with performances that continue to play today at the Ambassador Theatre.
	Hamilton	2015 (stage)	The production clearly tells an aged story in contemporary terms. Set to rap, R&B, and pop tunes, contemporary movement incorporates jazz, street, and hip-hop dance forms. Casting intentionally utilizes racially diverse performers as the Founding Fathers and other historical characters.
	The Greatest Showman	2017 (film)	This film is directed by Michael Gracey, choreographed by Ashley Wallen, and stars Hugh Jackman, Michelle Williams, and Zendaya. Both classic and modern, the contemporary choreography features unique camera angles, suspension methods, and dynamic ensemble production numbers.
	Mary Poppins Returns	2018 (film)	Emily Blunt and Lin-Manuel Miranda star in this film directed by Rob Marshall and co-choreographed by Marshall and John DeLuca. The movement is motivated by the story and features the energetically rhythmic and tune catching sequence "Trip the Light Fantastic," which features an ensemble of dancers and bikers.

fifteenth–nineteenth centuries	The transatlantic slave trade forced nearly 481,000 African individuals to North America.
1889	*Clorindy, The Origin of the Cakewalk* premiered as the first musical on Broadway to feature an all African American cast.
1903	*In Dahomey* featured the Cakewalk and starred iconic vaudeville performers George Walker and Bert Williams.
1920s	This era is known as the Jazz Age; the term "jazz dance" was coined; the Black Bottom and Charleston were popular vernacular dances.
1920s	Sherman Dudley created the Theater Owners Booking Association (TOBA).
1921	*Shuffle Along* opened on Broadway.
mid-1930s–mid-1940s	This era is known as the Swing Era; the Lindy Hop was a popular vernacular dance.
1930s–1950s	This period is referred to as the Golden Age of Movie Musicals.
1932	The Palace Theatre closed.
1936	George Balanchine choreographed the Broadway musical *On Your Toes* and was billed as the choreographer rather than the dance director.
1943	Agnes de Mille choreographed the musical *Oklahoma!* on Broadway.
1953	Gus Giordano established Gus Giordano Dance Center in Chicago.
1956	Luigi founded the First World Jazz Center in NYC.
1957	Jerome Robbins directed and choreographed the Broadway musical *West Side Story*.
1963	Gus Giordano Jazz Dance Chicago, known as America's original jazz dance company, was founded.
1966	The Palace Theatre reopened as a Broadway theater.
1975	*A Chorus Line*, directed and choreographed by Michael Bennett, opened on Broadway and ran until 1990, making it one of the longest-running musicals of all time.
1976	*Chicago*, directed and choreographed by Bob Fosse, premiered on Broadway.
1981	MTV first aired.
1982–1987	TV series *Fame* was featured.
1984	Decidedly Jazz Danceworks (DJD) was created in Calgary, Canada.
1990	Gus Giordano established the Jazz Dance World Congress.

8.3 Cont.	1990	Jump Rhythm® Jazz Project was founded by Billy Siegenfeld.
	1996	The Broadway revival of *Chicago* opened on Broadway and continues to perform today. It is billed as Broadway's "longest-running American musical."
	2012	The final Jazz Dance World Congress event occurred in Pittsburgh, PA.
	2015	*Hamilton* premiered on Broadway and quickly became a national hit.

8.4
Chapter 8 Vocabulary

authentic jazz dance	classic jazz dance	contemporary jazz dance
body isolation	commercial jazz dance	theater jazz dance
Broadway jazz dance	concept musical	triple threat
Cakewalk	concert jazz dance	
Charleston		

Reflective Prompts

1. What socioeconomic issues do you believe jazz dancers faced during the development of jazz dance?
2. Compare and contrast jazz dance with ballet or modern dance. How would you compare and contrast the characteristics of each? Can you find any parallels between their histories?
3. How would you describe jazz dance to someone who is not familiar with the genre?
4. What trends are current today in social dance? Can you identify characteristics of jazz dance within them?
5. Do you believe it is important for dancers to have their own individual style? Why or why not?
6. Explain the differences between the styles of jazz dance.
7. Have you seen any television shows or movies that include jazz dance? At the time you watched the show, were you aware that it was jazz dance? How did the dance impact the show as a whole?
8. Can you recall any television commercials that feature dance? Why would companies choose to use dance as a marketing ploy? More specifically, why might a company choose to use jazz dance within their advertisements or marketing events? How can dance, in general, be used to sell a product?

Movement Prompt

1. **Jazz Dance Movement:** Learn the jazz dance phrase on the companion website and try to execute the sequence.

NOTES

1 Lindsay Guarino and Wendy Oliver, eds., *Jazz Dance: A History of the Roots and Branches* (Gainesville, Florida: University Press of Florida, 2014), xv.
2 Takiyah Nur Amin, "The African Origins of an American Art Form," in *Jazz Dance: A History of the Roots and Branches*, ed. by Lindsay Guarino and Wendy Oliver (Gainesville, Florida: University Press of Florida, 2014), 36.
3 Sheron Wray, "A Twenty-First-Century Jazz Dance Manifesto," in *Jazz Dance: A History of the Roots and Branches*, ed. by Lindsay Guarino and Wendy Oliver (Gainesville, Florida: University Press of Florida, 2014), 12–14.
4 Nadine George-Graves, "Just Like Being at the Zoo," in *Ballroom, Boogie, Shimmy Sham, Shake: A Social and Popular Dance Reader*, ed. by Julie Malnig (Chicago: University of Illinois Press, 2009), 56.
5 Jacqui Malone, *Steppin' on the Blues: The Visible Rhythms of African American Dance* (Chicago: University of Illinois Press, 1996), 18.
6 Kirsten Harvey, "Jazz Dance in the Broadway Musical," in *Jazz Dance: A History of the Roots and Branches*, ed. by Lindsay Guarino and Wendy Oliver (Gainesville, Florida: University Press of Florida, 2014), 155.
7 Michael McStraw, "The Legacy of Gus Giordano," in *Jazz Dance: A History of the Roots and Branches*, ed. by Lindsay Guarino and Wendy Oliver (Gainesville, Florida: University Press of Florida, 2014), 107.
8 "About ODT," Odyssey Dance Theatre, accessed March 2020, https://odysseydance.com/.
9 Karen Hubbard, "The Authentic Jazz Dance Legacy of Pepsi Bethel," in *Jazz Dance: A History of the Roots and Branches*, ed. by Lindsay Guarino and Wendy Oliver (Gainesville, Florida: University Press of Florida, 2014), 75.
10 Guarino and Oliver, *Jazz Dance*, 27.
11 Melanie George, "Jazz Dance, Pop Culture, and the Music Video Era," in *Jazz Dance: A History of the Roots and Branches*, ed. by Lindsay Guarino and Wendy Oliver (Gainesville, Florida: University Press of Florida, 2014), 176.

CHAPTER 8 BIBLIOGRAPHY

"About ODT," Odyssey Dance Theatre, accessed March 2020, https://odysseydance.com/.
Boross, Bob. *Comments on Jazz Dance: 1996–2014.* Lexington, KY: n.p., 2016.
Gridley, Mark C. *Concise Guide to Jazz*, 6th ed. New Jersey: Pearson Education,, 2010.
Guarino, Lindsay and Wendy Oliver, eds. *Jazz Dance: A History of the Roots and Branches.* Gainesville: University Press of Florida, 2014.
Malnig, Julie, ed. *Ballroom, Boogie, Shimmy Sham, Shake: A Social and Popular Dance Reader.* Chicago: University of Illinois Press, 2009.
Malone, Jacqui. *Steppin' on the Blues: The Visible Rhythms of African American Dance.* Chicago: University of Illinois Press, 1996.
Stearns, Marshall and Jean Stearns. *Jazz Dance: The Story of American Vernacular Dance.* Boston, MA: Da Capo Press, 1994.

9 Hip-hop Dance

The year is 1978. A group of diverse teenagers gather on an asphalt covered corner of a park in the Bronx. The innovative youth form a circle as they shout out and raise their arms. Rhythms echo from a rectangular boom box. A closer look reveals that two individuals have centered themselves within the circle. One slowly steps back, hands on hips, chest quickly rising and falling. The other moves stealthily along the ground; weight is first on the hands; then the body spins on the back; legs whirl through the air. The body freezes in a peculiar, super-human position. Seconds tick by. The individual releases from the pose and stands as cheers erupt from the fellow group members. A winner has been declared. A battle has been won. However, the friendly yet competitive rivalry will undoubtedly continue. This was the true spirit behind the dance form known as hip-hop.

Unknown to many, the term "hip-hop" implies not only a form of dance but an expression of an entire culture, including style of music, fashion, speech, and behavior. The hip-hop culture emerged in the 1970s in the south Bronx, yet by the mid-1980s had found its way into the heart of mainstream America. What began as a cultural expression and form of communication among a diverse group of youth has since spread across not only the nation, but also the world. For some individuals, its cultural ties have remained intact, and its integrity has stayed strong. Yet in some outlets, hip-hop has become commercialized and fused with other forms of dance and expression; stripped of its original identity and provided with new meaning and intent. In either case, hip-hop has become a worldwide phenomenon that has amazed its critics by its continuing popularity. Today, hip-hop is a stand-alone genre of dance, performed on commercial and concert dance stages, in competitive venues, and in informal settings by amateurs and professionals alike.

HISTORICAL CONTEXT

Hip-hop as a form of street dance emerged initially in the 1970s on the East Coast within a borough of New York City known as the Bronx. The hip-hop culture developed among the African American and Latinx youth in these neighborhoods, providing a sense of strength and community among its participants. This dancing began on the streets, as opposed to the dance studio or European court, among multi-ethnic youth who felt frustrated by their socioeconomic position in life. Along with the other aspects of hip-hop, street dancing served as an outlet for expression, providing an emotional and physical release.

In 1955, the Cross Bronx Expressway was constructed, providing an additional route for people to commute to Manhattan yet resulting in dire consequences for many neighborhoods in the Bronx, which the Expressway now divided. Throughout the 1950s, middle- and upper-class families relocated to the suburbs, while lower classes were left behind in the borough. As above-ground portions of the subway were put into place, many homes, buildings, and businesses were torn down or destroyed. Tenement-style housing, which also became known as the projects, was developed and shaped the urban layout of the neighborhoods, which became populated by gangs and street

9.1
Breakdancing
in Washington
Square Park.
Leo Vals/
Getty Images

violence. These neighborhoods, comprised of primarily African American and Latinx immigrants, became severely overwhelmed and socioeconomically depressed throughout the course of the 1950s and 1960s: "between 1973 and 1977, the South Bronx lost 600,000 jobs, more than 5,000 families were displaced, and some 30,000 fires were set in the area"[1] Poor city management, a rampant drug scene, and corrupt police departments also contributed to the decaying urban setting at that time. Altogether, those factors left the individuals residing in these neighborhoods feeling unrepresented, frustrated, and with little power.

It its early years, hip-hop enabled individuals to express frustrations in a non-violent manner. During the 1970s, creative youth refused to remain passive victims of circumstance but, rather, became a creative agency of chance. They utilized their energy and spirit to generate a positive response to their socio-economic circumstances. For many, the hip-hop culture that emerged offered an alternative to violence. Breaking, the form of street dance that developed on the East Coast, emphasized crews instead of gangs and dance battles rather than street fights. B-boys, or break-boys, challenged one another to settle rivalries, and individuals danced for recognition. In the documentary *The Freshest Kids*, battle rapper Mr. Re highlights the fact that being a dance crew member and practicing for battles kept individuals occupied and out of trouble. "You were too tired to fight because you had been popping and locking all night. You were too busy learning how to windmill, than to rob and steal."[2] Popping and locking are dance forms discussed later in this chapter. In an article for National Public Radio, Lorenzo "Kuriaki" Soto, an original member of the Rock Steady Crew, discussed the preference of dance over fighting. "If I was dancing and somebody were to say, 'You're whack, man. You don't even got the good moves,' I'd tell him instead, 'Well, I'll battle you.' Right there, instead of me coming up and hitting him, I'd say, 'I'll battle you, see how good you are.' Whoever has the most moves wins."[3]

HIP-HOP: A CULTURE OF EXPRESSION

Hip-hop is a form of expression that is defined primarily by four elements: graffiti art, deejaying, emceeing, and dancing. Graffiti art is "the visual language of the hip-hop community."[4] Graffiti is also known as tags, and the individuals who create it are known as taggers. Graffiti artists leave their marks on anything and everything, from the spray-painted letters on the sides of cars and buildings to colorful designs on sidewalks and street signs. Tags serve as a form of personal expression and identity for taggers. **Deejays** (DJs), or disc jockeys, emerged as leaders within the communities. Through their mixing and sampling of music and the fresh beats they provided, DJs encouraged the innovative movements of the dancers, especially throughout the 1970s. DJs continued to experiment with the turntable, the record, and the microphone, finding new ways to isolate the breaks in music, mix various samples of songs together, loop beats on a continuous replay, and even create new songs. Emcees were the voice of the

9.2
A young male
breakdances on a
New York City street
as others watch.
Leo Vals/Stringer,
Getty Images

hip-hop community and could be considered as the first rappers. The **emcee** helped to continue the energy at dance parties, often working the crowds while delivering spontaneous rhythms of spoken word. These rhythmical chants later become rap music. The original street dance that emerged was **breaking**. This dance form was highly improvisational and focused on the dancer's individual style and flair. Breaking demands a high degree of skill and athleticism, which in turn requires hours of practice. As a result, those who engaged in breaking, by its nature, stayed out of trouble, because they did not have the time to engage in other activities.

Street parties, featuring interaction between the four groups (graffiti artists, DJs, emcees, and breakers), became a recurrent activity within the Bronx during the 1970s and 1980s. DJs would illegally plug their sound systems into streetlamps as dancers would lay down cardboard or dance right on top of asphalt. A shared theme across each of the four hip-hop elements was, and continues to be, that of competition in front of an audience. DJs, emcees, and dancers all desire to be the best in their area. Competitions, or battles, allow dancers to show off their skills and outdo one another, vying to be the best dancer. Creativity and individuality are key. Although competitions allow an individual or a group to dominate and rule, it is important to note that the dancers are generally quite supportive of one another.

Battles

Inherent within the hip-hop expression is a competitive spirit that has materialized in the tangible form as battles. Whether as graffiti artist, DJ, emcee, or dancer, individuals not only want to express themselves, but they also desire recognition. **Battles** are a means to challenge one another in a non-violent mode yet still arrive at a clear winner.

In the 1970s, street battles emerged among the African American and Latinx youth in the Bronx. Individuals in neighborhoods formed crews, also known as posses, that could be as small as six or upwards of ten or more individuals.[5] To gain entry into a crew, one had to prove oneself. Once one was in, crews acted as families, wherein older members would mentor younger members until they were ready to battle on their own. Members often named themselves after a dance movement or personality for which they were known. Dance became a hobby and was practiced regularly. Dance competitions were encouraged and settled rivalries between the crews. Each crew vied for the title of best dance crew and the prestige that came with that title.

During the later decades of the twentieth century, battles could occur anywhere: on street corners, in parks, in gymnasiums, and in community centers. Either the entire crews or individual b-boys/b-girls would compete, alternating series of movements until one side was out of moves, and a winner was declared. Dancers were judged on attitude, the way they presented themselves and performed, along with creativity and originality in movement. Of course, skill, execution, and athleticism were expected. Breakers strategically prepared battle tactics, as the goal was to take their opponent by surprise, often reserving their best moves for the final round of competition. As the crews took turns executing movement, they were responding to that of their opponents, ultimately having a conversation on the "dance floor."

Youth established themselves through the names they chose, the movements they created, the way they danced, and the battles they fought and won. Today, similar battles continue, both informally and formally. National and international competitions allow professional dancers and crews to vie for the title of best dancer. Judged by vote on established criteria and regulated

9.3
A dancer from the Red Bull BC One All Star Team competes at the Paris Battle Pro in 2019.
LUCAS BARIOULET/AFP via Getty Images

by a set number of rounds or time limits, competitions can be between crews or individual dancers, for male or female participants, and include a variety of clever themes, such as the "Bonnie and Clyde," which includes pairs consisting of a b-boy and a b-girl, or dance types, such as locking. One of the most renowned competitions is the Red Bull BC One, which is an international b-boy competition that occurs in a different location annually. Dancers must be careful not to steal or copy another's signature style or moves, an act referred to as a **bite** in the hip-hop dance community. This is considered extremely disrespectful to the original artist and would diminish a b-boy's reputation within the street dance community and possibly hinder the b-boy's chance of winning the battle.

The formation used in dance battles is most often the **cipher**. Here, the dancer performs in the middle of a circle of individuals. This configuration emerges spontaneously and can occur anywhere – in living rooms, in dance halls, on stage – and anytime, not just in competition. Ciphers can be small or large, and there can even be multiple ciphers occurring simultaneously. Depending on the specific setting of the cipher, anyone can participate, from the beginning mover to the more advanced breaker. It can be an opportunity to test one's skill, challenge one another, or simply encourage one another, much like a tap dance jam. However, the cipher can also be the place where a new member is initiated into a crew, an individual becomes recognized within the hip-hop community, or put back in check. Whether novice or professional, there is an etiquette to recognize for entrance into the cipher. Within a battle or a community cipher, dancers uphold ideals of peace, unity, and social enjoyment and share a respect and appreciation for skill among dancers.

BOX 9.1 ROCK STEADY CREW

Joe Torres, also known as Jo Jo, founded the Rock Steady Crew along with Jimmy D in 1977 in the Bronx. The group was named after the move "the rock," as a way to keep the dance going. The crew is credited with developing some of the original breaking movements and is also the first to have had a female in its ranks. Richard "Crazy Legs" Colon became president of the crew in the early 1980s and served as a spokesman for the group. He, along with other influential members of the group, such as Mr. Freeze, Ken Swift, and Frosty Freeze, helped to popularize breaking. The crew's biggest break occurred in 1981 when they battled the Dynamic Rockers outdoors at the Lincoln Center in New York City. The event was covered by *National Geographic* and *20/20*, garnering national attention. Throughout the 1980s, the Rock Steady Crew appeared in several films, including *Flashdance* and *Beat Street*. There are local chapters around the world today that continue to maintain membership.

9.4
Photo of Robert
"Crazy Legs" Colon
breakdancing at The
Ritz in 1982.
Ebet Roberts/
Getty Images

The Hip-hop Aesthetic

The hip-hop culture stems from an Africanist aesthetic. Professor and author E. Moncell Durden identifies the cultural characteristics of behavior tied to the hip-hop expression to include "individuality, creativity, improvisation, origin-ality, spirituality, stylization, dance posture (bending forward from the waist with the knees bent and the spine slightly curved), vocalization, pantomime, percussion, competition, polyrhythm, and polycentrism."[6] The elements of individuality, improvisation, polyrhythm, and polycentrism are unmistakably African. We also observe the competitive aspect throughout the development of tap dance, authentic jazz dance, and American social dances. Whether they were engaging in dance challenges or simply trying to push themselves creatively, new steps and dance crazes and trends emerged as the result of individuals trying to outdo one another. The innovations of dancers seeking to entertain audiences or gain recognition among peers has shaped the devel-opment of all four dance genres, each of which maintains roots in the African aesthetic.

Improv is HUGE

BOX 9.2 AFRICANIST AESTHETIC AND USE OF IMPROVISATION

Inherent within the African American tradition of music and dance is the improvisational aesthetic. In the hip-hop community, this is observed as b-boys/b-girls entering a circle and spontaneously breaking out into movement, DJs mix and spin tracks, and emcees rhythmically chant throughout parties. Think back to other chapters you have read thus far. In what other ways have we observed the improvisational aesthetic at work in the evolution of dance forms?

Hip-hop dance is a type of movement dialog. Dancers are responding in movement form to the world around them, whether in response to their socio-economic situations, an opponent's actions, or a crowd's cheers or taunts. It is important to realize that the dance serves as a form of expression, a way to communicate. Whether in a party setting or in a dance battle, the dancers are engaged in a conversation. Regardless of the type of dance, hip-hop dance as a genre uses each part of the body with purpose yet a fluidity that may be accented with sharp or smooth movement qualities. Isolated movement can be seen within the individual parts of the body, or dancers may move their entire bodies. Depending upon the type of dance performed, dancers may remain standing as they execute rhythmically and dynamically charged movement throughout space. Or, dancers may drop down and execute movement stealthily on the ground. In any instance, dancers present a strong attitude with their face, making the dance highly presentational.

TYPES OF DANCE

Hip-hop is an umbrella term used to classify many types of dance in much the same way as jazz dance is a genre with many sub-forms and styles. There are several dance forms that society as a whole has placed under the heading of hip-hop. Breaking was the original form of street dance that emerged on the East Coast. Two other forms, popping and locking, developed on the West Coast during the same time period and in similar socioeconomic environments. Popping and locking developed from the original subculture on the East Coast, alongside funk music, yet with their own creative pioneers, movement vocabulary, technique, and format. Of the various forms of dance that have emerged over the years, b-boying and party dances have been identified as the only true hip-hop dances. However, each dance style remains united within the global hip-hop community.

Hip-hop Dances

B-boying/B-girling

B-boying/b-girling is the improvisational street dance that kicked off the hip-hop generation. It is also referred to as "breaking" within the hip-hop community and as "breakdancing" by the media. It began in the early 1970s as a standing-only form of movement. Practitioners, known as breakers, b-boys, or b-girls, originally referred to the dance as "rocking," which was a term used to describe many things during the period and even today. For example, phrases such as "rock the mic" and "you rock" were frequently used during parties and battles to express something as highly entertaining, enjoyable, or effective. Rocking consisted of movement rooted in Latin, jazz and tap dance and emphasized patterns that swayed and rocked back and forth. As dancers continued to improvise and experiment with movement, their desire to outperform one another gradually led to the incorporation of the frenzied floorwork that is often synonymous with breaking. The terms "b-boying" and "breaking" gradually replaced "rocking," and then the media popularized the name "breakdancing" in the 1980s.

BOX 9.3 ETYMOLOGY OF BREAKING

Early jazz music is comprised of a section referred to as a break. It is here that individual musicians improvise a musical solo while the other musicians take a break from the melody. This idea has carried over into dance as well. In hip-hop, the term "breaking" stems from the technique utilized by DJs to isolate the breaks found in music and feature innovative beats during these breaks to which the dancers could improvise new movement. DJ Kool Herc is known as the father of hip-hop. A former graffiti artist turned DJ, he created his own rhythms by selecting his favorite beats from a range of records and then playing them back to back during the breaks. He noticed that dance floors became the busiest during the parts of the song when only the beats were being highlighted. He then continued to isolate and emphasize the beats, playing them continuously through the use of two record turntables, the first to do so. As a result, he was able to keep the crowd engaged on the dance floor. He also coined the term "break-boys," or "b-boys" and "b-girls."

Miss AVA
truly
coming
in clutch
Right
now
:)♡

B-boying consists of four primary elements: toprocking, downrocking, power moves, and freezes. Breakers begin with **toprock**, where movement done while standing introduces dancers and their individual style. The rhythmical footwork and relaxed and natural movement of the arms and torso engage the competition in a confrontational manner and serve as the breaker's entrance into the circle. The movement is then taken down to the floor through "drops," or stylized ways of transitioning the dancer to the ground. **Downrock**, or floor rock, was inspired and influenced by gymnastics and the martial arts films popular at the time and is also rooted in *capoeira*, a Brazilian dance form. It is in this portion of the dance that "strength, skill, creativity, and style" are cultivated within breakers as they transition fluidly through sequences of spins, slides, and swings of the legs.[7] During this portion of the dance, the third element of breaking can be seen, the **power moves**. These movements rely on speed, momentum, and strength from the breaker and are manifest in athletic or acrobatic skills. Head spins, windmills, flares, and swipes are all examples of basic power moves. Each requires power and strength and demonstrates an explosive movement quality. Power moves can awe an audience or humble one's opponent. The final element, the **freeze**, consists of a held position for emphasis. Here, the breaker uses upper body strength to suspend a stylized body position inches above the ground. A breaker may sequence several freezes in succession during the dance or may utilize a freeze to signal the end of the dance.

Uprock is a highly confrontational aspect of breaking. Uprock involves freestyle shuffles of the feet, spins, turns, and pantomimed gestures from both everyday and gang life. Integral within uprock are **burns**, gestures intended to pointedly deliver the equivalent of a verbal insult against the dancer's opponent, and jerks, the movement that prepares for the delivery of the burn. The challenge in uprock is for the breaker to freestyle the movement creatively, rhythmically, and artistically.

Party Dances

During the 1970s and 1980s, hip-hop party dances emerged parallel to the breaking battles and competitions. **Party dances** were light-hearted and fun, and while they did not require the athleticism and skill that breaking did, they were equally connected to the music and the culture in which they developed. As we learned in Chapter 1, social dance has been a continually evolving aspect of American culture. Throughout the decades of the twentieth century, an array of social dances emerged and vanished, often linked to the lyrics and reflecting the musical quality of a popular song. The Twist (1959), Robot (1960s), Whip and Nae Nae (2013), and Git Up (2019) are all examples of social dances. These types of dances, all heavily rooted in authentic jazz dance, are often relatively easy to learn, allowing a larger number of individuals to participate. A close study of some dances will reveal that several are not new innovations but, rather, reworkings of dances from previous decades. For example, the Moonwalk is a move said to be borrowed from the street dance crew the Electric Boogaloos and popularized by Michael Jackson, yet it can be seen performed by tap dancer Bill Bailey in a 1955 recording and traced back even earlier to performers in the 1930s.

BOX 9.4 "RAPPER'S DELIGHT"

In 1979, three emcees recorded the song "Rapper's Delight" with Sugar Hill Records. Within this track, rap was first presented as oral poetry, marking the rise of the hip-hop culture and the introduction of rap music in America. The song's lyrics reference the freak, the spank, and the bump, all hip-hop party dances.[8] The original version was fifteen minutes in length and recorded in one take; however, a seven-minute version was recorded by Sugar Hill to air on the radio. By the end of the 1980s and into the 1990s, rap music was still on the rise, with hip-hop party dances evolving to match the shifting rhythms of the music.

West Coast Funk Dances

Locking

Locking is a funk dance form that was created on the West Coast by Don "Campbellock" Campbell. Campbell grew up in Los Angeles and initiated the dance by accident. While many suggest he was inspired by a social dance called the Funky Chicken, it has been documented that he was influenced by the popular party dance known as the Robot Shuffle, which is a two-step movement of the legs and sway of the arms.[9] Upon attempting to execute the dance, Campbellock locked his arms, which resulted in a stop motion of the movement. This obviously was not the desired result but created a new movement trend, nonetheless. The resulting dance became known as Campbellocking, later shortened to locking. Campbell then developed more vocabulary for this style of movement along with the formation of a group of dancers called the Campbellock Dancers, later shortened to the Lockers. They performed on a variety of television shows, including *The Tonight Show*, *The Carol Burnette Show*, and *Soul Train*. Locking as a dance form has been featured in films, such as *Breakin'*, in music videos and tours, on television shows, and in national and international hip-hop competitions.

Locking encompasses its own vocabulary. There is a stylized way of doing each movement, from isolations of the limbs and movement of the body to a look of the head or a turn of the body to point in a direction. When performing movement, the dancer will briefly hesitate in a given position as if the movement is "locked" and then continue in the same tempo as before. The movement of the arms and hands is quick, while the lower half of the body, hips and legs, remains loose and relaxed. There is a contrast in the way the dancer uses both energy and time. The majority of the movement is performed standing, although knee drops and splits are incorporated into this improvisational dance. Locking may be performed with a comical or serious presentation by a single dancer or multiple dancers.

Boogaloo and Popping

Sam "Boogaloo Sam" Solomon created the dance known as the **boogaloo** in Oakland, California, in 1975. He moved his neck, torso, hips, and legs eccentrically and fluidly, adding in subtle contractions and pops to make his movement unique. The fluid circular rolls of the head, torso, hips, and knees are characteristic of the boogaloo style. The goal is to appear as though the dancer's body is without bones, somewhat animated in appearance. Popping stems from the sounds that Solomon would make as he danced. As his movement became popular among the youth, the popping elements were further developed in Fresno, California. In **popping**, the dancer's muscles hit, or tick, rhythmically with the musical beat by a consistent contraction and release while simultaneously executing movement. Both boogaloo and popping were originally performed to funk and disco music styles yet may be performed to a variety of musical styles today. Both forms appear in performance and competitions.

Additional Dance Forms

In additional to locking, boogaloo, and popping, other types of dance are included within the hip-hop community. Waacking is a West Coast street dance influenced by dramatic Hollywood actors of the 1950s and cartoon animations and includes a collection of striking arm motions, footwork, and posing. Voguing is a high-energy, ultra-feminine style of dance that features a model-style strut and posing. It emerged in the LGBTQ club scene in New York City. Tutting is a funk dance style that uses the limbs to create geometrical patterns through movement. House dance makes use of three primary elements: fast footwork; jacking, which is a repetitive rippling motion of the torso forward and backward; and lofting, which is similar to the acrobatic floorwork of breaking yet softer and sensual. The list goes on, and this discussion is intended only to provide a glimpse into the variety of dances that are now encompassed under the umbrella of hip-hop. Although hip-hop as a genre has a relatively short history, it has evolved to encompass a great many styles and forms that are still growing and popular today.

COMMERCIALIZATION OF THE ART FORM

Became more entertainment based and commercialized

Dance critic Sally Banes has identified two periods of breaking. The first involves amateur dancers comprised of inner-city youth from the Bronx. These individuals utilized social dance in lieu of fighting to demonstrate skill. The second period involves professional dancers once the dance form became commercialized.[10] The hip-hop culture emerged in the inner cities of the East and West Coasts during the 1970s, yet it was not until the 1980s that it began to gain national recognition.

During the 1980s, hip-hop dance forms appeared in commercials, television shows, documentaries, Hollywood films, and video instructional manuals, drawing national attention not only to the individual dancers and crews but also to the dance forms and community. In 1984, 100 breakers performed in the closing ceremony of the World Olympics held in Los Angeles. Many breakers felt further marginalized as their art was pulled from their original communities, commercialized, and exploited for the means of making a profit. On the other hand, the media exposure did help to create a national phenomenon surrounding hip-hop that has continued long past the expectations of critics.

AYYY what my Mia was on!

Randy Jackson, a former judge on *American Idol*, produced *America's Best Dance Crew* in 2008 as a competitive dance reality television show that ran for eight seasons on MTV. The series, hosted by Mario Lopez, featured national and international hip-hop dance crews that battled for a cash prize and a trophy. The dance crews were each provided with a challenge that followed a general theme for the episode. Based on the decisions of three judges as well as fan votes from across the nation, crews could advance to the next round. The show served as a platform to bring renewed national attention and energy to the dance crews and help springboard their professional endeavors. For example, the Jabbawockeez won the first season of *America's Best Dance Crew*, and their performance credits since include Universal Studios, commercial work, national and international tours, film cameos, and award shows. They currently have their own production in Las Vegas along with a clothing line and record label.

Today, hip-hop dance battles are found from local to international levels. Professional crews train hard, both in physical fitness forms and in the individual street dance techniques to battle in competition. Yet, hip-hop dance forms are not only presented in battle form; they also appear in music videos and live performances, commercials, movies, Broadway shows, and reality television, and on YouTube and digital apps. It is important to note that the hip-hop showcased in movies and reality television shows often does not depict authentic hip-hop but, rather, movement influenced by the hip-hop aesthetic that has been commercialized through its fusion with other dance forms or in its choreography. The hip-hop aesthetic is inherently improvisational. To create choreographed movement for performance on television or in film removes the original intent and meaning from the art form. The *Step Up* movies and the television series *So You Think You Can Dance* all display commercial forms of hip-hop dance. While they are highly entertaining, the performances are void of authenticity, as they utilize studio-trained dancers rather than dancers from the original community.[11] For example, in *America's Best Dance Crew*, authentic self-formed hip-hop dance crews appeared on the show to battle one another. However, on *So You Think You Can Dance*, a hip-hop dance is often performed by dancers unfamiliar with hip-hop dance. A ballet dancer may be paired with a ballroom dancer and then quickly taught a hip-hop routine to be performed the next week. In some settings, choreographers who have trained in other genres have borrowed movement ideas from hip-hop to incorporate into choreography and then add the hip-hop label to their work. As a result, many titles for movement, choreography, and classes have emerged, causing confusion among students and even those within the dance community. As dance studios offer classes in contemporary hip-hop, commercial street dance, street jazz, and urban dance, it becomes difficult to discern what is authentic and genuine hip-hop dance and what is a fusion or simply movement inspired by hip-hop dance forms. While it is exciting that dance studios are offering hip-hop dance within their curriculum, it is also important for students to recognize the distinctions between the authentic aspects of the dance and the blending of other cultural and dance-based elements.

9.5
Dance crew
Jabbawockeez
perform on Randy
Jackson's *America's
Best Dance Crew*
at Sony Studios
in 2008.
Polk Imaging/
WireImage,
Getty Images

9.6
The Rennie Harris
Puremovement
company performs
a hip-hop piece
from the dance
show titled *Facing
Mekka* at UCLA's
Freud Playhouse.
Vince Compagnone/
Los Angeles Times
via Getty Images

Hip-hop dance is also visible on the concert stage. Dr. Lorenzo "Rennie" Harris was the first to utilize hip-hop within the concert stage in his company Rennie Harris Puremovement (RHPM), founded in 1992 in Philadelphia. Harris, who grew up with exposure to street dance, has challenged the world of concert dance by utilizing vocabulary from hip-hop dance forms to explore the human condition. He has taken what was intended to be spontaneous, improvisational, informal, and participatory dance and placed it in choreographed form on the concert stage. In doing so, he has made thoughtful and exquisite statements of personal and cultural themes, encouraging audiences to discard preconceived notions of what concert dance must look like and what is high art in terms of dance.

TRAINING

Hip-hop can take a toll on one's body, specifically the power moves that are performed. Imagine spinning repeatedly with all of your body weight balanced on one body part. Or, consider the quick twists of the body as one drops to the floor followed by an immediate recovery back to a standing position. In fact, any of the eye-popping, jaw-dropping movements that you see a b-boy/b-girl or any other street dancer do can cause wear and tear on the body. Dancers risk a plethora of physical injuries after prolonged engagement in the art form, including the need for knee and shoulder replacements, hip problems, neuropathy in their hands, and neck issues.

There are many settings in which one can learn hip-hop dance forms. Many traditional dance studios offer some form of hip-hop dance classes, although, as mentioned earlier, these are often fused with classical forms and may or may not be pure in movement and musical approach. There are many online platforms, such as YouTube and other websites, that offer video instruction in various vocabulary and techniques. Lessons can be learned on the streets and in clubs in actual battles and ciphers. Many individuals will travel miles to study with a well-known b-boy/b-girl in the hopes of gaining insight and skill.

CHAPTER SUMMARY

Hip-hop dance is a powerful and energetic genre of dance. Similarly to tap and jazz dance, hip-hop dance forms originated in America. The authentic forms of hip-hop dance – b-boying and hip-hop party dances – emerged in the Bronx on the East Coast, and funk forms, such as locking and popping, developed on the West Coast. Hip-hop dance was established by African American and Latinx youth in marginalized, inner-city neighborhoods during the 1970s. These individuals were the pioneers and creators, the innovators and developers of this engaging art form. During the 1980s, the media helped to draw national attention to the various dance forms under the umbrella term of hip-hop as the dances were included in an array of Hollywood films, such as *Wild Thing*, *Beat Street*, and *Flashdance*, television shows, such as *Soul Train*, and music videos, thanks to the introduction of MTV. While many initial critics of the hip-hop culture expected the genre to disappear by the millennium, it has done just the opposite. By the end of the 1990s, the hip-hop culture, which includes not only dance but music, fashion, speech, and behavior, was still on the rise, with rap music, a component of the hip-hop expression, selling more albums than other music genres.[12]

Hip-hop dance forms continue to be taught on the streets and in mentor fashion but are also included in the dance studio setting. Some college and university programs are also beginning to incorporate hip-hop dance into their dance curricula. Movies, documentaries, television shows, online websites, and social platforms also feature hip-hop dance videos and resources. Hip-hop is a cultural expression that is rooted in an Africanist aesthetic and demonstrates yet another way that movement can be used in both social and theatrical modes to communicate powerful dialog between individuals.

9.1 Notable Individuals in Hip-Hop		
DJ Kool Herc (b. 1955)		Also known as Clive Campbell, DJ Kool Herc is considered the father of hip-hop. He was the first individual to make use of two record turntables and created the foundation for hip-hop. He coined the terms "break-boys," "b-boys," and "b-girls."
Richard "Crazy Legs" Colon (b. 1966)		Crazy Legs joined the Rock Steady Crew in 1979, later becoming president of the group. He is credited with inventing the backspin and the continuous backspin or windmill. He has been a spokesman for the hip-hop community and has won numerous awards for his work within the field, including a 1992 Bessie award for Best Choreography for the Rock Steady Crew.
Don "Campbellock" Campbell (b. 1951)		Campbell is the pioneer and innovator of locking. He assembled the Campbellock Dancers, later shortened to the Lockers, who performed on television, gaining national recognition. To some, he is known as the father of street dance. Highly respected, he remains involved in the community through teaching and judging competitions.

(continued)

9.1
Cont.

Sam "Boogaloo Sam" Solomon
(b. 1957)

Boogaloo Sam is credited with creating the boogaloo and popping dance forms. In 1977, he founded the Electric Boogaloos, a street dance crew that has helped to popularize the dance forms.

Dr. Lorenzo "Rennie" Harris
(b. 1964)

Harris founded Rennie Harris Puremovement, a concert dance company rooted in authentic hip-hop dance, in 1992 in Philadelphia. His work uses movement of the body blended with rap and spoken text and a variety of musical accompaniment as well as media visuals to convey social and personal themes. He is also the recipient of three Bessie Awards for choreography.

9.2
Notable Films
Featuring
Hip-hop Dance

1982	*Wild Style*
1983	*Style Wars*
	Flashdance
1984	*Beat Street*
	Breakin'
2001	*Save the Last Dance*
2004	*You Got Served*
2006	*Step Up* series
2007	*Stomp the Yard*
2008	*Planet B-Boy*, documentary

Notable Television Shows Featuring Hip-hop Dance

1984	*Graffiti Rock*, one episode
1990–1994	*In Living Color*
2008–2015	*America's Best Dance Crew*
2005–present	*So You Think You Can Dance*
2017–present	*World of Dance*

9.3
Historical Timeline of
Hip-hop Dance

1955	Cross Bronx Expressway was constructed.
1970s	Graffiti artists, DJs, emcees, and b-boys interacted with and inspired one another. Street battles emerged.
1975	"Boogaloo Sam" Solomon created the dance known as the boogaloo in Oakland, California.
1977	Joe Torres and Jimmy D founded the Rock Steady Crew in the Bronx.
1977	"Boogaloo Sam" founded the Electric Boogaloos.
1979	The song "Rapper's Delight" was recorded with Sugar Hill Records.
1979	"Crazy Legs" Colon joined the Rock Steady Crew, later becoming president of the crew.

9.3 Cont.	1980s	The media popularized the term "breakdancing." West Coast street dance forms gained recognition.
	1981	The Rock Steady Crew battled the Dynamic Rockers at the Lincoln Center in NYC.
	1984	One hundred breakers performed in the closing ceremony of the World Olympics held in Los Angeles.
	1992	"Crazy Legs" Colon won a Bessie award for Best Choreography for the Rock Steady Crew.
	1992	"Rennie" Harris founded Rennie Harris Puremovement, a concert dance company rooted in authentic hip-hop dance.
	2008	*America's Best Dance Crew* premiered as a competitive dance reality television show on the MTV channel, running for eight seasons.

9.4
Chapter 9 Vocabulary

battle	cipher	party dance
b-boying/b-girling	deejay	popping
biting	downrock	power move
boogaloo	emcee	toprock
breaking	freeze	uprock
burn	locking	

Reflective Prompts

1. How would you describe hip-hop dance to someone who has never seen it before?
2. Hip-hop dance has been described as a movement dialog between dancers or artist and audience. Describe how this dance form is used as a form of communication.
3. Do you believe that hip-hop dance should be considered as art or entertainment? Why? Be specific in your reasons.
4. Why do you think critics expected the genre to be short lived when it gained national attention during the 1980s?
5. Prior to reading this chapter, what was your personal experience with hip-hop as a dance genre? Has your perspective of the genre changed? If so, how?

Movement Prompt

1. **Hip-Hop Dance Movement:** Learn the movement exercise on the online video. Reflect on your experience with the movement.

NOTES

1 E. Moncell Durden, *Beginning Hip-Hop Dance* (Chicago: Human Kinetics, 2019), 74.
2 *The Freshest Kids: A History of the B-Boy*, directed by Israel (QD3 Entertainment, 2002), www.youtube.com/watch?v=RxoVVyGFSGuk.

3 Mandalit del Barco, "Hip Hop Hooray: Breaking into the Big Time," Present at the Creation,!Mira!, Columbia University, Spring 1984, www.npr.org/programs/morning/features/patc/breakdancing/article.html.

4 E. Moncell Durden, "Hip-Hop Dance as Community Expression and Global Phenomenon," in *Jazz Dance: A History of the Roots and Branches*, ed. by Lindsay Guarino and Wendy Oliver (Gainesville, Florida: University Press of Florida, 2014), 184.

5 Mohanalakshmi Rajakumar, *Hip Hop Dance* (Santa Barbara, California: ABC-CLIO, 2012), xxvi.

6 Durden, *Beginning Hip-Hop Dance*, 75.

7 Durden, *Beginning Hip-Hop Dance*, 78.

8 Durden, *Beginning Hip-Hop Dance*, 81.

9 Durden, *Beginning Hip-Hop Dance*, 88.

10 Rajakumar, *Hip Hop Dance*, 3.

11 Durden, *Beginning Hip-Hop Dance*, 84.

12 Rajakumar, *Hip Hop Dance*, 55.

CHAPTER 9 BIBLIOGRAPHY

Del Barco, Mandalit. "Hip Hop Hooray: Breaking into the Big Time." Columbia University. Spring 1984. www.npr.org/programs/morning/features/patc/breakdancing/article.html.

Durden, E. Moncell. *Beginning Hip-Hop Dance*. Chicago: Human Kinetics, 2019.

———— "Hip-Hop Dance as Community Expression and Global Phenomenon," in Guarino, Lindsay and Wendy Oliver, eds. *Jazz Dance: A History of the Roots and Branches*. Gainesville: University Press of Florida, 2014, 184–193.

Guarino, Lindsay and Wendy Oliver, eds. *Jazz Dance: A History of the Roots and Branches*. Gainesville: University Press of Florida, 2014.

History and Concept of Hip-Hop Dance: The Street Culture that Became a Global Expression. Directed by Moncell Durden. Dancetime Publications, 2009. 43 min.

Malnig, Julie, ed. *Ballroom, Boogie, Shimmy Sham, Shake: A Social and Popular Dance Reader*. Chicago: University of Illinois Press, 2009.

Osumare, Halifu. "The Dance Archaeology of Rennie Harris: Hip-Hop or Postmodern?," in Malnig, Julie, ed. *Ballroom, Boogie, Shimmy Sham, Shake: A Social and Popular Dance Reader*. Chicago: University of Illinois Press, 2009, 261–281.

Rajakumar, Mohanalakshmi. *Hip Hop Dance*. Santa Barbara, California: ABC-CLIO, 2012.

The Freshest Kids: A History of the B-Boy. Directed by Israel. QD3 Entertainment, 2002. 1 hr., 36 min. www.youtube.com/watch?v=RxoWyGFSGuk.

Part III
Behind the Scenes

INTRODUCTION

For many individuals, our observation of dance performance may be an unplanned occurrence, happening on the periphery of our daily lives. As we wait patiently between halves of a sporting event, dancers fill the arena. During the commercial break of our favorite television show, the movements of dancers energetically help to promote brands. While at an amusement park, characters and performers dance down the path during the afternoon parade. Sometimes, we make specific plans to go and see a dance performance, such as a dance concert or a Broadway musical. As technology continues to advance, dance performances become enhanced in unexpected ways, and the opportunities to view dance from the comfort of our own homes increase. While the ways we observe and encounter dance are varied, technology continues to change the dance landscape, the demands of a dancer's training are constantly evolving, science and medicine keep advancing, the dancer's life transforms over time, and career opportunities transform.

Just as technology has permeated almost every aspect of our daily lives, it has greatly affected the dance world as well. Film, television, internet, cell phones, and even virtual reality have influenced countless facets of dance, often in contradictory manners, as technology advances more quickly than the laws governing it. For example, video technology allows choreographers to "notate" or record their works relatively instantly, but then they must be wary of their work being copied or plagiarized. Social media has created a platform on which individual dancers may promote themselves, but trendy applications such as Facebook or Instagram can also circulate unhealthy training practices. Meanwhile, television and film industries have continued to help popularize dance by bringing performances and competitions into people's homes and on their desktops. Chapter 10 explores the multitude of influences that technology has had on dance and how directors, choreographers, and dancers have adapted technology to enhance their work across the field.

But how often do we consider what else happens behind the scenes or beyond the stage? How do individuals train their bodies to be professional dancers? Are there other options for an individual to pursue than a career as a dance performer or teacher? Chapter 11 looks at the training and educational perspectives of dance with a focus on the private sector, elementary and secondary education, and higher education. Chapter 12 explores dance from the perspective of the dancer, uncovering the journey of a dance performer. Chapter 13 discusses dancers' health and injury-related topics. Finally, Chapter 14 surveys a variety of dance-related career options. As we conclude our exploration of the art of dance, try to imagine stepping into the dancer's shoes, training, preparing, and building a career in this unique art.

10 Dance Media and Technology

Thousands of pixelated orbs of light dance with the live performers through the stage space, seemingly with a life of their own. As the dancers turn and leap wildly across the stage, the dancing light swirls around them as if caught in a great whirlwind, when suddenly, both dancers and light freeze simultaneously. The dancers take one deliberate step forward, triggering the drops of light to inexplicably lose their ability to levitate and rain down upon the dancers and stage floor …

Audience members in the movie theater breathe in with anticipation as the screen begins to display the beloved musical. Familiar music plays, but the dancing has been reimagined as it interacts with the camera. Dancers seem to turn right past you, jump over you, encircle you …

A group of young, aspiring dancers gasp and talk excitedly as they squeeze in tight around the smartphone to watch the principal dancer complete an awe-inspiring number of turns seemingly effortlessly. They rewind the Facebook video again and again, looking at every detail of movement the dancer makes, before attempting the turns in their kitchen …

The perpetually evolving technology industry continues to impact the world around us, how we communicate, where we obtain information, and our sharing capabilities. With powerful computers that fit in our back pockets, creativity has transformed to incorporate the digital world. All of this rapid advancement has called into question what art is, who can make it, and how it is shared with the world. Artists are sprinting to catch up with the tools now at our disposal while also inventing their own devices to suit their mediums. Technology has served as a catalyst for new artistic innovation. Dance on the stage, on the screen, and in the palms of our hands is progressing at an ever-increasing rate. This chapter will explore dance in live theater, on a variety of screens, and on smartphones and draw attention to the tidal wave of technological influence.

TECHNOLOGY IN LIVE PERFORMANCE

Technology in live performance encompasses a wide array of components and, as such, may be a bit of an ambiguous term. The term "tech," or technical rehearsals, refers to when dance rehearsals enter the performance space, and

10.1
A dancer performs at the Athens Digital Arts Festival's Extending Reality, CoExistence: Art, Science, & Technology.
Photo by Giorgos Georgiou/NurPhoto via Getty Images

theatrical elements such as lighting, costumes, sets, and props are integrated together for the first time. This chapter focuses more specifically on digital technology in live performance, which largely encompasses the lighting, sound, and artificial visual elements of dance performance.

Creates even more of a spectacle to see, enhancing visuals!

BOX 10.1 LIGHTING SAFETY

The importance of lighting dancers onstage was discussed in Chapter 3 as a concern of the choreographer in crafting a dance piece. However, technology and techniques for lighting dancers onstage have evolved tremendously over the centuries, affecting the way dance is viewed. For example, during the majority of the nineteenth century, ballets were lit using the technology of the era, gaslights, which allowed directors to vary the brightness of the instruments for the first time by supplying more or less gas to a pipe. However, this proved exceptionally dangerous, as it was not uncommon for ballerinas to brush their delicate, flowy tutus too close to the flames between wings, catch fire, and be burned alive. Other dancers backstage were unable to help because their skirts would be ignited as well. These accidents sometimes led to entire theaters burning down. Techniques were developed to prevent the tutus from igniting by first dousing them in a chemical bath. However, many dancers refused to wear tutus that had been treated because it made them look dingy. Some dancers chose to fight the safety measures that were developed for their very own safety.

In the 1880s, the recently invented electrical or incandescent lights were introduced to theater lighting. These instruments not only provided brighter light but also were much safer for performers, therefore ushering out the era of flaming ballerinas. It was during this time period that Loie Fuller began experimenting with light, colors, and fabric, as discussed in Chapter 6.

Projection Design

Just as choreographers use general theatrical lighting, costumes, sets, and, props, there is a whole new world of possibilities with the advancements in technology at their disposal to incorporate with movement to enhance communication with the audience. Similarly to lighting techniques, projection design has gradually become more prominent and advanced in recent decades. **Projection design** refers to the practice of projecting an image onto a surface as well as the use of monitors or screens to display an image. Projections can be cast on any number of surfaces, including a flat screen, a piece of scenery, a building, or even a dancer's body. Various techniques, equipment, and software are used to accomplish this, such as projection mapping.

Projections generally fall into one of two categories: either linear or interactive content. **Linear content** is predetermined and unchanging, for example, a pre-recorded video being projected onto a screen while dancers perform in the space. **Interactive content** is media changed by the performer as it reacts in real time to the performer's actions. Interaction can be carried out in a variety of ways. For instance, virtual costumes could be projected on the bodies of dancers while they are moving, or dancers may change the environment around them by triggering responses from the projections, in which case the projection "dances" with the human performers like a partner. In the latter example, a common piece of technology involves the dancer wearing a sensor that communicates with the projection software in order to create real-time responses from digital projections.

Projection mapping (formerly referred to as spatial augmented reality or video mapping) is the display of an image on a non-flat surface. Software is used to map the object on which the projection will be cast, including the height, width, and depth of the object, in order to account for any distortion of the image. Projection mapping adds dynamics to a surface and movement to a static object, and can create magic for the viewers. This technology was pioneered for public display by the Walt Disney Company with the creation of special effects on the Haunted Mansion ride in Disneyland® that opened in 1969. During the ride, a floating head was projected onto a neutral-colored dummy head inside a crystal ball using footage of a real person enunciating its speech. Later in the ride, singing faces were projected onto statues. Some experimentation was

10.2
Western Kentucky
University Dance
Company performs
Ils Vont Libérer in an
Evening of Dance.
Choreography and
video projection by
Meghen McKinley
and visual art
collaboration with
Marilee Salvator.
Photo by Jeff
Smith, WKU

done with this technology in the 1980s, but it began to really take off in the late 1990s. Disney has since taken projection mapping onto a much larger scale by projecting images onto Cinderella's castle in Walt Disney World Resort®. During the show, projectors cast familiar characters and special effects onto the castle, creating dramatic visuals such as waterfalls on towers, spinning turrets, and changing the façade to look like a birthday cake or gingerbread house.

Disney
loves
projection
mapping

Nowadays, projection mapping can be seen in theme parks, on landmarks such as the exterior of Notre Dame or the Sydney Opera House, on basketball courts during introductions of players and to build hype before the game, during the opening ceremonies of the Olympics, and of course in the theater. The musical *Sunday in the Park with George* (1984) was the first Broadway show to utilize projection mapping when casting an image onto a spherical surface on a sculpture. Artists are collaborating more than ever to create these digital effects and transport audiences into a world that blends reality with fantasy. Companies such as the Taiwanese Anarchy Dance Theatre and the Italian interdisciplinary company called fuse* continuously push the boundaries of combining art forms with projection mapping.

BOX 10.2 DANCING DRONES

Drones, defined as any unmanned vehicle, have also become an instrument in dance performance. Much like another performer on stage, drones are being used to create dramatic effects in live theater. Similarly to interactive projection, drones can interact with dancers onstage like a partner. Drone choreography was seen on a large scale at the opening ceremonies of the 2018 Olympic Games in South Korea. Dance companies such as Japan-based Elevenplay experiment with the possibilities of drones in their repertoire.

Shadow Dance

Similarly to the use of projection, shadow dance has become increasingly popular in the Western theatrical world. **Shadow dance** is dancing that is presented by throwing the shadows of dancers on a screen. It dates back to 200 BC in Chinese culture and echoes throughout multiple cultures. In modern Western theater, the shadows are cast by a bright light or projector at the furthest upstage point on the stage. The dancers perform in front of, or downstage, of the light, and their shadows appear on a screen between the dancers and the audience. The modern dance company Pilobolus was first to bring full-body shadow art onto the Western stage. This type of work started with a commercial for Hyundai, then an appearance at the Academy Awards, and eventually developed into the full-length performance *Shadowland* (2009), which portrays the narrative of a young girl cast into a surreal land of shadows and was the first production of its kind to tour the world.

Shadow dance presents unique challenges to the dancers. Unlike the traditional square or rectangular stage space, the dancers' performance space is a cone with the point being at the lighting instrument because of the way the light is thrown. In addition to the difficulty of moving around one another in this type of space, the dancers must be extremely precise with the shapes they are

10.3
A "behind the
screen" photo
of dancers in the
modern dance
company Pilobolus
creating an image
in their show
Shadowland.
Rune Hellestad –
Corbis/Contributor,
Getty Images

creating with their own bodies and in relation to the other dancers in order to create the desired effects on the screen. This often involves a bit of contortion and can be extra tricky when spelling out words, because the dancers see the reverse of what the audience sees. Additionally, sometimes the dancers wear sunglasses in order to protect their eyes from the bright light used to cast the shadows.

Shadow dancing performance groups have appeared on several television talent competitions, including *America's Got Talent* and *Britain's Got Talent*. Pilobolus continues to tour its production *Shadowland*, and other dance companies have emerged that are devoted to shadow dance, including Catapult Entertainment and The Silhouettes®.

Sound

As projection and lighting techniques continue to advance, so does sound mixing in live performance. For example, the tap dance company Dorrance Dance created revolutionary electronic tap boards to produce an entirely new auditory experience for the audience. In the company's evening-length production *ETM: Double Down* (an earlier version of this show, *ETM: The Initial Approach*, is pictured in Figure 7.16), these electronic boards allow the performers to generate a variety of synthesized sounds with different tap sounds, capture it, and then play it back or loop it. Associate artistic director Nicholas Van Young developed these electronic drum triggers with birch plywood in order to expand the compositional possibilities of a group performance. Though tap dancers have been experimenting with this type of technology since the 1970s, *ETM: Double Down* is the first time it has been carried out on such a large scale, essentially turning the entire stage into a musical instrument. Similar microphone technology has been used to manipulate, record, play back, and loop vocals instantaneously as well.

As technology, equipment, and software continue to evolve, so do live performance possibilities. Cutting-edge technology allows audiences to be transported into worlds of fantasy in real time. Three-dimensional projection interacts with performers like living and breathing dance partners, shadow dance projects the human body into new forms, and sound mixing generates unique compositional possibilities across forms of dance.

DANCE ON CAMERA *— Even more important bc of media and commerialisation*

With the advent of moving pictures in the late nineteenth century, it was possible to see dance movement in a setting other than a live performance for the first time. An endless list of new possibilities for dance was suddenly in the making. As technology advanced, choreographers adapted to harness the possibilities to portray dance in powerful ways never before seen. Artists began choreographing dance made specifically for the camera. This has manifested in a few different ways with varying terminology. For the purpose of this text, **dance on camera** relates to commercial use of dance on film such as on television and in movies. On the other hand, **screen dance** refers to the specific medium of dance created for video viewing, in which the film artistry equally contributes to the perception and intention of the work.

Film

Movie musicals helped to advance dance on camera techniques used to create illusion and spectacle. As discussed in Chapter 7, movie musicals took off at the end of the 1920s with the introduction of films with sound. During the height of the movie musical, Busby Berkeley, an American dance director of Hollywood musicals, pioneered many film techniques and left a lasting effect on motion picture choreography. After eliminating the use of the proscenium arch in dance films, he developed the use of overhead shots and the monorail to film dance sequences, techniques that are still utilized today. Berkeley is remembered for his dazzling film choreography, which included enormous chorus lines moving in geometrical patterns producing a kaleidoscope-like effect. His film credits include the 1933 musicals *42nd Street* and *Footlight Parade*.

Dance in all forms has remained or become prominent in films, such as the clash of ballet and hip-hop in the *Step Up* series (2006–2014), tap dancing animated penguins in *Happy Feet* (2006), a reimagining of the ballet *The Nutcracker* in the film *The Nutcracker and the Four Realms* (2018), and *The Descendants* series featuring the hip-hop dancing children of villains on the Disney Channel (2015–2019). New movie musicals continue to be created, like the hit *La La Land* (2016), which won Academy Awards for Best Actress, Best Original Musical Score, and Best Cinematography, while old films are also being remade, such as *Footloose* (1984 and 2011), *West Side Story* (1961 and 2020), and several Disney classics transformed into live action films, like *Aladdin* (1992 and 2019). Additionally, several movies with plots centered on dance themes have become classics in their own right. *Saturday Night Fever* (1977), *Dirty Dancing* (1987), and *Center Stage* (2000) all focus on dance as a central plot and were box office hits.

Television

As televisions became common household items in the mid-twentieth century, dance too found its way into the average American home. The new ability to watch dance performances in one's own living room drastically accelerated the speed with which various dances were popularized and spread across the country. From late in the 1940s through today, music and dance shows have been popular on network television, featuring variety shows, competitions, dramas, and docuseries.

One of the longest-running series, the *Ed Sullivan Show*, appeared in the coveted Sunday evening prime time slot from 1948 through June 1971. Sullivan's show presented a variety of talents, much as vaudeville shows had a generation earlier. Famous artists to appear on the show included Elvis Presley, The Beatles, and The Rolling Stones. Sullivan often featured Broadway casts on his show, performing hits from musicals like *West Side Story*, *Oklahoma!*, and *Cabaret*. Individual dance stars, like tap dancers Ann Miller and Peg Leg Bates and ballet dancers Rudolph Nureyev and Margot Fonteyn, also appeared frequently on the show. With outstanding ratings for such a long time on the air, the *Ed Sullivan Show* helped to pave the way for future dance shows on television.

The shows *American Bandstand* (1952–1989) and *Soul Train* (1971–2006) featured teenagers dancing to popular music. These platforms greatly influenced the spread of popular dance or social dance throughout their runs. Occasionally, dance contests were held on air that allowed viewers to mail in votes for their favorite couple, and the winners received an assortment of prizes. These small contests were a precursor to the dance competition shows that still air today. Both *American Bandstand* and *Soul Train* influenced the civil rights movement. *American Bandstand* appropriated African American style music to create a profitable show while refusing to allow African American teenagers in the studio audience. It was not until the program relocated from Philadelphia to Los Angeles that the audience was integrated; there were heated debates about the reason and timing for this change, but it no doubt influenced a generation. On the other hand, *Soul Train* featured mainly R&B, soul, pop, and hip-hop music and African American dancers from its inception. Sometimes it was referred to as the "black *American Bandstand*," creating conflict, though the show proved to be a huge success in its own right and celebrated African American art, including hip-hop at a time when it was most controversial. This model of a television show playing popular music and showing teenagers dancing was echoed repeatedly in shows including *Club MTV* (1987–1992) and *Dance Party USA* (1986–1992). Eventually, shows began airing the vocal artists' fully produced music videos, as this became a popular medium for artists. The choreography in these music

10.4
Dancers performing
the latest moves
on the long-
running television
show *American
Bandstand* in 1976.
Walt Disney
Television via Getty
Images Photo
Archives/Walt
Disney Television
via Getty Images

videos did then and continues to now influence popular social dance, as online dance "challenges" have emerged from certain videos.

Aside from pure entertainment purposes, several dance competition shows have succeeded on television. Nationwide talent searches such as *Star Search* and *America's Got Talent* include/d any type of talent in the competition, from dancing to singing to juggling to standup comedy. However, many dance-specific talent competitions have been largely successful on air. One of the earliest of these shows was *Dance Fever* (1979–1987), in which each week four couples competed for a cash prize by performing a short dance piece. Celebrity judges scored the couples in four categories, and at the end of the night, the couple with the highest average total score won. After four weeks, the previous four winning couples competed against each other for a larger sum of money, and after twenty-five weeks of competition, all the second-round winners competed against each other for the monetary grand prize.

Recent competitive dance shows include *Dancing with the Stars*, *So You Think You Can Dance*, and *World of Dance*; the former two both premiered in 2005. They have been able to last simultaneously for such a long period of time because of their very different content. *Dancing with the Stars* pairs real celebrities – like professional athletes, film stars, and political officials – with professional dancers, who always choreograph the routine the couple performs. Each week, every couple performs a predetermined style of ballroom dance. *So You Think You Can Dance* consists of individual pre-professional dancers competing with partners in genres such as jazz, ballroom, contemporary, Broadway, and

10.5
A group of dancers compete on the television show *World of Dance*. Jordin Althaus/ NBCU Photo Bank/ NBCUniversal via Getty Images via Getty Images

hip-hop and performing routines choreographed by leaders in the dance industry. Each show involves four judges and audience/viewer voting, but the procedures for elimination continue to evolve from year to year with the shows. *World of Dance* premiered in 2017; competitors can come from any age or dance genre background and include soloists and groups of any size. Each individual or group competes their way through four rounds of competition to reach the World Final competition for the grand prize of one million dollars. The three judges score every routine, which determines the winners.

As mentioned in Chapter 9, hip-hop had its own television dance competition series from 2008 through 2015. *America's Best Dance Crew* featured crews of hip-hop dancers that competed against each other weekly. Every week, each crew received a specific challenge that connected to an overall theme for the episode and had to choreograph a routine they made to fit the challenge. For example, one episode featured the "Music Video Challenge," in which each crew was assigned a specific famous music video and had to incorporate a signature dance sequence from the video into its routine that week. This show also combined three judges and audience voting to determine the winner.

Dance on television also features drama series and docuseries. *Fame* was a scripted dance drama series produced from 1982 to 1987 based on the full-length movie with the same name that was released in 1980. The storyline followed students and faculty in a performing arts high school set in New York City. The sixty-minute episodes often featured musical numbers highlighting the talent of the actors, including star Debbie Allen. *Fame* won several Emmys, including Choreography, Directing, and Cinematography. Other past television dance dramas include *Glee* (2009–2015) and *Dance Academy* (2010–2013). Television

So many TV shows are popular right now!

docuseries fall into one of two categories. The first are scripted docuseries that portray historical events or figures. For example, in 2019, the limited series documentary *Fosse/Verdon* aired on television with an intimate look at Bob Fosse and Gwen Verdon's personal and professional relationship as husband and wife and two leading figures in jazz dance. The second category of docuseries function more like reality shows, offering glimpses into the lives of performance artists, such as the show *Breaking Pointe* (2012–2013), which followed the lives of company members of Ballet West in Salt Lake City.

Not immune to the reality television show craze, dance has reality dance drama series that have aired on television, focusing on drama and scandal rather than fact. For example, *Dance Moms* premiered in 2011 and followed the Abby Lee Millor Dance Company's Junior Elite Competition Team based in Pittsburgh, Pennsylvania. The show follows Abby Miller, a group of young girls, and the girls' moms as they rehearse, travel, and compete in various dances. Show content has a reputation for featuring a very strict and screaming dance teacher, bickering moms, and upset young girls. *Dance Moms* has clearly been set up to capture highly emotional and often petty arguments on television. The images and interactions shown do not depict the average life of girls growing up at a dance studio. For instance, each week includes a segment in which six or seven young girls' headshots are taped to the mirror in a pyramid formation, supposedly depicting where each student falls in Abby Miller's eyes based on the girls' previous week of rehearsals, competition, awards, and their moms' behaviors. Following lawsuits and the departure of students, *Dance Moms* was slightly reconfigured and recast for the 2019 season.

BOX 10.3 RISE TO FAME

Maddie Ziegler was one of the original students featured on *Dance Moms*. Only eight years old at the time of the premiere of the show, Ziegler stunned audiences with her impeccable dance technique and passionate performances. In 2014, after seeing her on the show, vocal artist Sia cast Ziegler as the solo dancer in the music video for her hit song "Chandelier," which won the MTV Video Music Award for Best Choreography. Sia cast her again to perform in her music video for "Elastic Heart." This collaboration led to Ziegler performing live with Sia at several television performances and other live concerts.

Around the same time, Ziegler launched her acting career. She voiced the main character, a young ballerina, in the 2017 film *Leap!* She also has released a fashion line with her sister, models, continues to perform with Sia, and has judged *So You Think You Can Dance: The Next Generation*, the younger division of the hit television competition *So You Think You Can Dance*.

Documentaries

Dance history and icons have been captured in both television and full-length documentaries. The topics of these informative shows and movies vary in scope from individuals, to specific productions, to dance forms, and to the dance industry as a whole. These documentary-style films have been presented at film festivals, on cable television, and through streaming services like Netflix.

Dance artists who rise to fame often lead fascinating and dramatic lives, making them excellent topics in the documentary film genre. The film *Restless Creature* (2016) details the end of Wendy Whalen's prolific career as the longest-running performing artist with New York City Ballet after over thirty years performing with the company. Another ballet film tells the triumphant story of Misty Copeland, the first African American female principal with American Ballet Theatre, in *A Ballerina's Tale* (2015). Two examples of documentaries about modern dance masters discussed in Chapter 6 include Ohad Naharin and Pina Bausch. The 2015 film *Mr. Gaga* allows the viewer to enter the world of the brilliant modern dancer, choreographer, and director of Batsheva Dance Company, Ohad Naharin, who also developed his own movement language, for which the film is named. Additionally, German modern dancer and choreographer Pina Bausch is the sole subject of the cinematic eulogy *Pina* (2011), a film dedicated to her life and work in dance and theater.

Other documentaries take a broader look at specific dance forms. For example, from 1975 to 1976, Brenda Bufalino was able to gather master tap dancers from the early twentieth century, including the Copasetics, in order to capture the tradition of tap dance. The film features interviews and dance sequences from the tap elders who came before her and details moments from their lives and careers. The resulting documentary *Great Feats of Feet* is widely admired throughout the tap community as a treasure chest of information and personalities from a previous generation of tap dancers. A series of documentaries titled *That's Entertainment* celebrate song and dance sequences from MGM movies in the twentieth century. In 2011, former dancer Bess Kargman directed the documentary *First Position*, which follows six young ballet dancers as they train, rehearse for, and compete at the Youth American Grand Prix ballet competition in the hope of securing a spot at a prestigious ballet school. *Uprooted: The Journey of Jazz Dance* (2020) details the lineage of jazz dance's past and looks toward the future of the form, with interviews with jazz dance experts such as Debbie Allen, Chita Rivera, and Andy Blankenbuehler. Similarly, the documentary *American Tap* tells the story of this American art form and won the Audience Favorite Award at the 2018 San Francisco Dance Film Festival.

BOX 10.4 NOW STREAMING

Streaming services devoted to the performance arts offer video content dedicated to dance, theater, opera, music, documentaries, and shorts. Previous performances of leading dance companies such as The Royal Ballet and Paul Taylor Dance Company are available to watch, as well as Broadway musicals and several other dance performances. Platforms committed to this type of content include Marquee TV, the Stage Network, and Broadway HD.

SCREEN DANCE

Outside pop culture, artists have explored screen dance as a hybrid art form. In this mixed media form of dance and film, the camera is as much a part of the choreography as the dancing, directing the eye of the viewer and manipulating how the movement is seen. Critics argue that making dance into a video format made the work no longer an art form but a static object that would remain the same every time it was viewed; however, artists working in the medium believe otherwise.

Screen Dance Choreography

Screen dance production is a true collaboration between dance movement artists and videographers. Each must understand and appreciate the other's medium in order to capture the best shots for the film. Screen dance allows choreography to happen in endless possible settings for large audiences. While 200 audience members could not fit inside a ten-foot by ten-foot room to view a dancer portraying insanity in solitary confinement, the camera can fit in that space, record the movement, and then play it back an endless number of times for audiences. Dancers can perform through a church, crawling under pews and behind pillars, and the camera can capture all of it. Even though film flattens the performance and removes the kinesthetic connection to the audience, screen dance adds new dynamics to the work. Depending on the choices made for camera angles and movements, screen dance allows audience members to view the dance movement from entirely new perspectives as the camera moves around, over, under, or even through the dancer or dancers performing. In a harmonious creation, the dancer/s and camera act as partners, and highlight and complement each other in ways that enhance the viewing of the movement.

Since 1971, organizations such as the Dance Films Association have hosted film festivals specifically to screen dance films. Not only a platform to showcase and celebrate screen dance choreography, these festivals provide a networking opportunity for professionals in the field and inspiration for future projects. There are over fifteen dance-specific film festivals in the United States alone, from San Francisco to Oklahoma to North Carolina, plus nearly triple that number internationally. Higher education institutions continue to work to be at the forefront of this industry, offering classes in topics such as dance for the camera and even degree programs and certificates in screen dance.

BOX 10.5 DANCE FILMS ASSOCIATION

The Dance Films Association (DFA) is a nonprofit membership group dedicated to encouraging choreographers to explore the realm of screen dance. Founded in 1956, the DFA hosts the longest running dance film festival, Dance on Camera, and edits and publishes the *Dance on Camera Journal*. Members have access to benefits including shared resources essential for producing dance films.

Virtual Reality

Virtual reality (VR) poses a new screen format for dance. Though virtual reality was developed in the 1960s, it has recently become more feasible for dance with lighter equipment and software updates. There are, in general, two types of VR – desktop and immersive. **Desktop VR** can be watched on a computer monitor and provides arrows for the viewer to click to direct where the camera is angled in the 360-degree video. **Immersive VR** allows the viewer to wear a headset and move through space, interacting with and mobilizing through the environment as one does in real life.

Choreographers are faced with new challenges to compose dance works that are in the round and allow audience members to direct their focus, rather than the traditional proscenium setting in which the choreographer can use choreographic tools to direct the eye. This new medium for dance presents an opportunity to attract new audience members by experiencing it through this cutting-edge technology. Schools such as New York University Tisch School of the Arts, Duke University, and countless others continue to work at the forefront of this technology. Many programs have developed curricula that include courses and even degree concentrations in topics such as Dance Technology. Film festivals, including the San Francisco Dance Film Festival, now screen 360-degree dance films. Companies such as Pacific Northwest Ballet and Brian Brooks Moving Company are creating works specifically crafted for this medium. At the same time, documentaries filmed in immersive VR, such as *A History of Cuban Dance*, transport the audience to other countries and other cultures, creating a strong understanding of the subject matter.

VR has also been adopted into dance education. Applications like Dance Reality are sold online, promising to teach the buyer how to dance forms such as

Salsa, Samba, waltz, and hip-hop. When downloaded onto a smartphone, these applications can display videos of instructors seemingly in front of the student, and as the camera is pointed down toward the floor, footsteps appear on the screen for the student to follow beneath them.

COMPUTER TECHNOLOGY

In addition to the innovations driven by theater technology enhancements and the interaction of dance with cameras, the infrastructural developments of computer technology also continue to change the landscape of dance. The building of computers that can generate and cast enhanced CGI and the creation of the internet have each had sweeping effects on the art of dance.

Computer-generated Imagery

Another new possibility at the intersection of dance and technology is the use of **computer-generated imagery** (CGI) with dance. These special visual effects can be added in video production or postproduction using digital software. In essence, there are three ways to unite CGI with dance. The first is the creation of an entirely digital dancer or animated dancer that carries out the movement. This is the animation we are familiar with seeing in Disney and Pixar films. The other two ways to blend CGI and dance involve human bodies. In one case, technology similar to projection mapping is used to add visual effects around the human body. In 2011, Samsung produced a commercial with hip-hop artist JayFunk. In the video, JayFunk is seated in a chair behind a table, and as techno music begins playing, he begins to tut. While this is mesmerizing on its own, about thirty-eight seconds in, CGI is added. Geometric shapes, figures, and lines seemingly are produced by and react to JayFunk's tutting fingers, hands, arms, and head. The resulting futuristic dance scene was used to advertise a Samsung phone and went viral on the internet. Samsung later created a similar ad with a duet between JayFunk and Fiasko Daniels.

The final type of CGI utilized in dance production is **motion capture**, known as mocap for short. Mocap technology tracks human movement using a full-body suit with sensors and software. Data captured by multiple cameras is transferred to a 3D model so that the model performs the same movements as the person in the suit. When the process includes more detailed actions of the face and hands, it is often called performance capture. This is the technology that was used to create Gollum in *Lord of the Rings* (2001–2003) and the Na'vi in *Avatar* (2009). Motion graphic designers experiment with this technology to create surreal dance figures draped in liquid gold or made of multicolored fur. Other mocap effects include those similar to a long-exposure camera lens tracking dancers' movement through space and leaving traces of the movement behind. In many ways, artists and motion graphic designers are still on the frontier of this technology.

[handwritten margin note: Never heard of this in dance but sounds so cool and will def continue to become more popular with time]

10.6
Behind-the-scenes photograph of film crews recording the tap dance sounds of Savion Glover while he and a group of dancers wear motion-capture suits during the production of the hit 2006 film *Happy Feet*.
Entertainment Pictures/Alamy Stock Photo

Internet →Social Media!!!!

The internet and social media have reshaped society in more ways than any one person can count. Dance, too, has been affected by this pop culture and business shift. In addition to creating new performance possibilities and opportunities for dance, technology has made dance more accessible and brought it into entirely new realms, while social media has affected the manners in which dancers are seen, share their artistry, and interact with the dance community.

The revolution of online streaming has helped make dance performance more accessible. The internet has opened dance performances up to the possibility of livestreaming performances online. While it can pose an ethical issue of bypassing the purchase of theater tickets to see the show live, livestreaming dance immediately widens the audience for dance productions. This crucial connection has been used to broadcast performances to a global audience, share choreographic works with family and friends, generate interest in small or new dance companies, share festival works, and broadcast dance competitions in the private sector.

BOX 10.6 DANCING IN QUARANTINE

The effects on daily life brought about by the COVID-19, or coronavirus, pandemic in 2020 proved just how powerful the internet and livestreaming can be. As citizens all over the world were ordered by their respective governments to shelter in place in order to prevent the spread of this novel virus, dance classes and performances were cancelled on an unprecedented scale. Because the coronavirus was a respiratory virus that spread primarily through droplets from coughs, sneezes, saliva, or nasal discharge from infected people, social distancing protocols were put in place that shut down non-essential business and required six feet of space between people not of the same household. Thus, dance studios, performing arts venues, and college campuses closed.

Artists, however, rose to the occasion in order to continue offering classes and performances on online platforms. Dance teachers from private studios, professional schools, and colleges offered livestreamed or video recorded classes to their students online through platforms like Zoom and Instagram Live. Master teachers offered free online classes to the public for various levels of dancers in an effort of goodwill to share the joy of dance during difficult times. Additionally, professional companies like Alvin Ailey American Dance Theater and the Paris Opera Ballet published performances from their archives for limited times as an alternative to seeing productions while the live theaters were closed.

The 2005 launch of YouTube also forever impacted the dance world. As with any other technological advancements, industries could not anticipate all the repercussions of videos being so easily added to and viewed on the internet. Since the introduction of this platform, it has become common practice for dance students in any setting to ask an instructor for permission to film a step, exercise, or piece of choreography. Often, teachers allow it but warn students not to post the video anywhere online. Dancers and choreographers also run into trouble with music copyright laws if they ever post dance videos that play any type of recorded music, even though they are not profiting from it. However, YouTube also functions as an incredible learning tool for dancers. Countless videos lie in wait on the World Wide Web for a curious dancer to find one, watch it, and then watch twenty similar videos. Never has it been easier or more convenient to discover dance as it now rests at our fingertips. Unfortunately, some audience members abuse this ability at performances and attempt to take illegal video from their seats to share or post online later. When they are caught, theater staff will shine a flashlight on the individual's screen; if the device is not put away, it will be confiscated. This type of behavior is not only an insult to the artists onstage and the choreographers of the work, it also ruins the live theater experience for the patrons around them. As wonderful as new technology can be, it is up to consumers to use it responsibly and ethically.

Likewise, the development of social media has altered the world of dance. Performance companies, dance studios, professional studios, and university dance programs almost all employ social media in their marketing strategies. Facebook, Instagram, and Twitter serve as essentially free platforms to promote a business. Posters of performance seasons, sneak peeks of dance pieces, snapshots of rehearsals, upcoming classes, announcements, and simple day-to-day business can be shared with millions of people with only a few taps of a screen. That being said, managing multiple platforms with up-to-date information, creating stories, and responding to messages can quickly become a very demanding task; some companies have a social media specialist devoted to this work who also analyzes data from posts about how to reach the largest number of people most efficiently. Charts and statistics from research on the most strategic time to post items, how much text to include, photo format, and more are available to help guide operations.

These same tools are also all available to the individual dancer. More than ever, aspiring and professional dancers are marketing themselves through the use of social media and the internet. Many young artists have two accounts on any one platform – one that is their personal profile and one that they curate to represent a look or style that reflects their artistic voice. In a matter of a few years, talk about social media shifted from keeping everything you post absolutely private because your future boss may see it, to "Here's how to tailor your profile to make you appealing to potential future employers." Artists are able to use these social media platforms to showcase their diverse talents. Often, a professional dancer will have a separate account or include in their profile creative projects they create. These could be short videos of choreography projects they create, modeling photos, or their own photography. Social media functions not only to bring people together but also as a branding tool for artists. Many performers, choreographers, and educators have their own website, which includes headshots, biographies, resumés, contact portals, and reels of their choreography or video clips of them performing or teaching.

Internet technology has made smartphone applications (apps) the nuts and bolts of how we live. Nowadays, many would be lost without the map app in their phone. Finding out when and where an event is happening is as simple as asking the phone out loud. There are many apps available that are uniquely helpful to dancers. For instance, ballet terminology, being in pesky French, can be tricky, but there is a Ballet Dictionary app downloadable for free. Tap dance teachers may be unable to find music that is the perfect tempo for their intermediate students, but tempo manipulative apps are available to slow down or speed up any piece of music. Professional studios have their own applications that make it easier for students to look up the class schedule and view upcoming workshops or last-minute cancellations or register for classes online. Choreographers can download an app such as Choreo Lab and use it to draft formations for groups of dancers, complete with allowing the technology to work out the traffic patterns or pathways dancers need to move between formations.

CHAPTER SUMMARY

Though the onslaught of constant technology updates may feel relentless at times, it also permits dancers to experiment artistically. Mixed media such as projections in dance, dance on camera, and screen dance add new dynamics and texture to an already exciting art form. Media such as television, documentaries, and livestreaming bring dance into the mainstream and make it much

			10.1 Chapter 10 Vocabulary
computer-generated imagery	interactive content	projection mapping	
dance on camera	linear content	screen dance	
desktop virtual reality	motion capture	shadow dance	
immersive virtual reality	projection design		

more accessible to the public at large. Tools like projection mapping, CGI, and virtual reality transport dance to entirely new worlds. Meanwhile, the internet, social media, and personal websites provide a platform on which artists can share their work, promote themselves and their work, and support the work of other artists. As long as media and technology continue to develop, artists will have new frontiers to explore while continually developing and honing their craft and transporting audiences.

Reflective Prompts

1. Have you encountered dance online? Perhaps you have seen dance videos on your laptop or smartphone. What did you see? How did it catch your eye?
2. How does viewing dance on a screen compare with seeing it in a live theater? What are the pros and cons of seeing dance live? What are the pros and cons of viewing dance digitally?
3. Do you consider video dance to be a performance art or an artifact (an object that never changes)? Why?

- Online makes a big difference when a choreographer is thinking about how a routine will be viewed

- Tech can enhance visuals in a performance
  ↳ think our UDC routine with the ocean in the background

11 Training and Education

Throughout the twentieth century, opportunities in dance training and education have expanded immensely in the United States. Training in dance has broadened from the studio setting to academia, incorporating additional educational approaches aside from those focused strictly on the acquisition of technical skill. This chapter sheds light on the various ways in which dance training is offered in America and provides a concise overview of the evolution of dance in higher education.

Before we begin, it is helpful to distinguish between training and education. **Dance training** involves the acquisition of specific technical and practical skills. Dancers train their bodies and minds to perform movement with proper technique and style. **Dance education** includes information, theoretical concepts, and the application of that knowledge in a broad, general sense. Dancers study a range of dance-related topics, such as dance history and choreography, that shape their work as dance artists. One can become technically proficient by training in dance, but enhanced knowledge is power. Dance education provides a multi-faceted intellectual approach to the dance-making experience. It includes an understanding of the rich history of dance and the historical and social context in which it evolved (dance history courses); awareness and comprehension of human anatomy and kinesiology, specifically in regard to dance technique (dance anatomy and kinesiology courses); a familiarity with diverse musical genres (music appreciation or music for dance courses); and increased perception of how movement can convey meaning through carefully crafted phrases and sequences (improvisation and choreography courses). Furthermore, dance education fosters awareness of dance from a cultural and global perspective (dance in culture or world dance forms courses).

TRAINING OPPORTUNITIES IN DANCE

Training in dance happens first within the dance studio setting. Dance studios are found across America (and around the world) in a variety of formats: within the private sector, community centers, public and private elementary and secondary educational systems, institutions of higher education, and professional centers. In the United States, participation in dance class often begins as a form of recreation or as a hobby. There are differing modes of thought as to the age

11.1
Benefits of Dance

Engaging in dance has many positive benefits, which is why many parents enroll their children in dance lessons. The following is a list of many, though not all, areas in which one can experience positive results when participating in dance.

Physical	Basic motor skills
	Strength
	Flexibility
	Coordination
	Balance
	Control
	Endurance
Emotional	Self-confidence
	Self-esteem
Behavioral	Composure
	Following directions
	Respect
	Discipline
Cognitive	Creativity
	Expression
	Focus
Social	Sensitivity to others
	Cooperation
	Collaboration with others

at which an individual should begin studying each dance genre; however, training in dance is best initiated at a younger age (pre-adolescence), as the bones and muscles are growing and developing, and the body is still pliable.

Private Dance Studios

Dance studios within the private sector are often single-proprietor businesses and generally the first place one encounters the study of dance. The training taught at private dance studios is typically focused solely on technique, along with various modes of performance opportunities. Each dance studio is unique in that the owner determines the studio's overall approach to dance instruction, curricular design, genre and stylistic offerings, and dress code. Studios may be marketed for the recreational, commercial, and/or serious or pre-professional dance student. Training is typically offered at the pre-school age and extends through adulthood, yet some studios may also provide creative movement classes for toddlers/infants and parents. Dance studios follow a traditional, two-semester, academic calendar cycle wherein classes generally begin in August/September and end in May/June, and students have the opportunity to progress in level between terms or years.

Private dance studios require a fee for lessons, which varies from studio to studio and from city to city. There is often a registration fee along with monthly tuition fees based on the number of classes in which a student is enrolled. The student is typically expected to participate in the annual or bi-annual recitals, which may also require a participation fee and performance admission costs along with the purchase of costumes. Each dance could require a separate costume, and costs could range from $25 per costume to over $100 per costume depending on the age and level of the dancer and the costume needs of the dance. In addition to regular classes and recitals, many studios also offer performance and/or competitive ensembles or teams. These performance-based groups are often by audition or invitation and require a minimum number of weekly technique classes, rehearsals, and attendance and participation in scheduled performances and/or dance competitions. Competitive dance ensembles generally require individual choreography and costume fees. Events will also have separate registration and entry fees. Whether participating as a recreational student, a competitive dancer, or a pre-professional dancer, dance training, even at a local dance studio, can be as expensive as involvement in school athletics.

BOX 11.1 DANCE COMPETITIONS

Dance competitions have become nearly a genre of their own. Today, there are hundreds of companies that tour nationwide offering adjudication opportunities for young dancers. Most dancers compete as part of a dance studio team or ensemble. While some studios participate in the competition scene primarily for the educational aspect of feedback and performance opportunity, many studios dedicate considerable time to preparing for multiple weekends of competition with the goal of collecting top honors and dancer and/or studio recognition. Dancers will rehearse for endless hours perfecting their routines, filling the dances with difficult tricks designed to impress the judges and demonstrate their high degree of flexibility, strength and power in jumps and leaps, and ability to rotate endlessly in turns.

[handwritten note: Big problem in dance today!]

Dancers are divided into age divisions, with some competitions offering competitive opportunities for students from as young as four years of age up to over fifty. Dancers compete as soloists, duos/trios, small groups, large groups, and production groups (generally twenty or more dancers) in categories divided by age and a variety of dance genres. Dances are limited in length, typically restricted to three minutes or less. A panel of judges, usually professional dancers, choreographers, or educators, evaluates the performers on a set of criteria that may include technical execution, choreography, artistry/presentation, and costumes. Judges provide each routine with a score and sometimes a written or verbal critique. Awards are then given to those earning the qualifying number of points in each category.

While it can be costly, there are many benefits to training within the private sector. The curricula at dance studios often include a great range of dance genres to which a student can be exposed and which they may choose to study. Additionally, the curricula cover a wide range of ages and levels; attention is focused on the progression of the individual's technical growth from a beginning level through to an advanced level of skill. Perhaps the most impactful element is the mentorship that occurs within this setting. Many young dancers grow up training in the local private sector, and the hometown dance studio often becomes a second home for these dancers. Some children may begin dancing at a specific studio at the age of three or four and remain there until they graduate from high school. These dancers will have become a part of that dance studio's family, complete with a group of dance peers who have shared common goals and let-downs and dance teachers who have worked hard helping the individuals to develop dance abilities and lifelong skills.

BOX 11.2 (NO) STANDARD IN TRAINING: DANCE STUDIOS

The Western genres of dance lack a standardized system of training, although many professional dance schools and companies have devised their own certificate or certification programs. Private dance studios are not regulated by a national accrediting body or standard. While membership organizations such as the National Dance Education Organization (NDEO; see Box 11.4) and the National Association of Schools of Dance (NASD; see Box 11.5) exist to support dance education and promote standards, private dance studios, and even professional schools and institutions of higher education, are not required to seek membership in or thus abide by the teaching standards set forth by the organizations. Teachers do not have to be certified or receive dance degrees or certificates in order to open a dance studio or teach at a private dance studio. One is not required to gain specialized training in dance or dance education to begin instructing others in dance, nor is there a standard on how the dance curriculum within a studio or school is to be established. This lack of standardization creates a discrepancy specifically within early dance training. What one student may learn at one studio can be quite different in both scope and format from what another individual may learn at another studio.

[handwritten annotation: creates a TON of variation]

Professional Dance Studios

Several major US cities are home to professional dance studios. Similarly to the private dance studio, these businesses offer training in multiple forms of dance technique. The primary distinctions are that most classes taught are designed for the professional or pre-professional dancer and offered year-round at an individual class rate as opposed to a monthly-only tuition rate. The Millennium Dance Complex in Los Angeles, Broadway Dance Center in New York City, and

Visceral Dance Center in Chicago are all premier training facilities featuring master teachers in a variety of dance genres and levels. It is quite normal for the choreographer of an upcoming Hollywood film or Broadway show to teach class at a professional dance studio. Participating in dance classes at a professional studio is an excellent way for professional dancers to continue to train in various genres and styles, prepare for auditions, and network with other dancers, choreographers, and directors.

Many professional dance companies also have studios that coincide with a performance company. These studios have a dual purpose. Not only do they help financially support the company, but they also provide a funnel of trained dancers for the company. Individuals who have trained at the studio aligned with a company are best prepared in that company's distinct movement technique and style and are familiar with the company's directors, staff, and dancers. This familiarity and preparedness can often provide them with a "leg-up" during company auditions.

Supplemental Training Opportunities
Dance Conventions
Dance conventions began in the latter half of the twentieth century as traveling groups of leading dance educators who presented workshops and master classes in dance technique to students and fellow teachers of dance. From these early groups, an entire industry has since developed. Today, dance conventions are large-scale, company-run events that tour nationwide. These events provide an opportunity for dancers and teachers to attend a weekend of master classes in a range of genres and dance styles taught by nationally acclaimed dance artists and choreographers. Conventions are held in hotel ballrooms or event centers where participants are divided by age and level into multiple rooms throughout the event's classes. A sea of students from the city/state/region learn new movement and choreography together from an instructor who leads the class from a makeshift platform. Most events incorporate group warm-up sessions and closing award shows complete with a rental stage, production lights, and high-powered surround sound. These events are designed to generate excitement and enthusiasm among participants and often focus on the commercial aspects of dance. Some dance conventions have managed to stay in business for decades as new companies continue to come and go annually. Many exist today as convention/competitions companies, providing young dancers with both the master class setting and an adjudicated performance experience.

Dance Festivals
Dance festivals exist in America in a variety of formats. Most are dedicated to a specific genre and occur over a span of two to five days. During a dance festival, dance students, educators, and professionals from across the globe gather to participate in master classes, panel discussions, and performances. Leading

11.1
An instructor
teaches a hotel
ballroom full of
students during a
weekend of classes
at a RADIX Dance
Convention event.
Photo courtesy
of RADIX Dance
Convention

dance artists and choreographers teach workshop-style classes during the day. Performances often include informal concerts featuring student and amateur choreography and formal concerts presenting invited professional concert companies and/or individual renowned artists. There are festivals that occur across the country and internationally that focus on ballet, modern, jazz, tap, and hip-hop. Festivals are generally sponsored by a dance company or organization and possibly supported by other businesses, donors, or grants.

DANCE IN EDUCATION

Dance in K-12 Programs

Throughout the country, many public and private elementary and secondary schools offer fine arts components, such as curricula in music, art, theater, and dance. These programs may consist of a single unit of study or coursework consistently scheduled throughout the term. As debates over STEM (Science, Technology, Engineering, and Math) versus STEAM (Science, Technology, Engineering, Art, and Math) and state budget cuts permeate the education system, these programs often face challenges due to the resources required to implement and maintain their curricula. Teachers must hold dance certifications or licensures to teach within the public-school system, and suitable facilities and sound equipment must be secured. Additionally, students need access to appropriate dance attire and appropriate dance shoes (ballet slippers, jazz shoes, or tap shoes). Budget limitations often cause dance classes within some public-school programs to occur in gymnasiums on un-sprung floors with students not in proper dance shoes.

Dance may also be a featured discipline in magnet and performing arts schools. Because they carry the designation of specialized focus in certain areas, resources to maintain a stronger dance curriculum may be more readily available within these elementary and secondary schools. Such programs have additional funding available to them, and some may also maintain a connection to professional companies, which can further benefit students. The content of dance in K-12 public-school systems may vary depending upon the mandates and the standards of the state in which the school is located. Yet, an obvious benefit of dance training within K-12 schools rather than the private dance studio setting is that free access to dance instruction is provided for every student regardless of financial means.

BOX 11.3 TRAINING PROGRAMS AND CERTIFICATES

Many dance companies and organizations offer training certificates and certifications as an option for dance educators. While these do not replace a teaching license or certification within the educational system, they are attractive options to dance teachers and instructors. Dance teachers pursue certifications to further their intellect and ability as educators and instructors. Having a certificate also demonstrates to students that the instructor has received additional training in a specific area and thus is a way for the instructor to earn recognition among their students and become more marketable as a teacher.

Because the programs often take up as little time as one day to a week or two, many educators find them manageable to attend. Such programs are typically offered from beginning to advanced levels and concentrate on specific genres, styles, methodologies, age-ranges, levels, or aspects of teaching.

Dance in Higher Education

A Historical Context

At the turn of the nineteenth century, special teacher training programs were established within colleges to prepare individuals to instruct the newly implemented physical education curriculum within public and private schools. The development of these teacher programs in physical education helped pave the way for the incorporation of dance within higher education. Other factors occurring in the early years of the twentieth century, such as social and economic growth, progressive education, women's education and suffrage, and diverging practices in the performing arts, propelled society's curiosity about the body and the emergence of dance within physical education programs.[1] In 1926, a specialized major in dance was proposed and implemented within the women's physical education program at the University of Wisconsin. This marked the first undergraduate major in dance within higher education and brought greater recognition to dance within academia. Yet, to this point in history, the role of dance within higher education emphasized creative movement for children and was focused on dance as a form of physical education. Although theatrical dance forms appeared on stage and film, dance training for the professional artist had yet to make its way into academia.

During the later 1930s, a program known as the Bennington Experience occurred during the summers on the campus of Bennington College in Vermont, uniting hundreds of dance educators and professionals together in both class and concert settings. By bringing professional modern dancers and concert dance into the college setting, this program ultimately enabled the professional and academic aspects of dance to converge and shifted the focus of dance in higher education. The objectives of dance training at the collegiate level transitioned beyond those rooted in self-expression and physical well-being to a means for the development of the professional dance artist.

During the second half of the twentieth century, the presence of dance within higher education continued to grow slowly and steadily, due in large part to public policy and federal laws. The National Endowment for the Arts (NEA), established in 1965 under President Lyndon B. Johnson, made federal funding available for artists. In 1994, President Clinton signed into legislation the Goals 2000: Educate America Act, which was an effort to replace the Elementary and Secondary Education Act (ESEA) and the precursor to President George W. Bush's No Child Left Behind Act. Goals 2000 not only placed art as an equal to core subjects such as math, science, and language arts, but also identified dance as a separate art discipline. As a result, the National Standards for Arts Education – now referred to as the National Core Arts Standards – were developed, which consist of set standards in each of the arts, including dance, that students should not only know but also be able to do. These voluntary standards for state K-12 programs were devised to be assessed at grades four, eight, and twelve.

BOX 11.4 NATIONAL DANCE EDUCATION ORGANIZATION

The National Dance Education Organization (NDEO) was established in 1998 in Washington, DC, with the goal of supporting and "advancing dance education centered in the arts."[2] NDEO is a nonprofit, membership organization that publishes two dance education journals, hosts a number of yearly conferences uniting dance educators to further develop the field, and supports states in the pursuit of dance certifications. NDEO offers an Online Professional Development Institute wherein dance educators of all levels can further their education. Additionally, NDEO has produced standards in dance education that serve as guides for both students and teachers of all levels. Finally, the organization supports a National Honors Society for Dance Arts at the secondary and collegiate levels. NDEO is a recognized leader in the field of dance education, advocating for public policy, developing programs, and assisting dance educators within K-12, higher education, and the private sector.

Dance appeared as an academic discipline within physical education programs during the 1960s and 1970s. Yet, following the internal shift of those programs, the national momentum of public policy and federal support for the arts, and the discipline's emphasis on the professional molding of the dancer, dance programs migrated to fine arts departments, where missions were better aligned. Today, dance programs may be found as stand-alone departments or schools within the university setting or are combined with other fine arts disciplines, such as theater or music.

Colleges and Universities Today

Today, a range of post-secondary degree options are offered within institutions of higher education. University and college programs have become an excellent option for young dancers to hone technical and artistic skills, develop intellectual connections and understandings within the field of dance, and pursue additional areas of study prior to entering the professional world.

BOX 11.5 NATIONAL ASSOCIATION OF SCHOOLS OF DANCE

The National Association of Schools of Dance (NASD) was founded in 1981 and is the accrediting agency for educational programs in dance as recognized by the United States Department of Education. Today, the membership body includes both public and private institutions of higher education along with non-degree granting professional training programs, such as the Martha Graham School of Contemporary Dance, Inc. The organization currently maintains a membership of approximately eighty-two institutions, and as a governing body, NASD ensures that its members uphold the curricular and procedural standards that have been established by the association.[3]

The NASD has categorized dance degrees into the following categories: the liberal arts degree, such as the Association of Arts, Bachelor of Arts, or Bachelor of Science, and the professional degree, known as the Bachelor of Fine Arts. Graduate dance degrees include the Master of Arts and Master of Fine Arts along with a doctorate degree, a PhD or EdD. For students wishing to take a collection of courses in the field of dance but not pursue an undergraduate degree, the dance minor is also an option. Collegiate dance degree programs may choose how to focus and structure the individual program. For example, some degree programs may focus on a specific genre, such as ballet, while others may choose to require the study of multiple genres of dance. A degree program may emphasize dance performance or choreography or remain generalized in scope. Additional areas of emphasis within a dance degree may include pedagogy or dance education, management, therapy, history, or **somatics**, which is a movement discipline that emphasizes a mind-body approach. *soma= body*

On average, a dance degree curriculum will include a minimum number of dance technique and dance theory courses in addition to general education requirements. The required technique courses often align with the emphasis of the individual program. For instance, a program that is based in modern dance will most likely require a higher number of credit hours in modern dance technique with fewer hours of ballet technique required. Even fewer, if any, credit hours in jazz dance or other techniques may be included. Yet, a separate university dance degree program may require equal hours in multiple genres of dance.

Theory courses in dance can include choreography, dance pedagogy, dance media, and dance kinesiology, along with beginning to advanced sections of each course type. Dance theory courses may occur in a dance studio or in a traditional classroom setting and incorporate elements of standard lecture, discussion, and practical application of movement and study.

It is important to keep in mind that college dance programs also serve non-dance majors. These programs raise awareness of dance and the arts throughout the college and local communities, establish patrons and the audience of dance outside those enrolled within the program, and educate non-majors through humanities-related, dance-based general education courses. Dance within higher education can also fulfill physical education or wellness credits. Concerts produced by collegiate dance degree programs provide annual entertainment to campus and surrounding communities.

Dance within higher education continues to evolve with our ever-changing culture. Faced with technological innovations and inconsistent budgets, educators and administrators maintain ongoing discussion regarding curricular needs and concerns within the field of dance. Most university dance programs struggle to keep up with the rapid advancement in the area of dance and technology due to limited funding. The marginalization of jazz, tap, and hip-hop dance within institutions of higher education is heavily debated in an effort to provide equal opportunities for students to study these American art forms. These efforts to decolonize dance in academia carry over into curricular and course development, such as revisions to dance history courses, which currently discuss almost exclusively ballet and modern dance. Just as gender and equality issues are appearing in athletics, dance is confronting similar conflicts. For example, race and gender roles are being challenged in traditional works such as classical ballets. These are just a few examples of the areas being debated and considered within dance in higher education. As programs further develop and transition,

| dance education | dance training | somatics |

and the world of dance continues to evolve, it will be exciting to see where dance in academia will lead.

CHAPTER SUMMARY

Throughout the twentieth century, dance education has evolved significantly. No longer are dance studios the only setting in which a dancer can receive training. Today, dance education has achieved national recognition and federal support. Voluntary national standards have assisted states in the implementation of dance within their educational curricula. Many K-12 programs offer components of dance education, while college and university programs boast dance degree programs at the undergraduate, graduate, and doctoral levels. Yet, should one wish to study dance as an art form or simply participate in a dance class, the benefits that one can gain from experiencing this great art form are immeasurable.

Reflective Prompts

1. Assuming you are not a dance major, consider the degree that you are pursuing. Think about the different courses that your degree curriculum requires and why they might be included. Does it surprise you to learn that dance degrees require coursework other than movement classes? Why or why not? Did the reading alter your perspective? If so, how?
2. What was your experience with arts and education growing up? Were the arts included in your elementary and secondary education curricula? In what ways?
3. Do you think that utilizing dance can help a student learn better in other disciplines? Why or why not? Identify ways in which dance relates to your chosen field of study.
4. What are your beliefs on STEM versus STEAM? Do you think the arts, specifically dance, are necessary within education? Why or why not?
5. How can movement be used to teach other disciplines? For example, how could dance be used to help a child better comprehend a mathematical concept or a social studies lesson?

NOTES

1 Thomas K. Hagood, "Dance in American Colleges and Universities," in *The Dance Experience: Insights into History, Cultures and Creativity*, 3rd ed., ed. by Myron Howard Nadel and Marc Raymond Strauss (New Jersey: Princeton Book Company, 2014), 81.
2 "NDEO Advancing Dance Education in the Arts," National Dance Education Organization, www.ndeo.org/.
3 "National Association of Schools of Dance," accessed April 2020, https://nasd.arts-accredit.org/.

CHAPTER 11 BIBLIOGRAPHY

Bonbright, Jane M. "Agenda for Dance Arts Education: The Evolution of Dance as an Art Form Intersects with the Evolution of Federal Interest in, and Support of, Arts Education" (paper presented at the *Dancing in the Millennium Conference*, Washington, DC, 2000). https://s3.amazonaws.com/ClubExpressClubFiles/893257/documents/Evolution_of_Dance_in_the_Arts.pdf?AWSAccessKeyId=AKIA6MYUE6DNNN CCDT4J&Expires=1590701249&response-content-disposition=inline%3B%20 filename%3DEvolution_of_Dance_in_the_Arts.pdf&Signature=g4JsahXR53zbLG rQqJzPZlXTLfw%3D.

Hagood, Thomas K. "Dance in American Colleges and Universities." In Nadel, Myron Howard and Marc Raymond Strauss, eds. *The Dance Experience: Insights into History, Cultures and Creativity*, 3rd ed. New Jersey: Princeton Book Company, 2014, 77–96.

Kraus, Richard, Sarah Chapman Hilsendager, and Brenda Dixon. *History of the Dance in Art and Education*, 3rd ed. New Jersey: Prentice-Hall, 1991.

Nadel, Myron Howard and Marc Raymond Strauss, eds. *The Dance Experience: Insights into History, Cultures and Creativity*, 3rd ed. New Jersey: Princeton Book Company, 2014.

"National Association of Schools of Dance." Accessed April 2020. https://nasd.arts-accredit.org/.

National Dance Education Organization. "NDEO Advancing Dance Education in the Arts." Accessed April 2020. www.ndeo.org/.

12 The Dancer

Dance is a demanding art form, both physically and mentally. When watching a theatrical dance performance, you may have observed the dancers' extreme range of flexibility, agility, or stamina. The dancers' graceful motions and expressive portrayals may have been emphasized and featured. Or, you may have been whisked away into another realm of possibilities, stories, or concepts, full of dynamic movement and awe-inspiring physical feats. Yet, have you ever considered the mental aspect that accompanies the art form? How do dancers remember the sequence of steps, movement patterns, counts and rhythms for each movement phrase, and their placements on the stage? How do dancers prepare for auditions, and then once cast, what is their daily schedule? What types of stress might permeate a dancer's training and performance life, and how does this stress impact training?

Whether an individual chooses to dance as a professional performer or simply study the art form as a hobby, dance training challenges the human body physically as well as mentally and emotionally. Yet, dancers are willing to train hard in exchange for the joys that dance brings. As we have learned, dance is a form of communication that carries a great number of benefits to both the doer and the viewer. When performing, dancers have the opportunity to speak to an audience, to engage and connect with the audience on an emotional level. There is a sense of gratification that dancers receive, a deep sense of joy that stirs within them and propels them forward. This chapter explores the art of theatrical dance from the dancer's perspective. As we discover the arduous journey a dancer takes to become a professional and the challenges and happiness that accompany it, consider how your own chosen career path compares in these areas.

THE JOURNEY TO PROFESSIONAL DANCER

Proper training of the body is paramount regardless of the dance form which one pursues. Whether one is studying a Western theatrical dance, like ballet, tap, or modern, or another dance form, such as *bedhaya*, *kabuki*, or *capoeira*, disciplined and consistent training and conditioning of the body is a must. Each dance form has its own method of study, which is often dictated by either cultural patterns or tradition. Guiding principles outline the age at which one should begin instruction, the curriculum to be followed for proper progression, the standardized vocabulary to be learned, and the repertoire to be studied. Given the dance form and the culture, these principles may be standardized or generalized. Regardless, the training regimens for various dance forms can be fascinating to observe even if one does not wish to participate oneself.

The Western theatrical genres of dance detailed in Part II require similar yet distinct modes of study. While the paths may vary, training within the United States for each of these dance genres (ballet, modern, tap, jazz, and hip-hop) typically occurs within a dance studio setting, although it is important to note that these forms may also be learned within social and community settings. Dance studios are found throughout the United States in independently owned dance studios, professional dance studios, community centers, K-12 performing arts schools, and institutions of higher education. Dance studios become the home base for a dancer of any age or level; this is the training and conditioning ground for a dancer who wishes to advance to a proficient skill level. Every sport requires constant practice. Professional football players work basic passing and throwing drills on the football field. Similarly, a professional dancer must engage in regular dance class to ensure that the muscles stay toned and prepared for the demands of dance. It is through regular class work that young dancers learn the technique behind the dance form and gain the necessary skills to potentially advance to a professional level, and professional dancers maintain their technique and further condition their bodies as a form of injury prevention.

The Dance Class

The dance class includes more than simply learning the dance steps and positions. It extends beyond the technique of executing the dance vocabulary. The dance class provides opportunity for the dancer of any level to condition the body for the demands of dance and gain the discipline of a dedicated artist. As mentioned throughout Part II, the selected dance form determines the specific structure and exercises included within a dance class. Though instruction classes in all dance genres should include a warm-up and cooldown, the individual components of the class may differ. These components vary depending on the dance form, so that the exercises and movement are tailored to the groups of muscles and distinct skills that will be used. For example, consider the genres of modern dance versus tap dance versus *bharatanatyam*. Each form will use many muscles and body parts that probably will not be used in the same way in either or both of the other forms. Modern dance does not use the feet in the same way tap dance does. Or, the muscles will be used in a very different way and therefore will require practice in opposing movement patterning. *Bharatanatyam* makes use of the eyes, hands, and fingers in a manner quite distinct from modern and tap dance. The dance class inherently includes exercises designed to increase flexibility, strengthen the body, sharpen the mind, improve technique, and enhance artistry.

12.1
Dancers in the
University of
Oklahoma School
of Dance stretch
before a class.
Photo by
Noor Eemaan

It is imperative that the muscles of the body be properly conditioned so that they may safely move the body's bones from one position to the next. This is acquired through repetition and practice and under the watchful eye of the dance teacher. For example, the traditional ballet class begins with a *plié* exercise, which is a bending and straightening of the legs. This movement is integral to nearly every single dance vocabulary in all five Western theatrical dance genres. It is an essential position for a dancer to move through both before and after any jump or leap; it is used as a preparation into various turns; and the use of the *plié* can provide fluid transitions between movements. This movement, in isolation, serves as an exercise to loosen the joints of the hips, knees, and ankles and allow the dancer to establish proper alignment and placement within the body. Classical dancers will perform an infinite number of *pliés* throughout their lifetimes. Professional ballet dancers practice *pliés* as frequently as beginner-level dancers.

This is why you warm up slowly

Dance Conditioning

Strength and flexibility are equally important for dancers to possess, and exercises within the dance class are often balanced to promote the development of each. The muscles must be pliant, and a great range of motion is highly desirable. Dancers spend a great deal of time stretching the legs, hips, back, and feet so that they can move with great ease through a variety of positions and poses. Conversely, strength must be developed to balance and support the flexibility within the body and avoid injury. For example, a highly flexible and arched foot and ankle looks exquisite *en pointe*, but if the ankle is not strong, the dancer risks injury while dancing, as the muscles, ligaments, and tendons of the calf, ankle, and foot will not be able to support both quick and sustained

12.2
The Pilates reformer
provides a form of
body conditioning
for dancers.
ozgurdonmaz,
Getty Images

flexibility & strength required

movement of rising and lowering through the *pointe* shoe. A remarkably flexible back allows the dancer to execute a fully extended layout position in jazz dance, yet, if the muscles of the abdominals and gluteals are not strong, injury to the back could occur.

Additionally, the dance class works the coordination of the body through a variety of exercises and movement approaches. Exercises are designed to enhance the dancer's ability to organize the parts of the body and integrate movement throughout the body, enhancing a sense of mind-body connectivity. As a result, efficiency in movement is achieved. To further condition their bodies, dancers often engage in cross-training activities. Pilates, Gyrokinesis®, yoga, high intensity cardio, swimming, and strength training are examples of activities that dancers may choose to add to their daily or weekly routines to increase endurance and strength and reduce the risk of injury.

BOX 12.1 THE TAP DANCE CLASS

The tap dance class is unique in that primary focus is often applied to footwork and the production of proper sound. Conditioning, strength, and flexibility are approached differently than in the other dance genres. Just as the *plié* is included in the ballet class, the *shuffle* is a staple in a tap class. A basic *shuffle* is a swinging drop and lift of the leg as only the ball of the foot strikes the floor, making two sounds. *Shuffles* form the basis of a vast amount of tap vocabulary and are practiced for articulation, speed, and shading of sound. Tap dancers execute an infinite number of *shuffles* in their training. Stretching, in any form, may or may not be included within the lesson plan depending upon the philosophy of the instructor. Strength exercises often focus on tap dance vocabulary, with exercises intended to further develop the muscles of the feet, ankles, calves, and legs. Tap dance is not any less physical than other dance forms; it is just demanding in a different way. Classwork provides the opportunity to challenge the dancer mentally and technically and further enhance the dancer's artistry.

The dance class allows dancers – even professionals – to enhance and maintain their technique and skill and keep their bodies in shape for the demands of choreography and career longevity. Even dance teachers themselves, who may no longer perform, find it important to engage in dance class to help sustain their bodies and enable continued practice of the art form. It is through this type of consistent training that dancers are able to extend their dance careers and reduce the risk of injury.

Learning Styles

Individuals learn in ways that are unique to them, and dancers are no exception. There is no one set method in which a person acquires and comprehends new information. Researchers have identified three primary learning styles in which an individual best receives and understands information: visual, auditory, and kinesthetic. Visual learners must see or read the material. For dancers, this requires seeing the movement that is being taught. Auditory learners need to hear the information. To a dancer, this occurs when the instructor verbally explains the movement, naming the vocabulary, identifying the counting, and/or offering verbal sounds or scats that delineate the rhythm of the movement. Kinesthetic learners must engage in the material for themselves rather than simply seeing or hearing the information. These dancers must execute the movement themselves. They must be kinesthetically aware to internalize and understand the mechanics, sequence, and nuances of the movement.

Most dancers are kinesthetic learners; however, many dancers find that they also require visual and/or auditory methods. For this reason, it is important that dance educators are able to communicate movement in a variety of ways. An effective dance teacher will be able not only to demonstrate the movement, but also to clearly describe the movement using correct terminology and deliver the musical counts for the phrasing of the movement, or sing or scat the rhythms of the movement. Dancers are encouraged to perform the movement along with the instructor during the learning process.

Practice, Practice, Practice

Once dancers have learned a skill, a movement pattern, or an entire dance, they continue to engage in practice, practice, practice until the movement itself becomes second nature, or muscle memory. Just as the late master tap dancer Robert L. Reed would remind his students, "An amateur practices until he gets it right. A professional practices until he can't get it wrong." Dancers develop the muscle memory of the movement and technique and must then couple that with artistry. Yet, their jobs as performers do not end there. Dancers must also be prepared to meet the demands of the unexpected in performance. A missed entrance, a failed partnering lift, a mishap in the music, a botched scene shift, a costume malfunction, or forgotten choreography are all misfortunes that could strike during a performance. Yet, dancers handle these blunders with grace and composure in such ways that most audience members never realize they happened!

It is through the regular practice of dance that the ability to learn quickly is developed, memorization of sequence is enhanced, technical skill is increased, and artistry is honed. Training helps prepare the dancer physically; yet physical training alone cannot combat the mental stress that inevitably can affect a dancer of any level. Dancers are often faced with a variety of pressures throughout their careers. These pressures can result from concerns relating to body image, finances, employment, confidence, job security, skill level, scheduling, and injury. Just as dance can be a source of healing and therapy, it can also beget stress. This will be discussed further in Chapter 13.

The Age Factor — AGE DOES NOT MATTER

There is often the presumption that an individual must be young in order to dance professionally, and once they reach a certain age, they will no longer be employable. In some genres of dance, this may be true, but given the right training and the proper preparation, a dancer's career may extend much longer today than in previous generations. The growing fields of dance somatics and dance science have enabled dancers to learn more about how to keep their bodies dancing safely and performing longer. Some ballet and contemporary dancers believe it will be more beneficial to go straight into a performance career following high school. These dancers will often forgo college enrollment and instead begin apprenticeships with a dance company in the hopes of working their way up the ranks of the company. However, attending a college program first can help a dancer prepare for a career in performance in many ways. College not only furthers an individual's physical dance training but provides the individual with a deeper understanding of the art form, offering historical, theoretical, and cultural perspectives and methodologies that will shape their work as an artist. Many dancers do choose to pursue higher education and still enjoy successful performance careers post-graduation.

The length of careers can vary. While a dancer's entry into a performance company often occurs at a younger age, more and more dancers are able to sustain their careers beyond their twenties and into their thirties and forties and beyond. Often, tap dancers enjoy performing well into their later years. In general, dancers of all genres have learned ways in which to dance smarter and longer. Even after retiring from a performance career, dancers often remain active in the field, working as choreographers, teachers, or in one of the many other dance careers detailed in Chapter 14.

Ideally, dance training begins at a young age if one hopes to pursue a career in dance performance within the Western world, especially concert dance. However, male-identifying individuals are often an exception to this unwritten rule. There is a surplus of talented female dancers within the world. This fact alone works to the male's advantage in entering the dance field at a later age. Males are often able to begin training in dance at a later age and still find success, assuming they have good training and an inherent sense of coordination, rhythm, and flexibility. For those individuals wishing to simply enjoy dance as a recreational activity, many private and community-based dance studios welcome individuals at any age, even as adults.

It is true, though, that a dancer's performance career does come with an expiration date. One must consider the demands of the movement and how long the human body can sustain those demands. Each physical body is different, and the demands of each genre of dance are unique. While dance is a form of art, it is also a sport. It is athletic. And with any sport comes stress on the body. The strength and control of the ankle extended repetitively during *pointe* work, the extensions of the legs and the back in modern dance, the impact of the landing from various jumps in jazz dance, the slamming of the feet into the floor during heavy tap work, the spins and flips of the body on the ground during breaking, all demonstrate stress that the body withstands during dance. Therefore, consistent dance conditioning and proper training, along with knowledge of the body and awareness of injury prevention, are a must for a dancer. The next chapter speaks directly to injuries that can occur as a result of this stress.

BOX 12.2 DANCE: WORK OR PLAY

There is often a misconception that dance equates to play, and the life of a dancer must be one of fun and games within the studio. While it is certainly true that dancers do take great joy in performing on stage, sharing their love of dance with others, and exploring movement ideas within the studio, it is certainly not child's play. Many non-dancers may incorrectly assume that a dancer goes into the studio and merely spins, gallops, and frolics about in front of a mirror in fancy outfits. Many times, dancers are met with the response "oh that must be fun" when asked what they do for a living. This response is often interpreted as a condescending comment, where the word fun is often underscored with an implied "easy." Yet, dancers often find gratification in performance and discover it to be pure joy to be able to engage in one's passion for a living. But that choice does not come without sacrifice and hard work. Being a dancer, or even just engaging in dance training regardless of whether or not it is as a career, requires that the body be prepared to meet the demands of dance. Just as any athlete must train, so must dancers. On top of the physical skill, there is the artistic and intellectual level of skill that also must be acquired. Enjoyable, yes, but easy, definitely not.

Calling all Dancers

Dancers looking for a performance job can find information about upcoming auditions and casting notices via dance publications, such as *Dance Magazine*, and online websites, such as Backstage, which post audition notices. Professional dance studios as well as colleges and universities will also post audition notices. Finally, professional companies advertise auditions on their websites and social media platforms. These audition notices may include information on fees, what type of dancer they are looking for, and registration information. Dancers may also be invited to an audition or even a job offer based on who they know. The dance world is small, and networking is an important element in securing employment opportunities. The contacts and relationships made within the field can prove to be beneficial in gaining insider knowledge on upcoming events, auditions, or further networking.

Auditions may or may not require an audition fee, which could range from 10 to 30 dollars, but most typically require at a minimum that a headshot and a dance resumé be submitted. Some may require a photograph in a dance movement or pose in addition to a headshot. Research should be completed in advance of each audition. What is the job? What genre and style of dance does the company perform? What type of dancers does the company typically employ? The more information that one has about the company, the better the individual can prepare for the audition. It is also helpful to know whether one will even be a good fit for the company.

One must wear the proper dance attire and bring the correct shoes to the audition. For example, while it may be appropriate to wear a leotard, tights, and ballet skirt to a ballet company audition, one would wear something entirely different to a music video audition. After arriving early to an audition, one can then expect a long wait. Auditions are packed full of anxious dancers, hopeful for an opportunity to impress a director or choreographer and be offered their dream job, or perhaps any job. Many auditions are referred to as "cattle calls," in which a large sea of hundreds of dancers is in attendance. In some auditions, cuts may be made before the dancers even perform a step. In these instances, the group is narrowed down based on size and/or appearance and who might initially be "right" for a part. Movement combinations are taught, and then small groups of dancers perform the movement and more cuts are made. Some dancers are asked to stay and participate in more audition rounds, while others are thanked and dismissed.

An audition can be an extremely nerve-wracking experience for some or just another day for others. Depending on the structure and how long one is kept at the audition, the day can be unexpectedly short or quite long. For most dancers, the day ends with a disheartening "thanks, but no thanks." For the lucky few, on that particular day, a contract is offered, while others may be kept on file, or "in the book," to be called at a later date should a position open up.

I've got the job! Now what?

Dancers who seek a performance career train and train with the goal of presenting their art form onstage. With performing comes the enjoyment and gratification of entertaining and communicating with audiences. Dancers sweat through class after class preparing their bodies for each performance onstage to delight and engage audiences. Being a professional dancer can sound glamorous and exciting, but it is not without sacrifice and its own set of considerations. According to labor statistics, dancers on average make approximately 20 dollars per hour.[1] Many dancers are not employed full-time. A dancer may be hired for a single gig, or performance job. A one-time performance might only include a few hours of rehearsal and one hour of performance time. Dancers are often only paid for actual performance time but may also be paid for their hours of rehearsal time. When on contract with a company, dancers may be on salary or receive other benefits; however, those details differ with each job and contract.

Many dancers also maintain secondary jobs in addition to their dance careers. Squeezed in between their dance classes, rehearsals, and performances, most dancers are also employed in another field as well. Employment that works well with dancers' schedules includes working as fitness trainers, nannies, or in the restaurant business, administration, or merchandising. Many also teach dance. The life of a dancer is one of balance; a constant balance of rehearsals, performances, multiple jobs, and personal lives. Some contracts may only be for a single performance, whereas other contracts may be for six months or longer. Dancers are often continuing to audition even while they are currently under contract in order to line up their next job when their current one ends.

Within the world of dance performance, jobs are scarce, and roles are limited. One must train hard and be physically ready and in shape. Now more than ever before, there is the need for dancers to be versatile, meaning that they need to be trained in more than one style and genre of dance. They need to be prepared for anything and everything that a choreographer may throw at them or that a show may demand of them. In previous decades, a ballet dancer would train in classical ballet, join a classical ballet company, and perform classical ballet works. Today, that is no longer the case, as we have seen through discussions in Part II. Present-day companies, regardless of their classification, perform work outside their genre. Classical ballet companies regularly commission choreographers who work outside the genre of ballet, such as in jazz dance or modern dance. Therefore, classically trained dancers may find themselves performing contemporary work or choreography outside the classical ballet genre. It only makes sense, then, that dancers train for a variety of professional work so that they may be successful.

CHAPTER SUMMARY

The training of a dancer is long and rigorous. Should one wish to become a professional dancer, training starts at a young age, and it is necessary that many hours be spent in the dance studio taking class. Professional dancers consistently train in their craft. It is normal for a performing dancer to spend several hours daily in a dance studio in either class or rehearsals. The salary for a professional dancer is, on average, relatively low. Some companies only pay for rehearsal and performance time rather a steady salary. As a result, most dancers

12.1
A Day in the Life of ...

Below are sample schedules of what a dancer's daily weekday schedule may look like for dancers training in high school, dancers training in college, and professional dancers.

High School Dancer		College Dance Major		Professional Dancer	
6:00 am	Wake up/get ready	5:45 am	Wake up	8:00 am	Wake up with coffee
7:30 am–2:30 pm	School	6:00–7:00 am	Workout at gym	8:15 am	Pilates workout or meditation
3:45–5:15 pm	Assist children's dance classes	7:00–7:45 am	Breakfast/get ready	10:00–11:30 am	Company technique class
5:15–5:45 pm	Dinner	8:00–9:15 am	Tap technique class	11:45 am–1:30 pm	Rehearsal for upcoming performance
6:00–8:30 pm	Technique classes	9:15–9:35 am	Warm up, stretch, review classwork and company choreography	1:30–2:15 pm	Lunch
8:30–9:30 pm	Dance competition team rehearsals	9:35–10:55 am	Ballet technique class	2:15–4:00 pm	Continued rehearsals for upcoming performances
9:45–11:00 pm	Homework/study	11:10 am–12:30 pm	Jazz technique class	4:30–9:00 pm	Teach at local dance or fitness studios
		12:30–12:45 pm	Eat packed lunch	9:30 pm	Dinner
		12:45–2:05 pm	Dance Pedagogy class		
		2:20–3:40 pm	General Education class		
		3:45–7:30 pm	Dance Company rehearsals		
		7:45–8:30 pm	Eat packed dinner		
		8:45–10:00 pm	National Dance Education Organization Student Chapter meeting		
		10:15 pm–12:00 midnight	Student choreography rehearsals		
			Homework/study		

also maintain additional employment, which is often outside the field of dance. Between dance classes, rehearsals, performances, and additional jobs, the life of a dancer can be tiring and stressful. Why, then, do dancers engage in this field? Simply put, dancers love what they do. An artist creates because there is an inherent passion for the art, a passion and love for the art that is so strong that the artist cannot imagine doing anything else. Dance has the power to bring joy not only to an audience but to the one who is performing the movement.

Reflective Prompts

1. Why is it important for a dancer to study a variety of dance forms and styles?
2. Does it matter at what age one begins training in dance? Why or why not?
3. How does one prepare for a dance audition?
4. In what ways might a career in dance performance be stressful?

Movement Prompts

1. **Individual Challenge:** Challenge yourself to complete fifty sit-ups, a one- to two-minute plank hold, and ten minutes of deep stretches each day for a week. Some stretch ideas might include a runner's lunge stretch, sitting in a pike position and reaching toward the toes, or holding a downward dog stretch. Reflect on how the minor addition of strength and stretching exercises impacted your overall well-being each day. Imagine that this is just a fraction of the physicality required of dancers on a regular basis!
2. **Try Something New:** Seek out and try a fitness or conditioning class within your community. Try a Pilates, yoga, cycling, or strength training class.

NOTE

1   "Occupational Employment Statistics," U.S. Bureau of Labor Statistics, last modified March 19, 2019, www.bls.gov/oes/current/oes272031.htm#nat.

CHAPTER 12 BIBLIOGRAPHY

"Occupational Employment Statistics." U.S. Bureau of Labor Statistics. Last modified March 19, 2019. www.bls.gov/oes/current/oes272031.htm#nat.

13 Dance Health

The high demand of a dancer's training takes a toll on one's physical, mental, and emotional well-being. The sheer physical feats dancers are expected to perform tax the body even with sound training and technique. At the same time, high-stress situations such as casting, performances, and body image can affect a dancer's mental and emotional health. Educated dance teachers who promote a positive environment conducive to learning are paramount in protecting a dancer's health. Equally so, parents of young dancers must care for their children by being on the lookout for any signs of physical, mental, or emotional distress. Dance studios, teams, college programs, and professional companies have a strong sense of community, and dancers often are looking out for one another. Even so, the nature of the work puts an individual at risk for health issues. In this chapter, we will explore common dance injuries, nutrition concerns, and mental health.

DANCE INJURIES

As with any physical or athletic activity, risk of injury is unavoidable. Dancers tend to be more at risk than many of their athletic counterparts due to the artistic component of their work. For instance, a basketball player landing from a jump will naturally allow their joints to fold to absorb the shock of the impact; however, a dancer often will be expected to maintain their posture and will fold generously at the ankles and knees but hardly at the hips and maintain a straight spine, which places added stress on the joints absorbing the shock. The aesthetic demands of dance regularly increase pressure on dancers' joints even when they are properly executing the movement.

Dancers encounter four main causes of injury, and usually more than one is at play in the event of injury. First, dancers' physiques can make them more prone to injury. Either of the following extremes in body type will cause problems. A dancer who is malnourished and lacking muscular strength will be weak, which can cause joints to fail or accidents to happen. Likewise, a dancer carrying excess weight adds stress to the joints in every movement, also leading to joint failure or accidents. The second main cause of injury is technique errors. Though dance may seem unnatural at times, the techniques of each dance form have been developed in such a way as to allow the most efficient and safe movement practice in order to achieve the goal. As research continually develops and new knowledge is gained about the body, dance techniques adjust to avoid unsafe practices. Dancers who do not train regularly or properly put themselves at serious risk of injury. Dance instructors must be diligent in spotting errors in technique in their students, yet at the same time there is no magic wand they can wave to force the student to work the muscles correctly. Even if a dancer does correct a technique error, it is possible that the student will revert to old habits and muscle memory, causing error to occur again when the teacher is focused on a different student in the class. Ultimately, no one person is to blame in technical errors, but dancers must always be using their proprioception and concentrate to work safely.

The third main cause of dance injury is overuse. Dancers, especially competitive and professional dancers, train extremely frequently and for long periods of time. Exercises are done in training to maintain the strength to complete the necessary work, but repetition wears on the body. Similarly, when preparing for any type of performance, the choreography is repeated over and over again in order to polish the dancers, and often choreography will have more *battements* or kicks with one leg than the other, or land jumps on one foot more than the other. The repetition of these exercises and choreography often lead to overuse. Professional dancers may easily average forty-five hours of dancing per week; even when all technique is done properly, this takes a toll on the body. Issues such as nutrition or poor equipment, like non-sprung floors, can also lead to overuse injuries. Furthermore, dancers are notorious for ignoring or pushing through pain. Traditional culture in dance often taught dancers to "tough it out" in order to get through a semester or performance. This dance studio culture is shifting to urge dancers to listen to their bodies, and when they receive a bad pain signal, to rest and see whether further action needs to be taken. The fourth and final main cause for dance injury is accidents. Accidental injuries caused by a fall or a missed lift are the least common in dance. Unlike football players tackling each other and having little control over the force of the blows, dancers usually have control over their bodies, and accidents are less likely.[1]

[handwritten note: Technique can help keep you safe]

BOX 13.1 GOOD PAIN VS. BAD PAIN

[handwritten note: → can be the hardest part; telling the diff.]

Dance training is difficult. As strength and flexibility are developed, some pain will accompany the process. As dancers learn to listen to their bodies, they are encouraged to hone their abilities to discern the difference between "good" pain and bad pain. Dull discomfort or muscles quivering from fatigue are usually good or safe pains indicating that the muscles are being used to their maximum capacity. However, any sharp, shooting, acute pain that may or may not get worse over time is bad pain. Pain that is present at the beginning of an exercise and pain that causes any type of compensation or shifting away from correct technique is bad pain. Since teachers cannot feel the same sensation as their students, it is up to the students to alert the instructor if they are experiencing pain. If the student is unsure whether the pain they feel is safe or not, they can describe it to the teacher and talk through the situation. When bad pain is occurring, it is time to stop immediately. Depending on how localized the pain is and what causes discomfort, a dancer may be able to continue in class with slight modifications. The safer bet is to stop dancing until the dancer has met with a medical professional to diagnose the pain.

Foot and Ankle

Most dance injuries (around 60–80%) occur in the knee, ankle, or foot; in fact, about 50% of all dance injuries happen in the foot.[2] Great demands are placed on the lower body in dance. Even so, dancers have some of the least supportive footwear. This again is the aesthetic sacrifice of dance; ballerinas would not appear quite so light on their feet or be able to complete the line of the leg if they wore big chunky tennis shoes. Likewise, tap dancers would not be able to achieve the tonality necessary for their craft if their shoes had soft rubber soles.

Sesamoid bone injuries in the foot are common in dancers, specifically the medial sesamoid (by the big toe). A **sesamoid bone** is a small independent round bone that is embedded within a tendon or muscle; for example, the kneecap is a large sesamoid bone. Symptoms of sesamoid injury include tenderness around the bone and with movement, as well as pain when the toes are flexed. The diagnosis can be confirmed with sesamoid views or bone scans. A variety of problems could be causing the pain, including stress fracture, sprains to the ligaments on the bottom of the foot, dead bone cells, or degenerative arthritis. The most common treatment for sesamoid injury is rest, but sometimes surgery may be necessary due to fracture.

Fractures in the foot are also common in dancers. In fact, a fifth metatarsal spiral fracture (the long bone in the foot that runs from the little toe back to the heel) is commonly referred to as a "dancer's fracture." This type of fracture is usually caused by a dancer losing balance and rolling to the outside of the foot. Stress fractures in various locations of the foot are also common in dancers. **Stress fractures** are small cracks in a bone rather than complete breaks. They are usually caused by overuse but can also be caused by osteoporosis. Imaging such as a magnetic resonance imaging (MRI) or a bone scan is necessary to definitively diagnose a stress fracture. Treatment usually requires several weeks of immobilization.

Ankle **sprains**, or tearing of the ligaments around the ankle joint, are the most common acute injury in dancers. Usually, the ligaments at the front and side of the ankle are injured. Pain and swelling easily identify these injuries, but other possibilities should also be ruled out. Treatment most often only necessitates

13.1
Diagram highlighting common injuries for dancers.
Photo by Jeff Smith, WKU

I have had too many of these :-(

RICE (rest, ice, compression, elevation) but may require immobilization; rare cases require surgery. Physical therapy and rehabilitation are the most important factors when recovering from an ankle sprain. After the ankle heals, strength, flexibility, balance, and endurance will need to be rebuilt.

Knees and Hips

One of the most common knee injuries in dancers is patellofemoral pain syndrome, which describes pain around the front of the knee. This pain usually increases when climbing stairs, squatting, or jumping. Often, misalignment of the knee during physical activity and/or overuse cause the pain. Treatment relies mostly on rest, though physical therapy to strengthen the muscles around the knee may be needed.

A common danger in dance is **hyperextension** in the knees. Not everyone has the joint mobility to hyperextend, but the aesthetic of a hyperextended knee is often sought after in dance forms such as ballet and modern; those who have the range of motion are tempted to use it. On the other hand, dance teachers constantly tell students to straighten their legs, and to those with hypermobile range, the hyperextension feels straight and anything else feels bent. When the knee is hyperextended, the femur (thigh bone), tibia, and fibula (lower leg bones) are pushed back past the normal range of motion, which causes undue stress to the tendons and ligaments crossing the knee joint. Repeated damage to the knee may result in the need for surgery. While the line of a leg in hyperextension may be pleasing to the eye, hyperextension must never be used while the leg is weightbearing.

Snapping hip syndrome is so prevalent among dancers that it is referred to as "dancer's hip." This is a condition in which a snapping sound is heard or felt with movement of the hip joint. The snapping can be caused by a variety of tendons rolling over bony landmarks or muscle fibers in the hip joint. Usually, this condition can be diagnosed from history and a physical examination, though imaging may be necessary. Often, this snapping is not painful and requires no treatment. If there is pain associated with the snap, treatment may include RICE, anti-inflammatories, steroid injections, or physical therapy.

Hip labral tears are much more serious hip injuries in dancers. The **labrum** is the soft tissue that covers the socket of the hip joint, cushioning the joint and preventing the thigh bone from slipping out of place. Because dancers often use extreme range of motion in the hip and/or fast repetitive flexion in the hip, labral tears in dancers are most often caused by overuse. Symptoms of a labral tear include pain, a locking, clicking, or catching sensation in the hip, or stiffness. Diagnosis usually requires a physical examination and MRI. Treatment depends on the severity of the tear. Mild tears may be solved with a period of rest, but more severe tears often require surgery. For dancers, this surgery is risky, because it is not always successful, and they could lose range of motion in the hip joint. However, when it is successful, dancers are relieved of the pain and are able to continue dancing.

Back and Shoulder

Because of the extreme range of motion used in the back for many dance forms, dancers are at risk of several back injuries, including lower-back strain, stress fractures in the spine, and herniated discs. Overuse, poor technique, repetitive impact from jumps, and lifting other dancers off-center are all common causes of back injuries in dance.

Lifts are also a common cause of shoulder injuries in both male and female dancers. Dislocation of the shoulder joint (upper arm bone popping out of the socket), shoulder impingement (impinging of tendons or bursa in the joint), and rotator cuff tears (tearing of the muscles surrounding and supporting the shoulder joint) are all common dance injuries. Dislocation, impingement, and minor rotator cuff tears can usually be treated with rest, anti-inflammatories, and physical therapy. Serious rotator cuff tears may require surgery.

BOX 13.2 INTERNATIONAL ASSOCIATION FOR DANCE MEDICINE AND SCIENCE

The International Association for Dance Medicine and Science (IADMS) was founded in 1991 and is comprised of dance medicine practitioners, dance educators, dance scientists, and dancers. IADMS hosts an annual conference that includes presentations on current dance medicine, science, education, and research. With over 900 members spanning thirty-five countries, regional meetings are held in addition to the international conference. Furthermore, IADMS publishes the *Journal of Dance Medicine & Science*, provides quarterly newsletters, offers online forums, and sells dance medicine and science posters and publications. Topics at conferences and in publications include anatomy and physiology, biomechanics, general medicine, sports medicine and surgery, physical medicine and rehabilitation, physical therapy, dance education, kinesiology, psychology, and nutrition and dietetics. All these efforts serve to support the IADMS mission to "enhance health, well-being, training, and performance in dance by cultivating medical, scientific, and education excellence."[3]

NUTRITION

One of the most important steps in injury prevention is ensuring that the body is getting the proper amount of nutrients. However, a negative stigma has surrounded dance for generations that emphasizes low body weight over healthy ingestion of nutrients and fluids. This is fading as body-positive messaging is beginning to dominate the field. Emphasis is being placed on fit and healthy dancers, rather than skinny dancers.

Unfortunately, eating disorders have not been eradicated. Dancers spend several hours a day wearing skin-tight clothing in front of a wall of mirrors or surrounded by mirrors with constant concentration on their form and movement. This has contributed to dancers having a history of susceptibility to eating disorders such as anorexia nervosa (a pathological fear of becoming fat resulting in excessive dieting), bulimia nervosa (a disturbance in eating behavior characterized by binge eating followed by self-induced vomiting), and orthorexia (an obsession with eating a perceived perfect diet rather than attempting to maintain a healthy weight). Spreading knowledge of what healthy eating means for dancers and the risks of undernourishment could help combat these issues. Oddly, few college dance programs require any type of nutrition course for dance majors, and not many professional dance companies have a dietitian on staff.

Dancers need to fuel sufficiently for class, rehearsal, and performance. In an effort to be lightweight, many dancers do not take in enough calories to support the amount of activity they do each day. In other words, they are consuming fewer calories than they are expending. In order to achieve no change in weight, calories consumed should equal calories used, which includes exercise, activity, and resting, as our body still burns calories while inactive. Unless there is a health reason to lose or gain weight, individuals should strive for this **neutral calorie balance**.

Besides the ever-essential water, the majority of our dietary needs are made up of carbohydrates, fats, and proteins. In order to provide our bodies with fuel for activity, we need all three of these nutrients; dancers are no exception to this rule. Carbohydrates are essential for both muscle performance and recovery; they provide energy to muscle, energy to the brain, and a storage form of energy. Ideal times to eat carbohydrates are at mealtimes and within about a two-hour window before activity (to provide energy) and about a two-hour window after activity (to help recovery). For dancers, it is important to consume carbohydrates during long rehearsal days so that the muscles do not run out of energy; these can be consumed in a liquid format to also help with hydration.

Fats or lipids provide fuel to most cells and for contracting muscles. They also protect vital organs, provide structure for cell membranes, and form the base of many hormones. In regard to activity, stored fat will be used to produce energy for muscle contraction. As the body's backup energy, fat is used for endurance and is also important for dancers on long rehearsal days or performance evenings.

Proteins are a part of everything. They provide structure to all cells in the human body, largely make up the composition of muscle, skin, and hair, and provide structure for the minerals that make up our bones and teeth, and many are enzymes that increase the rate of metabolic reactions. Proteins also help repair muscle breakdown and work as reserve fuel. On average, the dancer's diet should be split into about 55–60% carbohydrate, 12–15% protein, and 20–30% fat.[4] Any exact dietary needs must be based on an individual depending on their current health status, body composition, goal, and activity.

BOX 13.3 VITAMIN D

Like many indoor athletes, dancers are at an increased risk of vitamin D deficiency. Vitamin D can be synthesized from sunlight, and the long hours that dancers spend in the studio may cause a deficiency. Vitamin D is important because it regulates bone density and influences muscle metabolism, both of which affect athletic performance. Low vitamin D levels will impair performance, weaken bones, and increase the risk of injury such as a stress fracture. Sources of vitamin D include fatty fish, tuna, cheese, and yogurt. Dancers may take supplements if they are not getting enough vitamin D from these sources, but supplements only aid vitamin D levels if there is a deficiency present.

MENTAL AND EMOTIONAL HEALTH

Dancers often find themselves in high-stress situations. Whether walking into the center of the studio to perform that long balance exercise again, preparing to rehearse a piece that addresses sexual abuse, entering a long day of technique classes without enough time to complete the necessary studying for other classes, standing in the wings before stepping onstage to perform a solo for the first time, or walking into yet another audition, there seems, at times, no end to the strain of being a dancer. Pressure is often high, as success depends on physically achieving what many people would find impossible. At times, the rehearsal process may involve confronting and/or portraying difficult topics. During all of this, the dancer must remember every nuance of choreography, class exercises, and their daily tasks.

As mentioned earlier, dancers must also face their own body image constantly. It is the medium for their art, and few people are more in tune with their bodies than dancers. Additionally, any type of injury that requires a dancer to sit out of class and rehearsal can take an immense emotional toll. Perhaps the only reason dancers are able to cope with all this strain is because dance can have an overwhelmingly positive influence on mental health as well. Multiple research projects have shown a correlation between dance and positive health. The movement triggers a release of endorphins, the creativity sparks inspiration, and the human connection can bring peace and joy.

However, it is important that any training institution or company take the mental health of their students or dancers seriously. Dancers are remarkable humans who endure uncommon challenges, and their mental health must be cared for just as well as their physical well-being.

CHAPTER SUMMARY

Maintaining dancers' health is paramount for their careers. Attention must be given to physical fitness, injury prevention, daily nutrition, and mental and

			13.1
hyperextension	neutral calorie balance	sprain	Chapter 13
labrum	sesamoid bone	stress fracture	Vocabulary

emotional well-being. The unique aesthetic strains of the art, in some ways, make these athletes more susceptible to injury. Injury is most common in the lower legs and feet. A balanced diet is key for a healthy and strong dancer. Simply focusing on counting calories, cutting carbohydrates, or anything of the sort will impair performance. Poor nutrition puts an individual at a higher risk of injury. A dancer's diet should include a healthy balance of carbohydrates, fat, and protein in order to provide muscles with sufficient energy. At the same time, the high-stakes environment of the performance world and emotional strain can take a toll on dancers' mental health. Care must be taken to attend to the physical as well as the mental and emotional well-being of the artists.

Reflective Prompts

1. What are the four main causes of injury in dancers and why?
2. What are three things a dancer can do to help prevent injury?
3. Consider your stressors as a college student. How might a dance major's stress be different? How might it be similar?

Movement Prompt

1. **Ankle strength:** Lie on your back with both feet on the floor. Pick up one leg and then trace the alphabet with your toes, only moving your ankle as if your big toe were a pen. Do one set with uppercase letters and a second set with lowercase letters. Be sure to do both legs.

   Young dancers often are taught to do exercises such as this to begin building range of motion and strength in the ankle joint.

NOTES

1. Stephen F. Conti and Yue Shuen Wong, "Foot and Ankle Injuries in the Dancer," *Journal of Dance Medicine and Science* 5, no. 2 (2001): 43–44.
2. Conti and Wong, 43.
3. "International Association for Dance Medicine and Science," www.iadms.org/.
4. Priscilla Clarkson, "Fueling the Dancer" (International Association for Dance Medicine and Science, 2005).

CHAPTER 13 BIBLIOGRAPHY

Clarkson, Priscilla. "Fueling the Dancer." International Association for Dance Medicine and Science, 2005.

Conti, Stephen F. and Yue Shuen. "Foot and Ankle Injuries in the Dancer." *Journal of Dance Medicine and Science* 5, no. 2 (2001): 43–50.

"International Association for Dance Medicine and Science." www.iadms.org/.

14 Careers in Dance

Endless options, and there is always a way for you to get into it if you want to

More often than not, people are unaware of the vast number of career options available in the dance world. There are not only opportunities in performance, choreography, and teaching but also a variety of career possibilities in dance therapy, writing, business, and production. Throughout this textbook, we have identified various roles in dance such as performers, choreographers, and teachers. We will now look more closely at these and other career opportunities in dance as we identify the functions and qualifications for these positions.

PERFORMANCE

Perhaps the most easily identifiable career in dance is that of a performer. These are the people seen onstage, on the screen, at sporting events, or in any other venue performing dance movement. Performance opportunities are often categorized into one of three types – concert, Broadway, and commercial. However, any one job or role does not necessarily always fit strictly into one category, and the similarities between each are greater than the differences. For the sake of this discussion, we will identify each individually.

Concert dance is dance performed for and to communicate with an audience, usually in a theater setting with choreographed movement and set music; concert dance pieces stand alone as separate works and may range from a few minutes to an evening-length piece. Performance in a theater is not a strict requirement for concert dance. As discussed in Chapter 3, decisions regarding venue, movement, and music are at the discretion of the choreographer. A concert dance piece may be designed to be set in a different venue than a theater, include improvisation, or have no music. A choreographer's intent may be better portrayed on the steps of The New York Public Library, with improvised movement, or in silence. Concert dance can be any form of dance. Dance companies falling into this category include Dorrance Dance (tap), Ragamala Dance Company (*bharatanatyam*), American Ballet Theatre, Rennie Harris Puremovement (hip-hop), Giordano Dance Chicago (jazz), and Paul Taylor Dance Company (modern). Artists working in this capacity often have yearly or seasonal contracts with a company to dance in all the company's concerts or events that season; it is common for artists to stay with one company for several years and perhaps move into a leadership role once they retire from the stage. Dancers

14.1
Commercial dance
is showcased on
board the Emerald
Princess cruise ship.
James D. Morgan/
Getty Images

may also work with several different companies at once or over the course of their careers.

Broadway dance is performed in a musical production as entertainment during the show and/or to help further the narrative of the story; Broadway dance is part of the greater whole that is the entire musical or production. Historically, ballet, jazz, and tap dance have been the leading forms in Broadway dance, including shows such as *Oklahoma!* (1943), *Chicago* (1975), and *42nd Street* (1980), respectively. Hip-hop has more recently become prominent on the Broadway stage in productions such as *In the Heights* (2005) and *Hamilton* (2015). In addition to the Broadway musicals running in New York City, there are regional Broadway productions in cities such as Chicago and Los Angeles and touring Broadway companies. Artists working in Broadway dance often work with a show for the duration of its run time on stage, which could vary from one week to several years, or complete an entire national or international tour with a production.

Commercial dance encompasses a wide range of venues and may be any form of dance done for entertainment purposes, including, but not limited to, entertaining guests at a theme park or sporting event or on a cruise; enhancing vocal artists' live concerts or music videos; or promoting the sale of a product. Common commercial dance forms in the United States include jazz and hip-hop. While most college dance programs have historically focused on concert dance, programs such as Studio School Los Angeles, Pace University, and Hussian College are beginning to add and offer undergraduate commercial dance degrees in order to prepare students specifically for this type of work. Artists working in this capacity may be on a seasonal contract at a theme park, complete one national tour with a vocal artist, or book individual gigs or performances. Commercial dance work entails a sense of entrepreneurial spirit in which the dancers must market themselves for various jobs. It is common for commercial dancers to sign on and work with a talent agency in order to secure jobs.

BOX 14.1 EQUITY CARDS

The Actors' Equity Association is a labor union that represents theater performers. The union protects workers by regulating healthy and safe working conditions. For performers, this means earning a livable wage, working in a theater that is up to code, being offered a break from rehearsal after a certain amount of time, a minimum number of hours of sleep between performances when on tour, and many other benefits. There are a few different ways for performers to earn their Equity card, including a points system by spending a certain number of hours working in an Equity theater or booking a specific type of show.

A major benefit of having an Equity card is being permitted to audition for Equity shows. As a rule, roles in Equity shows are only available to Equity members. Every now and then an Equity show will see walk-ins audition, but in order to be seen, a walk-in must arrive early to secure a place in line and then wait all day for the casting director to see the Equity performers first. At that point, there is still the possibility of being dismissed without receiving the opportunity to audition. On the other hand, once performers have their Equity cards, they are only allowed to audition for Equity shows, which is also limiting. Some touring and popular companies, such as Cirque du Soleil, are non-Equity only. Other labor organizations that protect performing artists' rights include the American Guild of Musical Artists and the Stage Directors and Choreographers Society.

In all three categories, the work of a dance performer includes rehearsals and performances. The rehearsal process will vary depending on the job, regardless of whether it is concert, Broadway, or commercial work. Some productions involve months of developing choreography, setting it on the dancers, and rehearsing and refining the work for weeks before performing it in front of an audience or filming. Other productions may only have a week or two or even a few days to do all of these same tasks. Performances vary in length and could be done anywhere from one time only, to six times in one day, to eight times every week for several months. For reasons such as this, dance performers must be able to learn and adapt quickly and persevere to keep work that is old to them new and exciting for audience members.

Individuals who wish to become dance performers most often have many years of dance training before they work professionally. A college degree is not required to work in the field; however, college dance programs such as a BA or BFA in dance are significantly helpful in preparing dancers for the demands of a performing career and help them learn to navigate the field. In any performance career, versatility is key. Being skilled in several forms of dance opens more doors of opportunity for an individual, and as previously discussed, almost all dance companies and shows perform a variety of styles of dance. A majority of the time, a dancer must go through the audition process discussed in Chapter 12 in order to obtain work as a performer, and these auditions are just as varied as the productions for which they are being called. Dancers may attend several auditions in one week, multiple auditions in one day, and continue auditioning

14.2
As part of the global "Keep It Moving" campaign, deaf dance instructor Christopher Fonseca teaches local deaf community members in New York, New York.
Craig Barritt/ Getty Images for SMIRNOFF

while working with a dance company or for a commercial gig in order to line up their next job after they complete their current contract. Dance performers may be paid a salary, for rehearsal time, per performance, or any combination of these. As discussed in Chapter 12, it is not uncommon for dancers to work multiple jobs at one time, depending on their income and time between productions. Often, dancers' second jobs will be in teaching dance, which allows them to continue to work in the field they love while keeping their own skills sharp and inspiring the next generation of dancers.

The entire training, auditioning, and rehearsing processes are extremely demanding of a dancer's physical, mental, and emotional abilities. The physicality of dance pushes the body to its limits. Detailed information on choreography, including counts, blocking (formations), sequence of movements, shape of the hand, direction to look with the eyes, constant notes to fix from the choreographer, and endless other details, taxes the mind. Moreover, the ability to put oneself on stage in front of an audience or camera crew and emote and communicate to an audience requires vulnerability and can be emotionally draining. The preparation to become a dance performance artist is all encompassing of the self. There is no career that quite compares to using one's own body as the medium for artistic expression.

BOX 14.2 DANCE FOR PEOPLE WITH DISABILITIES → The cooleft thing ever

As depicted in Figures 14.2, 14.3, and 14.4, dance classes and careers are not limited to those who do not have any disabilities. There are a variety of programs, schools, and companies that offer the same dance opportunities for people with a variety of disabilities, such as people who use wheelchairs, are legally blind or deaf, autistic, or amputees, and have learning disabilities or genetic conditions. These various dance opportunities address the functional needs of their participants. Moreover, some professional performance companies, like Infinity Dance Theater in New York City and Infinite Flow in Los Angeles, have artists both with and without disabilities and present high-quality dance works for audiences, further proving that dance has always been, and continues to be, for everyone.

14.3
Performers from the London-based Candoco contemporary dance company rehearse.
DANIEL LEAL-OLIVAS/AFP via Getty Images

CHOREOGRAPHY

In direct relationship with performing careers in dance, choreographers are needed to compose the works that the dance artists perform. Choreographers may work in the concert, Broadway, or commercial realm of dance, or even all of these areas. Any type of choreographer often has an assistant choreographer who aids the choreographer during the creative and rehearsal processes.

Concert dance choreographers compose works for the concert dance stage. Often, the artistic director is the most prominent choreographer for a dance company, such as Ronen Koresh of Koresh Dance Company and Mark Yonally of Chicago Tap Theatre, or as Merce Cunningham was of Merce Cunningham Dance Company. It is common practice for a dance company to have a **resident choreographer** who is "in residence" and contracted to create works for the company for a specified period of time that can range from one year to

14.4
Tap dance artist Evan Ruggiero performs a preview of *The One-Legged Song and Dance Man*, Vol.3.
Walter McBride/ Getty Images

several years. Resident choreographers are able to become familiar with the dancers in the company, which allows them to truly push the dancers to their limits. Plus, because of the job security, the choreographers can dare to take greater risks, which sometimes lead to innovation. Choreographers may also be commissioned to create and reset individual dance works for a dance concert, in which the choreographer is paid for teaching the work to the dancers as well as for the right for the company to perform their work, and sometimes even for each performance of the work.

Broadway dance choreographers are hired per production. The show's producer and/or director make the decision of who to hire to choreograph the dance movement for the cast. It is common for former stage performers to make the choice to transition to a leadership role and step into the position of choreographer when they are ready. Choreographers may also develop their careers by starting with small projects, and then, through the tiring process of presenting work in small productions, being seen, networking with other artists, and allowing word of mouth to spread, they may gradually be hired for larger and larger projects.

Commercial choreographers encompass the same wide variety of venues as commercial dancers. Similarly, the choreographers may be hired for individual gigs for product commercials or singular television show episodes, such as the Bollywood dance sequence in an episode in season four of *The Big Bang Theory*, and dance centered shows, such as *So You Think You Can Dance* and *Dancing with the Stars*. Many commercial choreographers work in this way and are called freelance choreographers. Work as a freelancer requires an excellent reputation and a lot of word of mouth in order to get hired from one job to the next. It is not uncommon for dance performers to also work part time as freelance choreographers. Cruises, theme parks, and sports dance teams often have choreographers who work for several seasons producing the entertainment for guests. Vocal artists such as Beyoncé often have their own resident choreographers, who will work with them for several years, choreographing their music videos and concerts.

Choreographer positions are sometimes funded by grants for the dance companies performing the work. Agencies or foundations, such as the National Endowment for the Arts, Jerome Robbins Foundation, and Andrew W. Mellon Foundation, offer competitive grants for companies to commission new works of art. Choreographers must be paid for their intellectual property, rehearsal time, and sometimes per performance of the work. Most often, choreographers are former dance students or professional performers who choose to step into a different role in the field of dance. College dance programs offer courses in choreography and composition. Though a degree is not required, a BA or BFA in dance is beneficial to aspiring choreographers, and there are several institutions that offer a Master of Fine Arts (MFA) in choreography. Choreography is a craft that is constantly refined in an individual artist. Creativity and an innovative and investigative spirit are crucial traits for an artist in this capacity.

BOX 14.3 AND THE WINNER IS …

Choreographers have the opportunity to receive awards for their work in distinguished national awards ceremonies. A few of the most prestigious are the following:

- Bessie Awards (Excellence in the field of independent dance artists in New York City)
- MTV Video Music Award for Best Choreography (Excellence in music video industry)
- Primetime Emmy Award for Outstanding Choreography (Excellence in television industry)
- Tony Award for Best Choreography (Excellence in Broadway theater)

TEACHING

As discussed earlier, dance training and education is multi-faceted and spans a broad range of levels and settings. Most dance teachers work in a private sector dance studio and may teach students from age two through to adulthood in a variety of dance genres. These instructors usually work in the evenings and on weekends and choreograph performance numbers for their students in addition to teaching their regular technique classes. No dance or education degree is required to teach in the private sector; however, professional collegiate training is ideal to ensure that proper and safe technique is being taught in a healthy class

14.5
The Louisiana State University dance team Tiger Girls perform during a basketball game.
John Korduner/Icon Sportswire/Corbis/ Icon Sportswire via Getty Images

structure in order to avoid injury in students. On the other hand, teachers in the K-12 division in public or private school systems usually are required to have a certificate in hand, which varies by state.

Middle school, high school, collegiate, and professional dance team coaches teach, choreograph, and rehearse their dancers. Competitive dance teams learn and drill a handful of dance routines with which they compete against other teams at various events. Walt Disney World Resort® hosts the annual Universal Dance Association National Dance Team Championship, where teams compete in divisions such as jazz, hip-hop, pom, and high kick. Non-competitive dance teams usually perform as entertainment at sporting events. For example, several teams in the National Basketball Association have their own professional dance teams, such as the Chicago Bulls' Luvabulls or Miami Heat's Heat Dancers. In both competitive and sports team cases, the dance coaches serve as the performers' teachers and work closely with them to train the dancers athletically and technically in order to present high-energy, precise, synchronized, explosive routines. College degrees are not required for these teaching positions but certainly aid in the promise of sound training, as they do in any teaching position. Coaches are expected to have had experience on a dance team in the past.

BOX 14.4 UNIVERSAL DANCE ASSOCIATION

The Universal Dance Association (UDA) is known as America's Dance Team Authority. Founded in 1980, the organization has always operated with the mission to offer high-quality training camps and clinics that include technique, choreography, and conditioning for high school and college dance teams.

UDA provides strict guidelines and rules for its competitions that specify duration of routines, costuming, and categorical requirements. For example, a high kick routine must include a minimum of sixty kicks, and at least half of the dance team must complete a kick in order for it to be counted.[1] These guidelines serve to create an equal playing field and protect the safety of the dancers by forbidding certain movements.

Some dance teachers work specifically in the convention or festival circuit. These teachers are faced with the challenge of teaching a ballroom full of potentially hundreds of students, often of a variety of ages and talent levels despite convention or festival guidelines. Conventions and festivals are usually structured to allow the participants to take class with as many teachers as possible, meaning that a teacher will most likely only have an hour or so to teach a group of students before moving into a different ballroom or studio and teaching a different class. Convention and festival teachers also rarely know any of the students in the classroom prior to class. Therefore, these instructors must prepare and deliver a quick-paced class to utilize their short amount of time effectively and be ready to adapt at any moment. Teachers in this capacity are often masters in their field or form of dance; this could mean that they have had prominent performance or choreographic careers or simply excel at teaching to the level of mastery.

Though they do not interact directly with the dancers, dance competition judges serve as a form of dance teacher as well. A majority of the time, judges speak into a microphone to record comments on the dance number and dancers as they are scoring them. At the conclusion of the competition, the performers receive these recordings and are able to hear verbal feedback about their performance in addition to the written scores. Judges often sit through hundreds of dances in one day and may work up to fourteen hours during large events. Since they only see the dancer onstage for about two and a half minutes, judges are able to offer a unique and fresh perspective to young dancers as they comment on both technique and performance quality. If there is a convention or festival happening in conjunction with the competitive event, the judges are usually also teachers for those classes.

Dance teachers may also work within a conservatory or higher education institution. Conservatory teachers usually boast prolific performance or choreographic careers and are brought in by professional training institutions to teach the next generation of dancers. These teachers may even return to the school in which they themselves trained out of a sense of loyalty. College degrees are not always required to teach at a conservatory, though some institutions may require an MA or MFA in dance. The MFA serves as the terminal degree in dance and permits an individual to teach at a college or university. Doctoral degrees in dance are also available and tend to focus on dance studies, education, or history, though few positions require them. Reasons to pursue a PhD in dance could include research interests or the desire to establish oneself as a prominent dance researcher and/or author. What exactly individuals will teach in university programs, whether or not they have an MFA or PhD, depends largely on the collegiate programs in which they work. Most professor positions require them to teach a variety of dance forms and/or at a variety of levels, as well as theory courses discussed in Chapter 11, such as dance history or dance pedagogy. In addition to teaching duties, university professors are expected to continue their own academic and creative research. The possibilities of research topics are endless; some focus on pedagogical techniques while others dive deep into dance history or dance in the cultural lens. Both conservatory and university teachers usually choreograph works for their students as well. In academia, choreography is considered part of the research and creative activity professors are expected to produce.

Teaching dance takes on many forms, and individuals often cross between multiple roles. For example, a college professor may also teach at a local private dance studio, or a dance competition judge may also teach at festivals. Many also serve the community in a variety of ways, such as teaching free classes for the local Boys and Girls Club or offering lessons for senior citizens. All teaching roles require creativity, intellect in safe dance practices, and that special spark teachers use to inspire students. The backgrounds of teachers are as varied as the many roles they may fulfill, but unique combinations of experiences prepare teachers for dynamic careers as educators.

THERAPY

With the physical demands placed on professional dancers and the therapeutic nature of movement, a variety of opportunities exist at the intersection of therapy and dance. In order to meet the needs of their students or performers, it is common for dance schools and companies to employ orthopedists, physical therapists, and/or massage therapists to tend to the dancers. At universities, it is not uncommon for dance program students not to have access to the athletic trainers on campus who serve the athletes. Because a dance program is under the umbrella of fine arts and not athletics, dance majors may not be able to consult the athletic department physicians. However, the students who perform at sporting events or compete with the dance team in the athletic department (which usually functions completely independently of the dance program) often do have access to these trainers. These physicians must have their degrees and licenses in order to practice.

As discussed in Chapter 1, there are many therapeutic applications in the practice of dance itself. Dance for health and dance/movement therapy (DMT) may serve a wide variety of constituents for any number of reasons. Sound dance training promotes physical well-being and social interaction, increases body control and awareness and self-confidence, and stimulates the release of endorphins. Dance may serve people with depression, arthritis, dementia, chronic pain, autism, Parkinson's disease, and many more conditions. Multitudes of studies have been done to examine and prove the benefits of dance in various patients. Dance for health programs are as unique as the constituents they serve. DMT is practiced by certified dance therapists who must have a master's degree in Dance/Movement Therapy. Dance artists and practitioners may also serve their communities with the health benefits of dance; these programs are different from DMT programs, as discussed in Chapter 1.

WRITING AND PRESERVATION

As in any art form, work is constantly being done to review, research, curate, and preserve dance. A myriad of publications exists to serve the general dance audience as well as small niches within the profession. Writers, authors, researchers, and editors all contribute to the written world of dance, while librarians and archivists work to retain the resources already available.

Various dance periodicals meet the needs of different audiences. *Dance Magazine* has been in print since 1927 and features a wide array of articles that include topics such as upcoming performance debuts, trends in dance, artist or company stories, dance news, and health tips, as well as dance fashion, history, and advice. It also publishes an annual college guide to aid students in search of degree programs in dance and an annual article called "25 to Watch" that features rising stars in dance choreography and performance and emerging companies and trends in dance. *Dance Teacher* publishes articles to aid dance teachers in their work, and *Pointe* magazine focuses on ballet, while *Dance Spirit* targets the younger audience. Each of these individual publications and many more requires the work of multiple writers, editing staff, a marketing team, and administrative staff to produce the magazines each month. Similarly, editors for dance research journals like the *Journal of Dance Education*, *Dance Research Journal*, and *Dance Chronicle* plan, revise, and coordinate material to be peer-reviewed and potentially published. Dance academics and researchers conduct their own studies to draft the articles submitted to journals and/or develop their work into a book.

Dance critics may be employed in a variety of publications. The dance magazines and journals mentioned in the previous paragraph, as well as newspapers like the *New York Times* and *The Guardian* and digital resources like *The Dance Enthusiast*, provide reviews written by professional critics who attend dance concerts and events, then contextualize and evaluate the work and write a summary of these observations for publishing. Critics will develop their own reputations and have a particular power to influence public opinion on works. There are no required degrees to be a dance writer; however, a strong dance background and writing skills are crucial.

Professional archivists and librarians work to preserve the history of dance. An archivist collects, treats, preserves, and catalogs artifacts to be stored safely yet available to the public for research purposes when need be. Artifacts could be any type of item, including programs, posters, newspaper articles, photographs, videos, drawings, journals, scrapbooks, costumes, shoes, and any other relevant material. Archives are often held in universities, such as the American Minstrel Show Collection at Harvard University and the Ballets Russes Archive at the University of Oklahoma. At the same time, librarians in city and university libraries maintain, catalog, and distribute dance materials such as books, newspaper articles, and film to preserve and distribute knowledge of the art form. The New York Public Library's Jerome Robbins Dance Division is able to boast its rank as the largest and most comprehensive collection of dance documentation in the world. Anyone with a valid ID may visit the library in New York City to view materials. The library also regularly curates and displays collections for public viewing in its lobby.

Being an ephemeral art form, a tremendous amount of dance would be lost without the work of a variety of writers, editors, publishers, archivists, and librarians. Degrees in dance, writing, archives, and library science from the bachelor to the doctorate level equip professionals with the tools to complete these tasks. It is through this preservation of history that artists and academics are able to look at the past, evaluate the present, and plan for the future of dance.

ADMINISTRATION

Any company or nonprofit organization must be structured and led by administration, and dance is no exception. Dance companies, professional studios, and nonprofit organizations have leadership and business teams devoted to various aspects of the organization, and all must be running successfully in order to keep the business going.

In a dance company, the **artistic director** fulfills the role of CEO and devises, develops, and implements the artistic vision for the company while overseeing the artistic staff, hiring and firing employees, and potentially also fulfilling the role of resident choreographer. Executive boards, including executive directors, assistant directors, operations managers, programs managers, education managers, and the like, coordinate their individual staff members with the rest of the teams in the company to ensure all jobs are carried out as needed. This is true for all dance performance companies, professional dance studios, organizations like NDEO, competition companies, and nonprofits. While a performance company is traveling, the company manager travels with the dancers to oversee day-to-day operations like meeting performance obligations and managing the welfare of the performing artists and the production team. Additionally, nonprofit organizations must work with their board of directors or board of trustees.

Other company staff include a marketing team in charge of promoting the company's performances or an organization's upcoming conference. The marketing manager and staff brand the company or organization with promotions that include logos, media campaigns, the website, newsletters, and programs for performances. A dance company publicist has the responsibility of writing and distributing press releases and photos to the media about upcoming performances, classes, or events. At the same time, communications and public relations managers plan the communication of the company with the public, working to foster a positive relationship with the public and maintain their public image. Fundraising managers coordinate efforts to raise money for the company or organization. This can include accounting, taxes, grant applications, and fundraising event planning.

BOX 14.5 APPLICATION DESIGNERS

As in any other profession, the advent of technology brings about new career opportunities. Chapter 10 discussed technological applications for dance at length. Application, or app, design for dance offers a distinct career opportunity with its own unique qualifications, challenges, and possibilities.

PRODUCTION

Earlier chapters have mentioned the various production elements that are involved in a performance. There are staff and employee roles devoted to each of these components, all of whom report to and communicate with one another in order to ensure a smooth run of the show.

The **technical director** oversees all of the technical elements of a production and helps to solve problems leading up to and during the run of the show. The **stage manager** acts as a ringleader in the theater. This individual sits in the tech booth at the back of the house during performances and tells the other technicians through a headset when to activate all of the sound and lighting cues throughout the performance. The stage manager is also responsible for the safety and well-being of the performers and crew while in the theater. The assistant stage manager communicates with the stage manager on headset from backstage and ensures that all performers are ready for their cues, often while helping as a stagehand.

The costume designer works closely with artistic directors and choreographers to carefully design costumes that meet the vision of the choreographer while still facilitating the necessary movement. The relationship between a choreographer and a costume designer is a two-way street; sometimes choreographers have very clear ideas in their heads of their desired costumes, which they outline for the costume designers, and other times the choreographer asks for more creative direction from the costume designer. The wardrobe head supervises all costume elements in a production, including accessories such as shoes, hats, and jewelry, and coordinates costume design, construction, and fittings. The head of properties manages all sets and props used in the production, including the design, build, installation, and upkeep of set pieces throughout the run of the show. The sound technician programs and controls the sound cues (in dance this is most often music) for the production, ensuring that all volume levels are as needed and all sound cues happen as directed. The master electrician oversees the wiring, hanging, and focusing of all the lighting instruments for the production. Meanwhile, the lighting designer designs the lighting used throughout the show under the direction of the choreographer or artistic director and programs the light cues into the control board. If the show calls for any projections or screens onstage, the projection designer oversees and designs these elements.

Additionally, the house manager coordinates all elements at the front of house, which include the lobby, box office, and ushers, as audience members arrive, purchase or pick up tickets, and find their seats. This individual also coordinates the start of the show with the stage manager, records data such as the show start and end times and number of people in the audience, and takes control of the audience in the event of an emergency such as a fire. Ushers greet patrons at the doors to the theater, take tickets, distribute programs, show patrons where they are seated, and in general help audience members navigate the theater. Finally, many dance companies hire a photographer to take promotional shots for shows as well as photographs during the rehearsal and sometimes performances to document the production.

There are many other members of the production crew who work under these supervisors. When each individual completes their tasks, the show will run smoothly. Each production requires a small army of cast and crew members to present the final product to the audience.

14.1
Summary of
Dance Jobs

Performance

Concert Dance

- Dance companies (all dance forms)

Broadway Dance

- New York City Broadway
- National and international tours
- Regional theaters

Commercial Dance

- Theme park
- Cruise
- Music concert
- Sporting events
- Product sales

Choreography

- Resident choreographer
- Assistant choreographer
- Freelance choreographer

Teaching

- Private dance studio
- K-12
- Dance team coach
- Convention/festival teacher
- Competition judge
- Conservatory instructor
- Professor

Therapy

- Company orthopedist, physical therapist, or massage therapist
- Dance/movement therapist

Writing and Preservation

- Magazine columnist
- Editor
- Researcher
- Critic
- Author
- Archivist
- Librarian
- Curator

Administration

- Artistic director
- Executive director
- Company manager
- Marketing manager
- Publicist
- Public relations manager
- Fundraising manager

(continued)

14.1
Cont.

Production
- Technical director
- Stage manager
- Assistant stage manager
- Costume designer
- Wardrobe head
- Head of properties
- Sound technician
- Master electrician
- Lighting designer
- House manager
- Ushers

14.2
Chapter 14
Vocabulary

artistic director   concert dance   technical director
Broadway dance   resident choreographer
commercial dance   stage manager

CHAPTER SUMMARY

With the development of dance as a field of study and the opportunities in dance education, many careers await those with experience in and a passion for dance. Performing, choreographing, and teaching are not the only career choices for a dancer. There are a number of ways in which an individual can merge other skill sets, talents, and interests with dance into an exciting, yet relatable, field in which to work. These options include jobs within dance therapy, writing and preservation, administration, and production. Yet, should one wish to study dance as an art form or simply participate in a dance class, the benefits that one can gain from experiencing this great art form are immeasurable.

Reflective Prompt
1. How might your career path relate to dance and dance artists?

NOTE

1   "2019–2020 UDA Competition Rules for School Teams," accessed October 21, 2019, www.varsity.com/uda/wp-content/uploads/2019/08/UDA-School-Rules.pdf.

CHAPTER 14 BIBLIOGRAPHY

"2019–2020 UDA Competition Rules for School Teams." Accessed October 21, 2019. www. varsity.com/uda/wp-content/uploads/2019/08/UDA-School-Rules.pdf.

Glossary

aesthetic   the perceived beauty in a work of art

artistic director   company executive who fulfills the role of CEO and devises, develops, and implements the artistic vision for the company while overseeing the artistic staff, hiring and firing employees, and potentially also fulfilling the role of resident choreographer

authentic jazz dance   movement that developed parallel to the music of the Jazz Age (1920s) and Swing Era (mid-1930s–mid-1940s) and features a grounded quality often coupled with fast footwork, polyrhythmic movements, and a high use of syncopation

avant-garde   characterized by unorthodox qualities that are new and perhaps surprising

awa   Dogon masking society

balance   an aesthetic principle of form; the equilibrium between sections of the choreography and within the work as a whole

ballet d'action   dramatic ballet; ballets popular during the eighteenth century where the dramatic action is incorporated into the dance itself without the need for speech or individual song

ballet master/mistress   the individual with the responsibility of instructing daily class for the ballet company and rehearsing the ballets that the company will be performing

barre   a stationary handrail that provides support during certain ballet exercises

battle (within hip-hop dance)   a means to challenge one another in a non-violent mode yet still arrive at a clear winner

b-boying/b-girling   improvisational street dance that kicked off the hip-hop generation; also known as breaking

bharatanatyam   the classical Indian dance that developed between 500 BC and 500 AD in the southern India region of Tamil Nadu

biting   term used when a b-boy steals or copies another's signature style or moves

body isolations   movement of individual parts or segments of the body

boogaloo   a West Coast funk dance created by Sam "Boogaloo Sam" Solomon that features circular movements of the joints making the dancer's body appear boneless

breakaway   the swing-out moments in the Lindy Hop where dance partners separate to individually improvise their own rhythmically charged moments of spontaneous movement

breaking   original street dance form that was highly improvisational, demanded a high degree of skill and athleticism, and focused on the dancer's individual style and flair

Broadway dance   dance that is performed in a musical production as entertainment during the show and/or to help further the narrative of the story; Broadway dance is part of the greater whole that is the entire musical or production

Broadway jazz dance   style of jazz dance that blends jazz dance elements with the movement vocabulary and stylistic aspects of other dance forms, such as ballet, modern, tap, and other dance genres; also known as theater jazz dance

Broadway tap dance   any style of tap dance that happens on the Broadway stage; often includes very specific choreographed arm and head movements that enhance the visual spectacle

buck dancing   an early form of tap dance comprised of flat-footed steps in which the feet remained close to the floor

burn   gesture in breaking intended to pointedly deliver the equivalent of a verbal insult against the dancer's opponent

Cakewalk   an African American dance born from African parody of the European minuets and other couples' dances

chance composition   the use of chance, such as rolling a die, and leaving some decisions up to random odds while composing dance choreography

Charleston   a social dance that emerged during the 1920s

choreographic concept   the idea, story, or intention of the dance as a whole

choreographic craft   the act of carefully selecting movements patterned in aesthetically pleasing and purposeful sequences and sculpting them into an overall form, or structure, that further enhances the choreographer's intent

cipher   circular formation used in street dance battles

classical ballet   a traditional formal style of ballet that utilizes standard ballet vocabulary

classic jazz dance   a blended style of jazz dance that formed the basis of studio training during the late twentieth century and was a component of the original movement of many early jazz dance companies

climax   an aesthetic principle of form; the point in a dance toward which the movement and energy of the piece have built

codified technique   guided by a delineated system of body and arm positions, defined movement vocabulary and terminology, and a methodical approach to movement execution

commercial dance   dance that is performed for the purpose of marketing a product or for venues in which a profit may be acquired

commercial jazz dance   a style of jazz dance performed for the purpose of marketing a product or for venues in which a profit may be acquired

computer-generated imagery (CGI)   visual effects added to a video in production or postproduction using digital software

concept musical   a show in which the dance is fully integrated into the storyline or overall concept, requiring greater depth in dance choreography within the musical

concert dance   dance that is performed for and to communicate with an audience usually in a theater setting with choreographed movement and set music

concert jazz dance   a style of jazz dance created for performance by concert-based companies with the intent to produce conceptualized choreography on the concert stage

concert tap dance   any style of tap dance specifically composed to be presented in a theatrical production in front of an audience with emphasis on the pure artistry of the form

contemporary ballet   a style of ballet rooted in classical ballet technique and vocabulary yet blended with modern dance technique, incorporating off-center positions, manipulations of the torso and body lines, and use of floorwork

contemporary jazz dance   a style of jazz dance rooted in jazz dance vocabulary that incorporates movement from other dance genres and often mixes in various jazz dance styles

contrast   an aesthetic principle of form; the dynamic opposition of how the subject matter or intent of the work is treated within the dance as a whole

corps de ballet   the lowest-ranking position within a ballet company and the level where most dancers enter the company

court dance   dance designed to demonstrate hierarchy and royal authority

cyclical ritual   a ritual that is general in nature and may be repeated each season

dama   a week-long ritual celebration of the Dogon people that ushers the spirits of the dead from the earthly realm into the spirit world

dance education   the information, theoretical concepts, and the application of that knowledge in a broad, general sense

dance for health   dance that is utilized as a vehicle with which to address specific health concerns and enhance quality of life

dance/movement therapy (DMT)   a modality of creative arts therapy focused on dance and movement as a psychotherapeutic tool

dance notation   the symbolic representation of choreographed movement

dance on camera   commercial use of dance on film such as on television and in movies

dance training   the acquisition of specific technical and practical skills

deejay (DJ)   disc jockey; one who mixes and samples music

desktop virtual reality   virtual reality that can be watched on a computer monitor and provides arrows for the viewer to click to direct where the camera is angled in the 360-degree video

downrock   element of breaking also known as floor rock; movement portion performed on the ground and often including power moves

downstage   the area of the stage that is located closest to the audience

emcee   the voice of the hip-hop community; could be considered as the first rappers, as they often worked party crowds while delivering spontaneous rhythms of spoken word

èmna   masks for the dancers of *dama*

energy   an element of dance; refers to the capacity for action or the build-up of power within the body

en pointe   rising onto the tips of the toes

ethnochoreology   the scientific study of dance that encompasses other disciplines, such as anthropology, musicology, and ethnography, to not only focus on the dance content but also reveal the social and cultural relationships

flash act   a high-energy upbeat act that combines tap dance with daring acrobatics

force   the way in which energy, or power, is expended through the body

form   the structure of a dance

fortification   an exercise in Horton modern dance technique with set counts and specific movements designed to achieve a training goal

freeze   a position in breaking that is held for emphasis

genre   a type of dance

harmony   an aesthetic principle of form; when all of the aspects of a work are appropriately coordinated and unified

hyperextension   the ability for a joint to extend beyond the natural range of motion

immersive virtual reality   virtual reality that allows the viewer to wear a headset and move through space, interacting with and mobilizing through the environment as one does in real life

Imperial Russian ballet   era of ballet history that occurred during the late nineteenth century in Russia

improvisation   the spontaneous production of movement

interactive content   media changed by the performer as it reacts in real time to the performer's actions

kabuki   Japanese dance drama

karanas   the traditional poses of the body the dancer moves through in Indian dance

labrum (in hip)   the soft tissue that covers the socket of the hip joint, cushioning the joint and preventing the thigh bone from slipping out of place

legacy company   a dance company devoted to preserving the history and vision of a particular individual, usually the former artistic director

Lindy Hop   an American social dance that emerged during the 1930s

linear content   predetermined and unchanging media content

locking   funk dance form that was created on the West Coast by creator Don "Campbellock" Campbell; dancer will briefly hesitate in a given position as if the movement is "locked" and then continue in the same tempo as before

mie   a codified pose in which the Japanese dancer will pause dramatically

minstrelsy   a form of American entertainment in the mid- to late 1800s that mocked African Americans and in which men dressed in blackface and performed variety acts

motion capture   technology that tracks human movement using a full-body suit with sensors and software and sends data captured by multiple cameras to a 3D model so that the model performs the same movements as the person in the suit

movement qualities the recognizable characteristics of movement that incorporate all three elements of dance resulting in the unique ways in which a movement can be executed

mudras the stylized gestures made with the hands in Indian dance

natya the portion of Indian dance that includes spoken word, movement, song, and scenery; implies both theater and dance

neoclassical a style of ballet in which traditional ballet vocabulary is used and *pointe* work is still emphasized, yet the narrative element is removed from the choreography and replaced with a modern, abstract approach

neutral calorie balance calories consumed equal calories used

onnagata female impersonator in *kabuki*

organic movement natural, free-flowing movement that is internally motivated by ease and efficiency

party dance a form of hip-hop dance that is light-hearted and fun, requiring less skill than breaking, yet equally connected to the music and the culture in which they developed

pas de deux a duet between the ballerina and her male partner that follows a codified format

political dance dance used as an instrument to display power and status among the ruling classes within a given society

polyrhythm multiple rhythms happening simultaneously

popping a form of West Coast funk dance where the dancer's muscles hit, or tick, rhythmically with the musical beat by a consistent contraction and release while simultaneously executing movement

post-modern dance a concert dance form that rejects classical dance constructs and considers all movement to be dance

power move movement in breaking that demonstrates an explosive movement quality and can awe an audience or humble one's opponent

principal dancers the dancers with the most important roles within a ballet company

projection design the practice of projecting an image onto a surface as well as the use of monitors or screens to display an image

projection mapping the display of an image on a non-flat surface

proportion an aesthetic principle of form; the quantity of dancers and sections within the choreography

***rasa* theory** the aesthetic, spiritual, and emotional response initiated through the performers and experienced by the spectator

répétiteur someone who teaches and rehearses choreography on a company in the event that the choreographer is unavailable or no longer living

repetition an aesthetic principle of form; the reoccurrence of a movement or movement phrase for emphasis and meaning

resident choreographer a choreographer who is contracted to create works for the company for a specified period of time

rhythm the arrangement of the movement within the musical beats

rhythm tap dance a style of tap dance characterized by intricate footwork with extended musical phrasing, complex patterns, and syncopated heel drops

ritual dance dance designed to please or placate the gods or to ask for favor or blessing from the spirits

Romantic ballet era of ballets choreographed between the years of approximately 1830 and 1870; ballets emphasized the individual and emotions

screen dance the specific medium of dance created for video viewing in which the film artistry equally contributes to the perception and intention of the work

sequence an aesthetic principle of form; the arrangement of movement phrases and choreographic sections

sesamoid bone a small independent round bone that is embedded within a tendon or muscle

shadow dance dancing that is presented by throwing the shadows of dancers on a screen

Shim Sham Shimmy recognized as the national anthem of tap dance, this short tap dance routine is comprised of four sections and is often performed as a performance finale

social dance dance that functions as a means for social interaction or social display

soft shoe a style of tap dance characterized by elegant style, graceful movements, and light tap sounds usually performed at a slower tempo

somatics a movement discipline that emphasizes a mind-body approach

space an element of dance; the three-dimensional area through which a dancer can move

specific ritual a type of ritual done only one time and for a very distinctive purpose

sprain tearing of the ligaments

stage left the left half of the stage when viewed from the dancer's perspective

stage manager ringleader in charge of the production while in the theater, who calls cues for performances and is responsible for the safety and well-being of the performers and crew

stage right the right half of the stage when viewed from the dancer's perspective

stimulus a person, place, thing, or idea that provides inspiration for a choreographer; a catalyst for movement

stress fracture a small crack in a bone

style the way in which a genre of dance is performed

syncopation an emphasis of the weak beats within music rather than the strong beats

technical director person who oversees all of the technical elements of a production and helps to solve problems leading up to and during the run of the show

tempo the speed or pace of the beat

theater jazz dance   style of jazz dance that blends jazz dance elements with the movement vocabulary and stylistic aspects of other dance forms, such as ballet, modern, tap, and other dance genres; also known as Broadway jazz dance

theatrical dance   dance performed for a non-participating audience with the intent to communicate or entertain and supported by production elements

time   an element of dance; refers to the duration of time in which a dance unfolds and the various tempos and rhythms that are used within the dance

toprock   element of breaking; movement done while standing to introduce dancers and their individual style

transition   an aesthetic principle of form; the way in which a dancer moves from one movement or movement phrase to the next and the way in which sections of choreography are connected

triple threat   a performer who demonstrates the ability to sing, act, and dance

unity   an aesthetic principle of form; wholeness of a dance; all aspects of the choreography working together in agreement

uprock   highly confrontational aspect of breaking that involves freestyle shuffles of the feet, spins, turns, and pantomimed gestures from both everyday and gang life

upstage   the area of the stage farthest away from the audience

variety   an aesthetic principle of form; the multiple ways in which a movement or movement phrase can be manipulated, changed, or altered throughout a dance

vaudeville   a form of American entertainment in the late 1800s and earlier 1900s that featured variety acts in a family-friendly setting

vernacular dance   dance that naturally forms within a culture and is learned without the instruction of professional teachers

Index

Note: Numbers in **bold** indicate text within a table. Numbers in *italics* indicate text within a figure.

■ Index

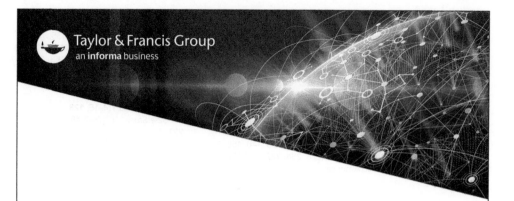